George A. Corrigan

Calked Boots
and
Cant Hooks

II

Calked Boots and Cant Hooks

George A. Corrigan, Author

L. G. Sorden, Editor

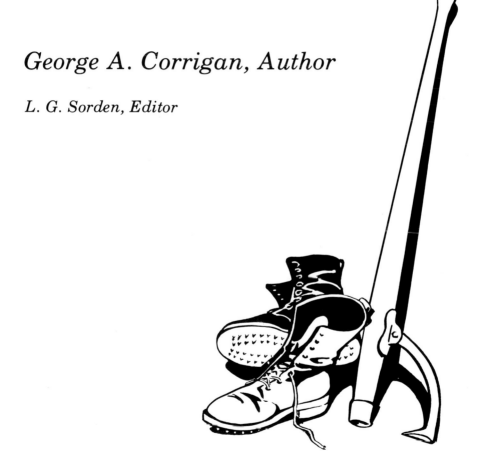

Dedication

This book is dedicated to my children, Bonnie, Shirley, and Clayton.

It is also dedicated to all the woods workers in Northern Wisconsin and Upper Michigan. These workers were a hardy lot and they were productive. In summer they fought the mosquitos and black flies. In winter they waded snow, sometimes three feet deep, in temperatures recorded as low as 54 below zero. In spring they worked in rain and slush, often wet to the skin. It was hard work and often dangerous. Many lumberjacks were killed or were badly crippled as a result of logging operations. Wages were low but generally spirits were high.

It is the hope of the author that these timber men will never be forgotten for the contributions they made in the building of the Great Midwest.

George A. Corrigan
Saxon, Wisconsin

VI

Contents

Preface IX

Introduction XIII

Area Map XVIII

Foster-Latimer Logging Area Map XX

1   Making of a Logger 1

2   Move to New Company 11

3   Move to New Camp 29

4   Another Camp Move 39

5   Camp Move and New Job 49

6   First Trip to Hurley to Hire Men 55

7   Danger In The Woods 61

8   A New Challenge 71

9   Summer of 1919 85

10 New Challenges 103

11 Hired Out To New Company 119

12 Logging In Native Home Area 127

13 Interesting Items of Logging Camp Life 149

14 Another Camp Move Deeper In The Wilderness 161

15 A New Part of a Logging Job 169

16 The Peak of the Depression 187

17 Contract Logging In Michigan 193

18 Camp 2 At Crooked Lake, Michigan 211

19 Camp 3 At Tamarack Lake, Michigan 221

20 Camp 4 At Beaton Spur, Michigan 227

Tanneries 237

George Kennedy, Camp Cook 239

Preface

This is a true account of the logging history of Ashland and Iron Counties of Wisconsin and Gogebic County of Michigan "as it was" in those counties from 1912 to 1937.

What I am writing is not a success story. I am setting down this information because no one else has come forward to do the job. I am proud of the years I spent in the logging industry which has played such a large part in the economic and social life of this area and in the building of our nation.

Living and working in the woods for most of my life, I can truthfully say I have worked at almost every job known in the logging industry, especially in the work of the old days. At one time, while working for the Foster-Latimer Lumber Company of Mellen, Wisconsin, I was paid the top wage rate in order to be available at whatever job needed to be done. Sometimes I worked in two different camps on the same day.

I was used much as a utility ball player on the baseball team is used, and I enjoyed most of the jobs assigned to me. I do want the readers to know that it is written from experience with humility.

Much of it was humorous for me at the time as I was very young when starting out in the industry. If it were not for the humor while working in logging camps, there would have been little enjoyment in the old days.

I wish all to understand that when I mention nationalities they should not be offended. Few men have had more respect for all nationalities, races, creeds, or colors than I have, and the best and most enjoyable crews I have worked with were crews of all nationalities.

A little illustration comes to mind. While I was a partner in the Corrigan-Organist Logging Contractors on the Beaton Spur out of Watersmeet, Michigan, in the thirties, Sandy Murphy, conductor on the C. &. N.W. freight train which did our switching at that time, was asked at Watersmeet Depot one morning what nationality predominated at our camp. Sandy replied, "They have all nationalities out there. They even have an Irishman or two." I think we had eleven or twelve different nationalities at the time in a crew of around fifty men.

The story that I will tell can be proved easily at this time as some men who figure in it are still living around Mellen, Ashland, Hurley, and Saxon, Wisconsin, and Ironwood and Ontonagon, Michigan, who I lived and worked with for many years. A few are still living who were neighbors of my family when I was born on April 3, 1896 at Mineral Lake, eight miles west of Mellen when it was real wilderness.

A thing to remember about old logging camp days is that there were always new experiences, for the logging industry was making great changes at the start of the twentieth century.

Until around 1910 to 1915 the great virgin pine forests of the north central states were being destroyed without any thought of the future, so the gradual change in thinking about the forests as national resources is part of this story.

According to the Wisconsin Conservation Department and the Wisconsin Historical Society, the first commercial sawmill in the state seems to have been built in 1809 at DePere on the Fox River, followed by mills on the Wisconsin River in 1831 near Portage and at Sheboygan in 1835. The Civil War made commercial logging big business in Wisconsin. There were mills mostly in the eastern Lake Michigan counties during the war with markets in Milwaukee and Chicago. Following the Civil War and the opening up of the prairie states through railroad expansion, the logging companies pushed on throughout Wisconsin forest land with miles on all the rivers both west and north. The "Golden Age" of Wisconsin lumbering had begun. The great era in northern Wisconsin lumbering began after the railroads came into the area in 1870. Before the railroads and during their development, millions of board feet of pine were driven down the rivers to mills in the developing cities. In addition to the lumber cut in Wisconsin, millions of feet were driven down the Mississippi to mills on that river. Agricultural development and settlement followed lumbering rather slowly in the north, leaving much unused and uncared for cut-over lands. While lumber companies offered such land to settlers at low prices, much wasn't suitable for agriculture and was acquired by greedy speculators who sold it to unwary city people. The fire danger also was greatly magnified by the vast acres of unoccupied Wisconsin logged land. These problems were ignored for years until pressure from the College of Agriculture, conservationists, recreational concerns, and the general public brought it to legislative attention in the late twenties and thirties.[1]

While our family lived at Bibon, Wisconsin, in the first decade of the twentieth century, Lever Lien had a fair-sized sawmill on the White River, and Hines Lumber Co. had one of the largest sawmills, if not the largest, in Wisconsin at Mason in Bayfield County on the White River. The Mason mill sawed around 500,000 feet of pine lumber every twenty-four hours in two ten-hour shifts. The Bibon mill sawed around

---

[1]The Wisconsin Conservation Department and the College of Agriculture have excellent literature on this subject. Particularly interesting is the booklet "Forest Fires and Forest Fire Control in Wisconsin."

200,000 feet in two ten-hour shifts. Considering the fact that there were hundreds of mills in Minnesota, Michigan and Wisconsin all sawing pine and producing at similar rates, you realize that this was a staggering amount of lumber.

In this era a few lumbermen began looking ahead at the prospect of sawing hemlock and hardwood lumber, especially in Michigan and Wisconsin where some of the finest hemlock and hardwood forests in the nation were located. This new look at a different type of timber, along with the wood for the veneer plants and for the pulpwood industry, extended the growth of the lumber industry in Wisconsin. It remains today as a thriving and essential element in the economy of the state.

XII

Introduction

As far as I have been able to determine, my family's branch of the Corrigan clan immigrated to Wisconsin from Canada, arriving near Eau Claire in the 1880's. Six of the seven Corrigan Brothers of Orilli, Ontario, on the east side of Lake Simcoe, left home to see if they could better themselves in the newly-opening logging operations of the midwestern United States. Hugh settled in the Eau Claire area, Pat and Tom in northern Wisconsin, and Henry, Jim and Mike went to the far west in Washington state after several years in northern Wisconsin. Oral tradition in the family has it that only "Curly" Bill remained at home in Orilli. Of the five sisters, at least two left home for the United States; Rose to settle in Detroit, Michigan, and Maggie to go to Washington and Alaska. All the Corrigan boys worked in the woods and mills, married, raised families, and settled permanently in the areas of their choice.

My father, Patrick, married Johannah Hoffmeister in Chippewa County in 1888 and their first child, Ida, was born in June, 1889. They came north to Drummond in Bayfield County after their second daughter, Ann, was born in November, 1891. The young family soon moved to Mineral Lake in Ashland County where Pat began working for the newly re-organized Mineral Lake Lumber Company as a lumber piler. In April, 1894, their first son, William, was born. At this time, Hannah also had her three sisters join her in the north country. Pat continued his work at the mill in the growing little community. The Corrigan family grew also with the birth of George (the author) in 1896 and that of a third daughter, Frances, three years later.

The personal life of our family was busy, content, full, and warm in those years. There was hard work but it was satisfying. But before continuing the family chapter, we should take a look at those working conditions which kept my family at Mineral Lake, eight miles west of Mellen, Ashland County, Wisconsin.

Henry Sherry, a large lumber operator from Neenah, Wisconsin, had purchased pine stumpage in the Mineral Lake area. After bad luck in having a new mill burn as he began operations, Sherry formed the Mineral Lake Lumber Company in 1890 which built up an extensive logging and lumbering setup at Mineral Lake.

The company built the mill, hotel, store, office and houses for the employees. They logged heavily during the winter of 1890-91 in order to have a log inventory for the summer of 1891. The mill started operation in the spring of 1891 with a sawing capacity of 15,000,000 board feet a year, which is a lot of lumber. At the time this mill was running, only pine logs were cut. Old-time timber cruisers told me that these were of the finest of the famous white cork pine, which was getting scarce and in great demand. The Mineral Lake Company had a large amount of this fine pine stumpage.

The mill site was on the northeast end of Mineral Lake where a public access road now leads into the lake from the National Forest Road north of the Mellen-Mineral Lake-Marengo-Sanborn Road. The main office, company store, warehouse, blacksmith shop, and utility buildings were on the south side of the spur which ended where the gravel pit is now located. The hotel of about sixty rooms was on the hill just south and east of the office building.

The dwelling houses (all company owned) were located on the edge of the lake, northwest of the sawmill around the bay at the end of the lake, and east along both sides of the railroad spur entering the village. There were at least twenty-five dwellings.

The school house was on a little rise on the east side of the main road and north of the railroad track. The foundation of this building still can be easily located by persons who lived in Mineral Lake at that time.

After the closing of the mill in 1897, several of the unused buildings were sold to homesteaders coming into the area but the balance burned in the forest fire of 1911.

The Mineral Lake Lumber Company had logging camps in the area which housed many men. A logging camp in those days was made from logs with lumber for roofs, floors, and doors. The lumber was toted a long distance over rough trails with a lumber wagon. Sometimes the lumber was hauled out in the winter on sleds to prospective campsites to be built in the spring and summer. Logging roads were also made. There were about two hundred men in a large logging camp.

In about September of each year the logging crew moved in with ox and horse teams to cut, skid, and deck the pine logs on sleigh roads or on river banks. The logs on sleigh roads were then hauled on 12 to 16 foot bunk sleighs with four-horse teams on ice roads many miles to the mill or to the river banks where they were driven to the mill on high water in the spring breakup. The river drive was always looked forward to by the majority of lumberjacks as it was very exciting but dangerous work. For many, however, it meant getting out of the woods for the first time in a year, as many of those men went to the woods in the spring, helped build the camps, make the log roads, cut, skid, and decked logs in the fall and winter, then went down with the drive to the mills.

The Mineral Lake Lumber Company drove logs down the Brunsweiler River, an inlet to the lake. A dam was built on the Brunsweiler above the lake. The company also drayed or sleighed many pine logs to the bank of Mineral Lake and boomed them to the mill.

Many logs which had some small defects which let a lot of water soak in are still at the bottom of Mineral Lake. These would still be good for lumber but it would probably cost too much to salvage them.

The skidding was done with ox teams, with horses used only in the cross-haul for decking or loading onto sleighs and in sleigh hauling.

All the woods work in those days was done by hand labor as there were no steam or gas engines in general use yet. The roads were made with axes, cross-cut saws and shovels; the railroad ties were hewn on two sides with a broad axe.

Since there was no refrigeration, storage of fresh foodstuffs was a major undertaking. Sometimes oleomargarine or lard was kept in a spring or creek but in the very early days, no attempt was made to keep butter. Fresh meat was part of the diet in summer, but camps did serve venison or moose in the fall in areas where there was a surplus of those animals. In the winter the companies were able to tote in frozen meat of all kinds. In the summer the cooks used screen houses to keep what meat they could receive. A screen house is a building with a rectangular roof to keep the sun from shining too directly on it, built about four feet off the ground on blocks. The walls were built of boards about three feet up, then about four feet of screen wire all around to keep out flies and other insects. The building had long eaves so the sun's rays couldn't get in and the air circulating through the screened sides would keep the meat hanging on hooks dry, with very little spoilage, especially of smoked meats. This method worked quite well (although, of course, you could not expect to keep meat over long periods of time) and was the storage method in general use until about 1940 when some camps began to have ice boxes and refrigeration.

Root houses, excavations in the side of a hill, supported by double tiers of logs with a solid door, located as near the kitchen as possible, were used for storing potatoes, turnips and other root vegetables for use in the fall and winter months.

The teamsters driving the tote wagon teams which supplied the camps and kitchens had to be picked carefully, as this was a very important job. Roads were very rough and wagons had to be loaded to capacity to save extra trips whenever possible. The teamster needed to be a man with very good judgment who knew how to treat horses fairly and to build his loads well to save trouble on the road.

While Pat was in the mill as a lumber-piler, they lived in one of the company houses. A short time later, Pat and Hannah bought a 160-acre homestead about one-half mile from Mineral Lake in Section 12, T44, N-R4W. Although he continued his mill work, they now began clearing their land for farming as most people did at that time. Two of Pat's brothers, James and Henry, also worked at the mill in these years, while three of Hannah's sisters also lived with them. Ida did dressmaking, Mae worked in the company office, and Nell was a school teacher. Although the working hours and weeks were long, this was a happy time. The young people, married and single, enjoyed Saturday night dances and Sunday outings and picnics. At the Saturday night dancing club affairs, Pat Corrigan and John Tobin played the violin and did the calling. Pat played by ear and it is said he could play a whole evening without ever repeating a song. When in Ashland or Mellen, he listened to the latest tunes and returned home with them in his head and ready for his violin.

Their seemingly secure life was jolted, however, when the mill closed suddenly a few years later in 1897. What had been envisioned as a long term operation ended abruptly because other companies came in and purchased the stumpage the Mineral Lake Company intended to log but had not acquired. At the time of the closure, the Mineral Lake Lumber Company hired Pat Corrigan to be the mill watchman so the little family moved back into town to be near the mill. My older sisters and brother had fond childhood memories of playing in the abandoned mill homes during this period.

About 1900 there was another flurry of activity in Mineral Lake as it looked as though mining operations would be begun at last. This activity, including prospecting and sinking of shafts, continued through 1902.

Pat Corrigan, however, suffered a heart attack and died in January, 1902, at age 39. The next three years were particularly hard for Hannah; her oldest child was 13, the youngest 3. She stayed on in Mineral Lake and operated a boarding house for the mine crew while a young nephew of Pat's, John Corrigan, took over the watchman job and helped her with the homestead and the children. The Mineral Lake Lumber Company estate cut the wages for the watchmen in late summer of 1902 so my mother found it impossible to stay on and keep Johnny there.

My mother, a marvelously courageous woman, was not daunted, although a widow with five young children to support. At the urging of my uncle, Mike Corrigan, we moved to Bibon, another sawmill town, where Mike had a thriving saloon and restaurant. My mother ran the restaurant and we settled down to life in Bibon for almost three years.

Ironically, the sawmill at Mineral Lake burned down in October, 1902, just two months after we ended our millwatching job and moved. We were the last family at Mineral Lake Valley.

During this time at Bibon, Hannah became engaged to James Doyle, a widower with five children by his first marriage; however, only one son, Leo, was with him in Bibon.

James Doyle was a great horseman and was barn boss at the Lever Lien sawmill at Bibon. He and Hannah planned to be married as soon as possible, but Hannah and the family went back to the homestead in the spring of 1905 to put in the garden. We also bought cows, chickens, and a driving horse. Ida, the oldest girl, left for Alaska at age 16 to work for Pat's sister, Maggie, and her husband in Valdez.

During the winter of 1905-1906, my mother and we four children lived alone at the homestead. My brother Bill and I, aged 11 and 9, sawed with a cross-cut saw all the wood needed for our log cabin home. Henry Hanson, a neighbor would file the saw and fall the trees. My sister Ann, 14, helped my mother with all the chores and with the care of Frances who was six.

In June, 1906, Mr. Doyle came down from Bibon and he and Hannah were married. He brought a team of work horses. They farmed and did some road work that summer and fall. After the crops were in, he hired out to a logger in Marengo for the winter. He came back home in March but came down with pneumonia while working on clearing land and readying the ground for the crops. Although he was taken to the hospital in Ashland, he lived only two weeks. My mother was again a widow and we were again without a father.

The only time I ever remember seeing my mother almost give up was in April of 1907, when the roads were impassable for team travel and she arrived in Mellen from Eau Claire where Mr. Doyle was buried. She was walking home to the homestead from Mellen on the old Mineral Lake road alone, eight miles, all wilderness, when a band of timber wolves started howling near her. She said it did not bother her at all as right at that time she did not care what happened to her.

She got over that despondency in a short time, but we had to leave Mineral Lake again. This time moving to Mellen where my mother worked real hard trying to give the family an education. Through it all she always kept her humor and her stability.

I was only 11 when we moved to Mellen but kept busy for the next five years doing chores for families and working as a printer's devil in the Mellen Weekly printing office. My mother went on to marry a third time and you will encounter her again from time to time in this book. My brother Bill also appears; he had a long, active woods life also. His death occurred at age 79 in February, 1974. My sister Ida died in December, 1971, in California, after spending 37 years in Alaska. My sisters, Ann and Frances, are both still living in California at this writing, Ann in Modesto and Frances in San Fernando. Ann's daughter, Pat, (Mrs. William M. Graham of Oakdale, California) has been my editorial assistant in this project of writing my history.

Map of the
orthern Wisconsin - Upper Michigan Area
which is the setting for
"Calked Boots and Cant Hooks"

ONTONAGON

Silver City

White Pine

Rockland

64

Bergland

45

28

Bruce Crossing

Wakefield

OD

28

Marenisco

Gogebic Branch

Beaton Spur

2

MICHIGAN

WISCONSIN

Watersmeet

Crooked Lake

Tamarack Lake

Land O'Lakes

Conover

45

51

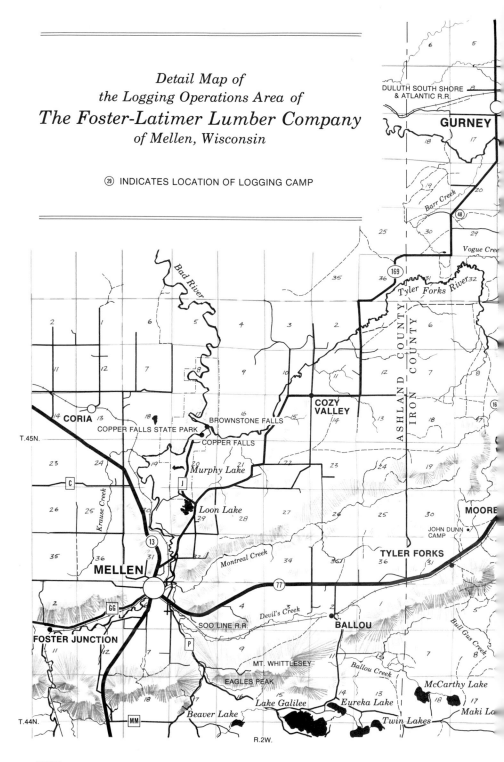

Detail Map of
the Logging Operations Area of
The Foster-Latimer Lumber Company
of Mellen, Wisconsin

㉙ INDICATES LOCATION OF LOGGING CAMP

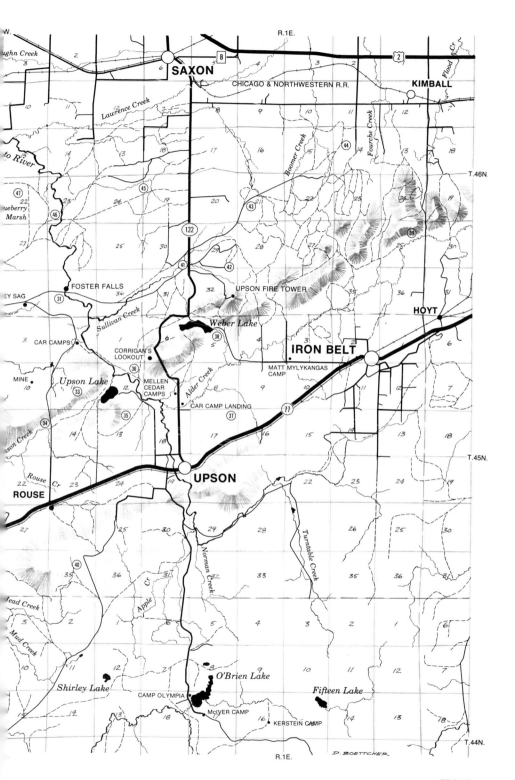

XXII

Calked Boots and Cant Hooks

A 25-year history of my logging experiences in Northern Wisconsin and Upper Michigan.

George A. Corrigan

1

Making of a Logger

The big decision of my life being no surprise following such a background as I have outlined. Such involvement was almost inevitable -- the only question seemed to be -- when?

The decision came in the spring of 1912, while I was still able to have more time to participate in sports, especially baseball and basketball which were my favorites. I decided to quit school, a poor decision from my adult way of looking at things, but reasonable to me then. My mother urged me not to do it, but I really did not wish to see her work so hard, so I went to work.

At that time, it was legal to quit school and go to work at the age of sixteen. I was sixteen on April 3, 1912, so I decided to try for a job at the Foster-Latimer Lumber Company Flooring Factory at Mellen, Wisconsin. Having grown up in that area which depended on logs and lumber for its living, I naturally saw the lumber industry as my own way to independence. It would fit in with my growing love for the outdoors and the woods. Also my older brother, Bill, was already working as a teamster and I felt I, too, could help take the load from my mother by full-time earnings. Here, therefore, began my life-long attachment to the woods industries.

I had made application at Foster-Latimer on my sixteenth birthday on Saturday, and was hired to start work on the following Monday morning, April 5, 1912. I was to tie flooring into bundles. The pay schedule was 16.5 cents per hour, ten hours per day, and six days per week with no coffee breaks. If you ate a lunch, it was on your own time, or you ate while working.

Anton Trolson, flooring factory superintendent, was average size, a very quiet man and wore glasses at all times. He did the mill wright work and filed the saws used in the flooring mill. A very busy man.

He did his work without showmanship and had the respect of his crew at all times. A sure sign of a good foreman.

Some of the men who are still living in Mellen who were working there at that time are Reinold Henke,[1] Mike Fisher, and Joe Cramer. It was hard work, for the lumber used for flooring stock in those days was hard maple and yellow birch, with the greatest percentage in long lengths. The rough lumber was taken from the yard, put into dry kilns from where it entered the factory. At one end it was unloaded onto conveyors, carried to the planer, then to the ripsaw where it was cut into 2½" or 1½" widths, then through a molding machine where it was grooved. The lumber then went through end-matchers and was trimmed from where it was loaded onto carrier trucks, then moved to the flooring platform where it was graded into grades of F. & S.[2]: the best, clear; the second best, common, third best and factory, the lowest grade. It was then tied into bundles of all the different lengths from 1½' to 16', the 2¼" widths in bundles of eight pieces and the 1½" widths in twelve pieces to a bundle. It was tied with a lightly tarred binder twine.

The younger workers were almost always started out on tying flooring as their fingers were supple and their reflexes quick for placing the different lengths of flooring in the correct racks. They also had to keep a good lookout in order not to get hit by a stick of flooring from the grader. Today work is much more simple and less dangerous in a flooring factory since much more of the work is done with machinery.

I stayed with my job until November, 1912, when Mr. and Mrs. A. J. Sullivan, who had a hardware store and a clothing store where the supermarket and the old post office buildings are, offered me a job as a janitor and helper in the stores. They thought it would help me get a new start, but that winter was misery for me; I did not like that kind of work at all -- not enough activity.

So in the spring of 1913, I went back to the flooring factory and sometimes unloaded lumber onto the conveyors from the piles coming out of the dry kilns. It was heavy work but did not require much know-how. I still liked tying and grading of flooring when one of the better breaks came for me.

Roy Welch had been working as a camp clerk in the railroad construction crew for the Mellen Lumber Company, west of the town in the Potter Lake area. The boarding cars were located on the shores of Potter Lake. Roy was going back to school and he recommended that I take his place, to Gust DeLene, the woods superintendent for the Mellen Lumber Company. Roy knew I was aching to get working in the logging camps. I made a quick decision to accept the job, even though I knew it would only last about two months. I was sure that by the end of the two-month period I would be able to take some other job in one of the camps.

[1]Word of Reinold's death was received as the book was going to press.

[2]Flooring grades were not marked the same as lumber. F. & S. means Firsts and Seconds -- the best grade.

The wages for clerks at that time were $30 per month and board ($1.15 per day and board which amounted to about 35 to 40 cents a day). If a cook was unable to keep under the 40 cents per day maximum for feeding a man, the company would soon be looking for a new cook. Of course, if a crew was under fifty or sixty men, the company would allow the meals to cost a little more, as the larger the crew the more economical. The average number that most cooks preferred was around 100 men. In addition to the cost of the kitchen supplies and equipment, the wages of the cook and his helpers such as cookees and chore boy, plus the wood, the blankets, and other housekeeping supplies were all charged to the cook camp.

Boarding cars owned by logging companies expected many years of operation were especially built to fit their needs. That was the case at the Foster-Latimer Lumber Co. and the Mellen Lumber Company. They had large blocks of timber stumpage which would take years to log and were planning heavy private railroad logging operations.

Where timber was in large blocks of solid heavy stands, suitable for railroad logging, it was the cheapest way to get logs to a mill. In logging hemlock and mixed hardwoods in those early days, it was very necessary to log the cheapest way possible.

They would build boarding cars to their own specifications or needs. They were able to build the cars wider so as to utilize space better.

The Mellen Lumber Company boarding cars were built to their own specifications.

The kitchen car was built for a kitchen crew to handle up to about 60 men. It had a ventilator on the roof with windows which could be opened with a long pole by the cook or cookees. There would be room for two good-sized regular camp ranges, with 50 gallon barrels attached so as to have plenty of hot water at all times.

There would be a bake-off table for pastry. All cooks of that period did their own baking of pastry, pies and bread. The only pastry furnished was crackers, ginger snaps and hardtack.

There was a large rack to hold large bread pans, cookie sheets and other cooking utensils for fruit, meat and vegetables.

There was also a large sink for dish washing and drying. The knives, forks, and spoons would be put in a large bean sack after a thorough rinsing in very hot water. Then the two cookees or cook and one cookee would take a hold of one end of the sack, shake it good, then dump it on the dining room table to be sorted and placed for the next meal.

The dining car would connect with the kitchen car on one end of the car and be wide enough to hold ten to twelve tables of six men to a table. The tables would be placed with one end to the side of the car with five or six tables on each side. An aisle was left for the men to walk through the center of the car coming in to take their place at the table. Also there was room for the kitchen help to serve the tables.

There were two sleeping cars with single bunks built three-tier high with a ladder between each tier to get to the second and third bunk.

Those first boarding cars of the Mellen Lumber Company used boards lengthwise for springs. Straw or conifer boughs were used for mattresses whichever the sleeper preferred. They were not bad. I slept in one bed for two months with no aftereffects. I used a sack part filled with bran for a pillow.

Another car, a little smaller for the office crew and Wannigan, was attached to one end of the kitchen car. This made five boarding cars in all.

The company planned one move a year for the cars. In that way, there was no moving in the busy season to interfere with railroad building.

The busy season was from April to October and a cleanup and repair job on the cars before boarding up for the winter.

A set of boarding cars on private railroad of the Mellen Lumber Company running out of Foster Junction about 2 miles west of Mellen to the Mineral Lake, Lake 3, Morgan Creek, Marengo and Sanborn area.

Used building railroads in the spring, summer and early fall. Each car 24' long, 12' wide and 8' high.

The cars were well-lighted with windows over the tables in the kitchen and dining room. Kerosene lamps and lanterns were first used. Gas lamps and lanterns were used after World War I.

The cars were used entirely for railroad building, except for a few bark peelers when the company had a scattered patch of hemlock trees to be peeled. This was done to save the peelers a long walk.

A screen meat house was set up and a roothouse was built at each location.

The foreman of the railroad crew where I was located was John Carlson, a self-made railroad man with a ready Scandinavian wit.

John Carlson was a short, stocky man, not boisterous, but he let the crew know who was boss. He carried himself well at all times. He was the serious type, did no kidding at any time, and did not expect to be kidded by others.

He and I had fun keeping track of a crew of Greek workmen who could not understand English, although they did understand John's calls for handling ties and rails. The names of these men were so long and complicated that we wrote them once on a time sheet, then issued numbers to each man which we used for keeping time and commissary charges.

The railroad crew was always composed of some good, experienced railroad men to help get the rail grades ready and to keep the ties and rails in order. Most of the railroad grades were made by station workers who got so much per 100' of grade to grub trees, level the grade ditch, and other clearing jobs; the work was all done by hand except where a cut or fill had to be made; then horses were used on slush or wheel scrapers.

Lawrence Wangard, who lived in Glidden, was steam shovel operator at that time. The railroad was laid in the McCarthy Creek, Brunsweiler River area and over toward Cayuga. Most of the present Chequamegon National Forest roads are now on those old railroad grades.

While I was clerking, I had an interesting experience. John Carlson, the foreman, was allergic to condensed milk, and because he was a good, steady foreman the company furnished a cow during the summer for his convenience. There was a bullcook, also known as chore boy or shanty boss, by the name of Jack Hamilton, who was caring for and milking the cow. One day, while splitting wood, Jack cut one hand real bad and there was no one to milk the cow. Having done some milking while living at Mineral Lake, I volunteered to do it -- and what a mistake. It was a big Holstein which gave about sixteen to eighteen quarts of milk to a milking. She was a hard cow to milk. The milk was so much like water, we had to put condensed milk in it to tell it was milk, but that cow furnished almost enough for the entire crew. Knowing Jack Hamilton, I believe he cut his hand on purpose. I know if the job had lasted much longer, I might not be writing this history now.

When the boarding cars closed for the winter, I started to get my real logging experience.

Bill Richardson was the foreman at Camp 6 of Mellen Lumber Company. Bill was the step-father of Clarence Carlson and Needa Carlson Shoveland. Clarence Carlson and I had been boyhood friends. Clarence had also left school and was driving team at Camp 6 for his dad. He told me to ask Bill for a job. Bill said okay -- to report at his camp when the cars closed on Saturday, November 1, 1913.

Bill Richardson was just the opposite to John Carlson. He was a freckled-faced man, medium height, of slight build. He was pleasant most of the time with an abundance of wit, which he could use in sarcastic terms when he thought the occasion deserved it.

Bill had a knack of using his wit to good advantage and could get a lot of work out of the crew without driving them.

He laid the work out well for the crew, then expected them to do their part. After the workday was over, he was just one of the crew.

In those days an inexperienced worker in a logging camp was given an axe, told to sharpen it and start work as a swamper, clearing out trails for horse teams.

The Sunday afternoon before I started to work, the foreman gave me a brand new four-pound double bit axe, as they were short of lighter ones. Most axes were three and one-half to three and three-fourth pounds. A fine, old hard-boiled lumberjack named Charles Ewoldt took a liking to me and said, "You turn the grindstone, I will hold the axe." Well, when we finished, I had a very sharp axe on both bits, but one side was not quite as sharp as the other. It would hold up better when cutting limbs from dry peeled hemlock logs which the crew was skidding to the railroad track for shipment to the J. B. Nash Paper Company (now the Nekoosa-Edwards Paper Company) at Port Edwards and Nekoosa, Wisconsin.

At that time a skidding crew consisted of two teamsters and teams, four swampers, and a tail-down man at the skidway at the railroad track, seven men in all. At Camp 6 there were five of those seven-man crews when I started to work. Each seven-man crew was expected to skid out two flat-car loads of logs each day. This would be from 75 to 100 logs for each team or from 6,000 feet to 7,000 feet (board feet) of logs on each car load or an average of 13,000 feet of logs for each skidding crew. This made a total of around 65,000 feet of logs per day. This was a very good average for a crew of that size.

In addition to the skidding crews, there was a crew of six men and two teams skidding out and loading hemlock bark onto cars which were shipped to tanneries for tanning hides.

There were eight or ten gangs of log cutters of two men to a gang. In addition, there were single contract workers cutting and skidding pulpwood, cedar, poles, ties, etc.

The crew at Camp 6 averaged around one hundred men.

Bill Richardson, the camp foreman, was one of the better all-around camp foremen that I have had the good fortune to work for, and believe me I have worked with and for some real characters.

Bill had a way of laying out the work for a crew so the men would have plenty to do, but at the same time, be able to do it. Other foremen I worked with would lay out more than he knew a crew could do, thinking he would get more work done that way. It would not work out that way, as the good men would get discouraged, and the mediocre men would not care, so the net result would be lower production. Bill knew how to talk to men with authority and he also knew when to use humor without losing the respect of the men.

On Monday morning, November 3, 1913, (I remember as well as if it were yesterday) Bill Richardson told me to go swamping for Clarence Carlson, who would tell me what to do. I followed Clarence out with his team and took instructions from him, although I knew enough about the work to make a start. Each teamster would put one of his swampers on a separate skidding trail. He would then make a trip with one or two logs from each swamper to the skidway on the railroad if railroad skidding, and on log road if decking for a sleigh haul.

After a couple of hours of work, Clarence said, "Now you take the team, as you have to learn how to take advantage of hooking onto logs so as not to get hurt. I know you will be driving team before long." To drive a team in those days was considered quite a promotion. It gave you prestige and generally a little higher wages. He didn't have to urge me. I took the team with a log from Clarence, who was swamping in my place, then I would get a log from the other swamper, then back to Clarence. To my horror, I found that Clarence had almost severed part of one foot with that sharp axe. We all pitched in to stop the flow of blood, applied a tourniquet to his leg, and carried him to the railroad track to be hurried to Mellen for a doctor's attention. It took eighteen stitches to close the cut.

"Well," I thought to myself, "guess that ends this job," as I was sure I would get my walking papers. But when Bill arrived, he said, "You're not to blame; it could happen to anyone. Take the team for the balance of the day. Take your time and be careful." He then gave me some instructions on skidding logs so as not to get hurt.

I finished the day driving team without incident and was very proud driving into camp that evening. It was a very good team. Of course, most all the companies had good big horses to enable them to do that kind of work. These horses were purchased from farms in the corn belt. They would weigh from 1,700 to 2,000 pounds. I spent the evening cleaning the horses and talking with the teamsters in the barn. If you didn't take care of the horses, you would not be a teamster very long.

The next morning I went back swamping, but only for the day, as the following morning a teamster wanted to have a few days off so I drove that team a few days. By that time another teamster wanted a vacation. At the end of two weeks, I had driven five different teams and Bill said, "Now you can drive this team steady as they are a good, steady, reliable team." They certainly were, and I was matched up with Ed Bidgood, a Mellen native and a good teamster and worker. We got along very well and would work our swampers so that we would get back to our long skidding as soon as possible. In that way, the steam loader would start to empty the skidways each forenoon when the railroad cars were spotted. Each skidding crew was expected to have the two skidways filled for the next day. By taking as much long skidding as you could, you would get back to your maximum distance, generally forty to fifty rods. Then if the loader was ahead of the loading schedule one day, you could take some of the short skidding. It was just a matter of work planning and was no problem when teamsters were working steady. Sometimes, though, teamsters only planning to stay a few days would try to grab off the short hauls, but Bill would be on to that kind of teamster in a hurry.

Bill Richardson, the foreman, was always ready to do a little joking at the right time, especially with the younger members of the crew. So when someone got a barb back on him, it was always enjoyed. One afternoon he looked through the bunkhouse and there were two new men sitting in the camp. Bill said, "I imagine you are looking for work." When they said, "Yes," Bill asked, "What kind of work do you prefer?" One said he generally drove team and the other said he liked to use a cant hook. "Okay," Bill said, and told the teamster to go out to the barn after supper and he would show him which team to take the next morning.

That evening all of us teamsters were cleaning and bedding our teams when Bill arrived with the new man, showing him the team. It was a good team, but one horse had a slightly large leg from an old injury. The man walked around the team a couple of times, then said, "It isn't a teamster you want for that team, it's a veterinarian," and went back to the camp. Needless to say, we all got a big kick out of it, even Bill who could take it as well as give it out.

Another time a young man working there said, "Gee, my whiskers are getting long and are affecting my face." Bill said, "I'm staying at camp this weekend, come into the office Sunday morning and I'll shave you." Sunday morning shortly after breakfast, the lad went over to the office. Richardson was ready. He set the fellow in a chair, lathered his face good, went to the drawer holding the shaving utensils, took a razor out, opened it up, then went to the stove pipe and starting stroking the razor up and down on the pipe. The fellow jumped up out of the chair, saying, "You're not going to shave me; you're crazy." He didn't know that Bill had two razors, one for paring corns and one for shaving. The lad didn't wait to find out either. Such incidents were common.

By working with the men in the woods and listening to them in the evenings, I began to understand and respect most of them as they were trying to help make the work easier for me and also trying to keep me from injuries.

After I had been driving team two or three weeks, I was going toward the skidway with a medium sized log when the end of the log caught a big tree root. It glanced over suddenly and knocked me down pinning one of my legs under the log. I hollered, "Whoa," and luckily the team stopped quickly. Since the ground was soft, my leg wasn't broken, but I was pinned. Ed Bidgood, the other teamster and skidway man, got a hand spike, raised the log a little so I could get the leg out. It hurt a lot but I told Ed and the other man not to tell the foreman or he might take the team away from me. They kept the secret long enough so that I didn't lose the team. The leg was sore, black and blue for a week, but no broken bones; I survived the first test.

There was a good crew of men at that camp, all willing to do their share and more, too. Harry Henneback was engineer on the steam loader with John Lundquist, top loader. Also, two hookers and a handyman helper, and a McGiffort jammer. This loader raised the wheels to let empty cars through. It was very heavy and had lots of power. It would load one end of a flat car with four bunches of logs. There were about nine logs to the bunch.

John Lundquist would always try to empty the skidways with each car. In the evening the teamsters would say, "You emptied our skidways today, but I bet you won't tomorrow." They would put extra logs on the skidway the next day. Most men were proud of their work.

Of course, in those days the only pastimes crews had were card playing, arguments on boxing, wrestling, and other sports, or horseplay. With the long hours out-of-doors, men didn't have much time for recreation in the evenings as the chore boy put the lights out at 8:00 to 8:30 p.m., and they were up at 5:00 a.m. Most men got enjoyment out of their work, if they got enjoyment at all. I often wondered at so many men following the woods work for steady employment. For some, it was enjoyment, and for others it was a necessity as they didn't have too much of a chance.

Around the first of the year in 1914, a funny little incident happened which showed how seriously some of the woods workers felt about their jobs. The ground was frozen and a little snow had fallen. The foreman wanted to get at some of the longer skidding left for just this kind of weather. He told Ed and I one morning to take out two small drays[1] with our crew to one of those locations where we put our swampers to work. Ed, the older teamster on the job, had the privilege of putting his team on the dray haul and I bunched the logs at a loading place. We looked for a fairly level spot with a little raise in the ground where we could spot a dray. We then rolled the first two or three logs

---

[1]The small round nosed dray used for this purpose was made by the wood butcher by cutting fairly small hardwood saplings with a natural crook in the roots, so the tow runners about four feet long would widen out to about forty-two inches.

onto the dray, then used spiked skids to roll one or two small logs on top. We then put on a wrapper. The dray team left an empty dray to be loaded while they took the load to the landing. By hauling on drays, the team made good time to the railroad so we had to hurry to have a load ready when they came back. The foreman and Ed had told me not to skid far as it was much easier to move the loading place than to skid an unreasonable distance. All went well for a few days, but then a swamper, August Roloff, got teed off when I told him we were moving to a new bunching place. He said, "You kids drive team a short time and then think you know it all. What do you know about a bunching place?" I said, in a calm tone and not smart-alecky, "Mr. Roloff, it doesn't take years to learn how to turn one of these drays around. If you have some objections to taking orders from me, tell the foreman; I'm just following his instructions."

You know, August was fine with me after that. In fact, he worked for me a lot when I got to be a camp foreman.

One weekend in the early part of January, 1913, a few of us young fellows decided to walk to Mellen after supper. It was a distance of about eight miles. Sunday afternoon Bill Richardson, the foreman, told one of the men that he and a few men had come to town on the pump-lever railroad handcar and our group could take it back if we wished as he was going to ride back with a few men from one of the other camps on another handcar. Although you could make a little better time with a handcar, it was hard work pumping one, especially on a frosted trail.

The two handcars were supposed to leave at the same time from Foster Junction, two and one-half miles from Mellen, but our group arrived on time and the other group was late. We waited a short time, but it was cold and since all were there to go on our handcar, we decided to pull out. It was a clear, cold moonlight night and the wild animals were on the move, especially timber wolves. When we passed English Lake, we heard a pack making a lot of noise and moving at a swift pace so we kept on the watch. We were sure they were chasing a deer. Sure enough, we had not gone far when looking back, we saw the deer cross the railroad track with one long jump. Right behind it came the pack of about twelve timber wolves. Only a minute or two later we heard them catch the deer as there was a terrible noise made first by the deer and then the wolves. I guess it has to be that way in the wild as all animals seem to have been put on this earth for a reason.

Often while working alone for days at a time in the wilderness, I would sit down on an old log or rock for a rest or lunch. My thoughts would wander about the trees, flowers, weeds, high ground, low ground, swamps, creeks, rivers, animals, birds, insects, etc. How could anyone think there isn't a Supreme Being?

The fall and early winter of 1913-1914 was unusual. There was very little snow. In fact, we walked in from camp to Mellen for Christmas kicking up dust all the way on the railroad track.

2

Move to New Company - Iron County

I drove team after Christmas until about January 20, when I received another break. While home one Saturday evening, I was approached by Otto Pearson, Office Manager for the Foster-Latimer Lumber Company. He asked if I was interested in a clerk and scaler position with the company. I had the early fall experience as a clerk but knew very little about scaling, but I had watched closely when logs were being scaled when I was driving team. I had ambitions to be a log scaler. Otto said it would give me a good chance to learn something about scaling logs. I always appreciated Otto's interest in me, as there were men with more experience looking for these jobs. I think some of Otto's interest was that he knew how hard my mother was working to make it go. I didn't let Otto down as I worked hard and long hours.

Otto Pearson had lost a hand in a mill accident at the age of eighteen, then went to business college at Wausau. Following this, he took employment in the Foster-Latimer Lumber Company at Mellen, where he worked up to a salesman and office manager.

It was necessary for me to go out to the Foster-Latimer Lumber Company camp as soon as possible so I walked out to Camp 6 of the Mellen Lumber Company on Sunday to get what clothes I had. I then walked back to Mellen -- about fourteen miles round trip.

On Monday morning around January 25, 1914, I reported at the Foster-Latimer Lumber Company office where I was met by Otto Pearson. He turned me over to Dan McDonald, the Woods Superintendent.[1]

Dan McDonald was a man of average size, very wiry with a sandy complexion and tough as they come.

[1]The Foster-Latimer Lumber Company officials at that time were George E. Foster, President; H. I. Latimer, Vice-President; E. J. Gilhooley, Sales Manager; Otto Pearson, Office Manager and Salesman; Andrew Pomeroy, Accountant; Fred Fuller, Timekeeper; Gertrude Earl, Office Secretary; Dan McDonald, Treasurer and Woods Superintendent; Joe Landry, Yard & Main Line Railroad Superintendent; Joe Jordon, Superintendent of Shop and Maintenance.

You could tell he came up through the ranks of the logging industry the hard way. He was a man of many moods and could change from one mood to another very fast.

He was very blunt or sarcastic at times. Underneath it all, he had a more sensitive side and would overlook faults of employees in his charge.

At Camp 29 Dan turned me over to George Taylor, the camp foreman. He was a very active man about forty years of age. He was short and well muscled and had no excess weight. A very good man with an axe or cant hook. He had heavy wavy hair prematurely gray.

One day a member of the train crew was kidding him about his gray hair. He answered, "You know a gray horse is just as good as a black or brown one."

We got along very well and I worked with him as a clerk and scaler, saw-boss and many other jobs over the next two years. With a crew of one hundred men to look after, George Taylor didn't have much time to spend on a clerk or scaler, so Dan told Aristo David, the "handy-andy" for Dan in the woods, to break me in. Aristo lived with his widowed mother in Mellen for a good many years. He helped his mother educate his brothers and sisters and he did well for himself with only a limited education. Aristo later became a good civil engineer.

David was a big help to me as he realized I was rather nervous and over-anxious to make good. He told me not to hurry and that if I got behind in my work, he would help me.

The instructions I had received from Bill Benninghouse, the log scaler, while driving team out at the Mellen Lumber Company camp began to pay off. Aristo could see I had received some basic instructions on scaling logs.

Even though I had grown up in the woods, I had not paid too much attention to the different species of trees. Of course, I knew hardwood or deciduous trees had leaves and conifers were trees with needles. I did know the conifers fairly well but would get mixed up sometimes on balsam and spruce after they were cut into logs and I could not see the needles. I also knew the maple and birch hardwood species fairly well.

Dan McDonald was one of the old-time timbermen having come up the hard way from woods worker to foreman, woods walking boss, to a partnership in logging and milling operation in the Newberry area of Michigan. When the Foster-Latimer Lumber Company went through a reorganization about 1910, they brought Dan in as a stockholder and woods superintendent -- a decision they never regretted. On the exterior Dan was rough and tough but after you got to know him you could see he had a more gentle side. It took me two years to get to know him. I wasn't around him much, only when he would stop once-in-a-while at the camp for dinner, or stop overnight to go over logging problems with his foreman.

The first two years, from January 1914 to April 1916, that I worked for the Foster-Latimer Company was a very depressed time in the timber industry. During that period I scaled logs in the daytime and in the evening did many things such as keep up time sheets, make out daily reports, sell wannigan supplies such as work clothing, shoes, rubbers, tobacco, etc. for the 100 to 150 men. In addition, I got the cook supply orders ready two or three times a week. We got up at 5:00 a.m., had breakfast at 5:30. In the early days the crew was turned out at 6:00 a.m. and they worked until 5:30 p.m. Supper was at 6:15 or 6:30 p.m. with lights out in the bunkhouses at 8:30. After World War I, camps let the crews leave the woods at 5:00 p.m. and they had supper at 5:30 or 5:45 p.m. When weather was too bad to work in the woods, I had time to catch up on the office work. Those hours were long -- eight to ten during the day and at least three hours in the evening. For this I was paid $35 per month and board, with board figured at about 40 cents per day. Thirty-five dollars per month divided by 26 days came to $1.346 plus 40 cents or roughly $1.75 per workday and I was glad to get it. It was not that I couldn't get another job, but better jobs were few and far between. Woods workers during some of that period were paid at a rate as low as $8 per month and board. Very few were paid that low however, because the foremen were ashamed to do it, but $12 to $16 per month, plus board, was a common wage from 1913 to 1915.

When I started to work in large logging camps, they were building more camps to hold up to 200 men. Of course, they were logging virgin pine. Most of the logging was carried on in the fall and winter season. It was a crash production.

I had seen some of those large camps of the pine days around Bibon and Mason before I started to work in the woods.

At the time I started to work in the woods, the only companies in this area with 200-man crews were the Stearns Lumber Company at Odanah on the Bad River and the Schroeder Lumber Company of Ashland, Wisconsin.

The Foster & Latimer Lumber Company, east of Mellen, and Mellen Lumber Company, west of Mellen and around Glidden, were building for about 100-man crews.

Those two companies were logging virgin hemlock and mixed hardwood, also cedar products, such as poles, shingle bolts, and posts.

With some variations, most all of the companies of that period built camps very much alike. When a company was able to build for a full two-year setup, they could build for more comfort.

The companies who had been logging virgin pine soon found out it was an entirely new situation to log hemlock and mixed hardwoods.

The virgin pine grew to a larger size, real tall trees, with not much underbrush. Pine was much lighter in weight than hardwood. A lot of stands of white pine would average three or four logs to the thousand feet. Hemlock and hardwood would more often run ten to twelve logs per thousand board feet. There was much more underbrush and small sapling trees in mixed hardwood stands.

White pine was more in demand in the forest industries for the building trade and therefore demanded a better price.

Many of the companies who had always been in the pine were unable to cope with the situation and closed very quickly. The companies who started out in the hemlock and hardwood timber were more successful as they made it a point to figure out the difference in the cost of the logging and milling. They knew they would have to cut cost corners wherever possible, in order to be successful.

The Foster & Latimer Lumber Company started out with a sawmill to cut conifer and mixed hardwood logs. Then added a planing mill soon after. The flooring factory was added a few years later.

The sawmill was built to cut an average of 75,000 feet per ten-hour shift of conifer logs or 40,000 feet of mixed hardwood logs. When sawing mixed hardwood and hemlock at the same time, an average would be about 50,000 feet per day.

The Foster & Latimer Lumber Company ran a well-managed organization from logging to the finished product.

The one place most all the large companies fell down on around 1910 was not looking far enough ahead. A few large companies were making plans to selectively cut their stumpage at that time. Some who did so are still in the lumber business. Looking back is always easier than looking ahead.

If the Foster-Latimer Lumber Company and the Mellen Lumber Company stockholders had looked ahead at that time, it was possible there would still be a good industry in Mellen. They had the stumpage to do so. Foster & Latimer did cut the larger percentage of their stumpage while the Mellen Lumber Company at Mellen and Glidden shipped out all of their logs.

Selective cutting would have made a tremendous difference for Ashland and Iron Counties.

I am not looking back to criticize, but I do like to look ahead, then try to do better the next chance I have. It is a good pastime at least.

A set of camps for logging was arranged a little different than boarding cars. There was not much difference in a kitchen, only larger, of course. The kitchen and dining room were in one building in camps.

A combination dish up table with drawers holding bread, pastry, pies, etc., separated the kitchen from the dining room. An opening was left in the center of the building to carry food to the tables.

The dining tables were placed lengthwise with two tables to hold up to 60 men each or three tables to hold 36 men each.

There was a roof ventilator over the kitchen and another smaller one over the dining room.

There also was a store room for kitchen supplies and a bedroom for the cook off the kitchen end of the building.

A meat screen house and a root-house would be built separate.

There were two or three sleeping shanties with a washroom on each end of the shanty.

There would be two large box or barrel-type heating stoves, with hot water barrels attached. Hot water was always available at meal time.

Sleeping conditions were not good in the old-time logging camps. It was beyond a doubt the worst part of the logging camps until around 1937. Imagine 60 men sleeping in one shanty with double bunks, two high, two men to a bunk. The bunks were end to end the full length of the sleeping part. A hallway was left open through the center of the building for stoves and walking.

Camp buildings were made of one tier of lumber covered with tar paper. The roofs had one tier of lumber with a medium heavy roofing paper to cover. The floors were one tier of hardwood boards only.

There were long poles on each side of the heating stoves, held with wire from the ceiling ridge poles. The poles could be used for drying mitts, socks, etc., when wet.

A nice bunch of heavy draft horses and large set of camps. I believe this is the last set of camps of the Mosinee Lumber Company or Underwood Veneer Co., at the border of Michigan and Wisconsin, Town of Oma.

Just imagine the wet mitt and socks perfume daily. Combine that with blankets, sometimes washed two times a year. All heavy rough cotton blankets were used. If you wished a sheet blanket, buy one!

Then to add a little more misery in the wintertime, two men in each bunk. The man next to the wall would be cold and the man on the inside would be too warm, especially near the stoves. The floors were always cold. I thought the upper bunks were better for winter.

I slept three months in one such camp, but I was lucky enough to get a bunk a medium distance from the stove.

To complete a large set of camps to be used for two years, additions would include a blacksmith shop, a barn for 10 to 15 teams of horses, a barn boss shack so the barn boss could keep spare harness parts and repair harnesses, lanterns, etc.

An office big enough to sleep four men, partitioned off so the time clerk could keep a plain set of books, keep work clothes, boots, shoes, tobacco, etc., to be sold to the men. It was a necessity to stock work clothes.

Sometimes a logging camp office would be called a wannigan (a word used more on the pine log drives). It would be on a large raft and follow behind the log drive.

An important service in a logging camp was the mail service in and out of camp. At least it was important to me. In camps where there was railroad logging, it was not a difficult problem. You had to expect mail to be at least one day late. The logging train would leave too early in the morning for that day's mail.

There were always a few men who worked steady for one company who subscribed to a daily paper. I was one of them. I subscribed to the Milwaukee Journal since 1918. Before that I believe it was the Milwaukee Sentinel. Other men would subscribe to different papers and all would exchange them.

I give daily newspapers credit for part of my education after quitting school in my sophomore year, April 1912, to work in the forest industry.

After my day's work was finished, I would read the newspapers through like a book, then go to bed. It would help me fall asleep quickly. It would help me keep up on news so I could talk on current events with visitors we would have at camp and others when in town. It also helped to keep up on grammar, which was much abused in camps.

I also studied mathematics and spelling.

Radios came into use shortly after I started to work in camps, but the battery situation did not lend to good radio service. It was in the 1920's before they were successful.

I take my hat off to the newspaper people. My wife and I subscribe to two daily newspapers and three weekly papers. Also, many magazines especially on forestry. I do not have time to read them as much as I would like. I do have quite a complete forestry library.

There were very few good hard roads, just tote roads to some of the camps where horse teams and farm wagons or sleighs were used to tote in the supplies. It was real tough going at times, especially during a wet season. Most of the existing lumber companies had privately owned railroads running into their timber holdings and were able to log winter and summer. They ran railroad branches into the virgin timber stands where the soil conditions would hold up train loads of logs and pulpwood. Sometimes they had to leave blocks of timber where ground was rough, hilly, or too swampy to build a railroad. In such cases, the logs were cut, skidded and decked on skids on a winter log road and later hauled by teams on large sleighs made for large loads on an ice road to a railroad landing.

The swamp timber was cut after the cold weather set in, skidded to log roads, and put directly on sleighs and hauled to railroad siding where they were loaded on railroad cars and delivered to the sawmills or to pulp and papermills. Some of the sleigh haul logs were decked on long roll ways at the landing to be loaded out during the spring breakup when it was impossible to skid logs in the woods. This was generally

A steam engine log hauler used extensively in northern Michigan and Minnesota on long sleigh hauls. Not used much in Wisconsin; horse teams on ice roads were much more economical.

from the middle of March to the middle of May or first part of June. In the summer they were able to cut and skid directly to the well-built railroads on higher and more solid ground, loading directly onto railroad cars with steam loaders. At the time I first started to work in the woods, the only machine equipment used were steam loaders, steam shovels, and steam skidders, in addition to the railroad steam engines. Steam skidders were few in the hardwood forests of Wisconsin. They were more generally used in the large timber of the west. A few steam haulers were used for pulling sleighs in the more level land of northwestern Wisconsin and Minnesota, but they were never a great success. Eventually gasoline tractors were used with more success.

The cook at Camp 29 when I started to work was George Killarney. He was a big Polish man who had changed his name from Kilarski to Killarney a few years previously when he was cooking for a railroad building crew. The crew was made up of almost all Irishmen and he got along so well with them that he had his name changed to Killarney. After getting well acquainted with him, I could understand why as he was full of deviltry at all times.

I will never forget one of Killarney's April Fool jokes. Charles Johnston and Fred Bowers of Mellen had a bark skidding and loading job at the camp. They were seated at the table at a set-up which included George Taylor, the foreman, John Pollock, the hoister, Hans Wagner and myself. While making pancakes that April Fool's Day morning, Killarney decided to cut some cheese cloth in the shape of pancakes which he placed between two thin pancakes after browning one side. No one could tell the difference by looking at the dish of pancakes. We all took two pancakes on our plates, applied the syrup or bacon grease, or both, then each took our knives and fork to take a bite, but we could not cut them. Well, George Taylor and I thought about April Fool's Day at once so kept quiet until the other four men had tried theirs. We all had a good laugh. Then the cookee brought a dish of regular pancakes which we would not touch so we were fooled the second time.

At noon time we went back in to dinner not thinking the cook would spend extra time to fool us again, but I guess we didn't know him well enough. All went well for the main meal and then he put in front of us a nice looking apple pie. George Taylor was through with his regular meal first and took a piece of pie only to find out it had a heavy dose of red pepper in it. He didn't say a word until the rest of us had taken a bite. By that time, the cook could stand it no longer and stepped out the back door where he was doubled up laughing. Taylor took his piece of pie in his right hand and slapped it to the back of Killarney's neck. Needless to say, the crew had a lot of enjoyment that noon.

The cook put another pie at our set-up, but again no one would touch it. By that time a lot of other men in the crew wouldn't touch the pie either so he didn't have to make many pies the next day. He was a great morale builder around camp.

One of the cookees at Camp 29 at the time was Steve Ferkovich, a sixteen year old, slim, red-headed lad who had just come over from Yugoslavia to make his home with Joe Ferkovich who had a boarding house on Division Street in Mellen. Steve couldn't speak English when he first arrived, but he was very alert and smart so learned quickly. Steve said when the cook wanted him to get a can of vegetables or fruit from the warehouse, he would give him an empty can with a picture on it.

Steve first worked as a swamper and then tried driving team, but he had his eye on a kitchen job all the time so when a vacancy showed up in the kitchen, George Taylor gave him a chance. It worked out well as George Killarney could understand and speak Steve's language some and helped him get a good start by teaching him the cooking trade. Steve got to be a good cook in a few years and cooked for the Foster-Latimer Lumber Company most of the time until they closed operations in 1933. In fact, he cooked at their last camp, Camp 49, near Gurney.

Steve took his first cook's job in one of the Mellen Lumber Company camps in 1915 or 1916, when he replaced George Padjen of Mellen who had taken the job of cook at Lake Galilee for the Mellen Unit of the Wisconsin National Guard just before World War I. Steve was eighteen years old at the time. He says he baked at night in order to make good, so was a cook from then on.

When I started to work at Camp 29 near Mellen, there was a crew of about 100 men. In May when the hemlock bark peeling season started, another 50 men were added. There were many tanneries in Wisconsin until the mid-twenties, including a large one in Mellen. The tanneries had to have hemlock bark for the tannic acid that could be extracted from it. [1]

Bark peeling, therefore, was a very important job from around 1900 until about 1925, when other chemicals began to be used for tanning hides.

The tannery at Mellen employed around three hundred men at one time. There were tanneries at Lugerville, Medford, Phillips, Prentice, Rib Lake, and Tomahawk, in this general area. Only bark peeled from hemlock trees was used in Wisconsin and Michigan, although much oak and chestnut bark was used for tanning in the northeastern United States in the early 1900's.

During the bark peeling season, usually from mid-May to mid-August, unless a hot, dry summer caused a shorter season, the sap runs freely through the trees making it easy to peel the bark.

Hemlock bark peeling was all hand labor. The men worked alone or in two-man gangs. It was all piece work, so much a cord for the bark and so much a foot for cutting the logs. When the demand was up for hemlock bark, the company didn't let the job of cutting logs until after the peeling season was over. The men felled the trees with either a one-man or a two-man saw. Some good axe men felled trees by chopping,

[1]See addendum on tanneries at the end of the book.

using only the axe and no saw. The bark was cut in four-foot, four-inch lengths. The men ring-cut around the tree with the axe at the desired length and split a straight line lengthwise on the tree through the bark. Then they took a bark spud, a sharp rounded cutter blade with a twelve to eighteen-inch handle, which could be managed with one hand. They helped move the sheet of bark with one hand and used the spud with the other hand. They often wished they had two more hands to fight off flies and mosquitoes. I have honestly seen mosquitoes so bad that you could hardly tell if a man had a shirt on or not. Some people ask how the men stood it. It is a good question. You just had to become immune to them. Some homemade lotions helped, such as pine tar and lard. Skunk grease was good too. Later there began to be some patented fly dope available. It took real men to peel bark successfully in those days.

The bark peelers worked long hours and earned their money. When the bark dried, which took about twenty-four hours in dry weather, they put it in piles of one, or three-quarter, or one-half cords. If trees were scattered, the company allowed one-quarter cord piles if piled two feet wide and four feet high. Bark peelers were required to pile the larger piles where trees were thick as it was much better for the bark to keep out the rain or snow and easier to get a jumper load when skidding.

In order to preserve bark it was necessary to place good skids on the ground to pile the bark on, and good end sticks to keep the pile straight up and down. It was always piled with the rough side up as the cambium, the tissue between the bark and the wood, was what was needed to make acid in the tanneries. When piling bark it was necessary to lay out the wider and unbroken sheets until finishing the pile, then put a couple of layers of the good sheets for top cover. When bark was piled right, it would keep a long time. In fact, I know where there are some bark piles from the early 1920's, which escaped the forest fires that are in fairly good shape today.

It was very important that the camp foreman and bark scaler watch bark peeling closely as the peelers were paid by the cord and the company was paid by weight when sold.

Bark peelers were required to pile the bark four to six inches over the four foot high and eight foot long pile to be scaled as a full cord, the smaller piles had to be scaled in the same way. It was also necessary to see that the bark didn't get too dry before piling or the thinner sheets would curl and be like a stove pipe. When piled, it might be four feet high but would only contain about two feet of bark.

Good bark peelers took pride in doing a good job and generally had a little extra bark in the pile. In those days, if the bark scaler was a fair man, the expert peeler might get a little extra to his credit, but the poor bark peeler would have to be docked according to condition of the pile. There were always some workers, then as now, who figured they could outsmart the foreman or scaler by piling around a stump or rock or by camouflaging in some way. Once in a while they would get by with it.

I remember one case of very good camouflage which I saw at Mellen Lumber Company Camp 6, when I was driving team in the fall of 1913. Charles Leighton, who many old timers around Mellen will remember as running a livery stable and dray line in Mellen, had a bark skidding and loading job at Camp 6 that fall and winter. One night he said to Bill Richardson, the camp foreman, "Come out where we are skidding bark tomorrow morning; I want to show you something." Bill went out there and the bark piles where they were skidding all looked perfect. Charles took Bill over to a bark pile and took off the top two or three tiers of good bark. You could look down to the ground. The bark peelers had piled good bark on the pile top but had broken bark piled in short pieces on each side. It looked to me as though it probably took as much time and work to camouflage the pile as it would have to do it right, but they outsmarted someone. It was a good lesson to me because after that it was always my job to scale and look after bark peelers. Some summers I scaled as much as three to four thousand cords of bark. I would be a taller man today only I wore off a few inches walking from pile to pile during those seasons.

Bark peeling is a lost art today, though some hand peeling of aspen or poplar for pulpwood is still being done. The bark, however, is just waste and a fire hazard. It is peeled off the easiest way and left on the ground. The paper mills prefer the peeled pulpwood as it saves on freight charges and can be kept in piles to be used in the winter season when wood is frozen and bark comes off hard.

During that first winter at Camp 29, the Foster-Latimer Lumber Company didn't have much railroad built. The winter of 1913-1914 was a fine winter for logging -- not too much snow. They wanted to get all the logs they could out of the woods.

There was a fair sized ravine east of the camp with a nice slope on the south side so Dan McDonald decided to extend the railroad branch past the camp into the ravine. Since it was mid-winter he didn't try to lay the steel then, but he knew he could in the spring. However, he and the foreman decided to dray logs the balance of winter and to deck by hand off the slope on the south side of the proposed railroad spur, then load onto cars after the railroad was built. It worked like a charm and almost 500,000 feet of logs were decked there by spring with a very cheap decking cost. One man did most of the log decking with what help I would give him. I scaled the logs, and decking was a good way to keep warm.

A tall, thin Scotchman, Harry Frost, was the one man decking the logs and what a man he was with a cant hook! A good wind from the front or back would have blown either one of us over, but a wind from the side would likely miss us. Harry Frost could make the rolling of logs easy with a cant hook. He would have the first dray loads come in the low part of the slope the length of the landing, then would have drays come in higher up and use small hardwood saplings to roll out over the first bottom on the rollways. It was really a work of art and by spring, I too was able to do a fairly good job with a cant hook. To this day, I have not forgotten how to do it.

When the camp broke up in the spring around March 15, I got my first responsible log scaling job. A contract logger by the name of Tom Nephew owned a piece of timber near where he lived west of Highway 169, across from where the Richard Kretzschmar farm is located. The main line Foster-Latimer Railroad crossed that area. If you look closely while car riding, you are still able to see some of the old railroad grade.

I used to pump one of the track speeders to and from work a distance of about eight miles one way. It was on this scaling job that my bosses found out whether I was learning anything about the value of logs. Using a log scale rule is simple, but to know how much to deduct for rot, crook, and other defects, judgment has to be used. Although I still had a lot to learn, I made the grade. One old, witty lumberjack said to me one day, "You should have a lot of judgment because you never use any" -- good-natured banter. That was sixty-two years ago in March and I'm still learning something about logs and growing new crops of trees. It never loses its interest for me.

After the spring breakup, I clerked and scaled at the same logging camp all summer and another winter, so you can imagine what kind of timber was on those lands. That camp averaged a million feet of logs a month or ten million feet a year for two years.

Topics of conversation in those early days in logging camps were the condition of the United States, new trends in the log and lumber industry, the Workmen's Compensation Law, which turned out to be a very big gain for the woods worker, and other new laws that were pending.

Newspapers were scarce but some of the office crew would always subscribe to a daily newspaper which would be passed on to the bunkhouse where it would be worn out in handling.

One topic was the center of conversation. The winter and spring of 1914 was Henry Ford's proposal that he was going to raise all his factory workers to a $5 per day rate for a ten-hour day. This was really exciting as general hourly wages were running in the $.18 to $.30 an hour bracket in the woodworking industry.

Henry Ford was ridiculed and laughed at by many intelligent people with remarks such as "Henry Ford, who has been a success up until now, has finally found a way to go broke."

The companies tried to build camps so crews wouldn't have to walk much over a mile to the cuttings. Quite often, though, you had a corner or block of timber where you walked a mile and a half one way. The camp location where they had summer and winter logging generally was planned to log four sections of timber, which averaged around five to six million board feet to the section.

I remember one extremely fine 40 of hemlock and mixed

hardwood, with considerable yellow birch, which Dan McDonald wanted scaled separately to see what it would cut. It was on the southwest side of what is known to this day as Casey Sag. I had the privilege to scale and keep track of what was cut off of that 40 acres. It was an unbelievable 900,000 feet of about equal hemlock and hardwood. Not many 40's would yield that much. Where there was mostly all hemlock, some 40's might cut more.

Where a logging camp was both for summer and winter logging, it was generally a two-year location. When located for winter logging only, it sometimes was for one year. The winter camps were generally all sleigh haul camps with a railroad to the landing, so the forest products could be loaded on cars for delivery to the sawmill, tannery or main line railroad. In this case, it was at Mellen, Wisconsin.

When I started to work, the Foster-Latimer Lumber Company railroad crew was made up as follows:

The main line crew, daily out of Mellen, was composed of Joe Taylor, engineer; Mert Taylor, fireman; and August Anderson, conductor. In the winter when there was lots of switching, snow plowing, etc., the crew would have an extra brakeman. During the first winter, he was Fred Martin of Mellen. The No. 1 engine at that time was a large rod-driven engine. It was a very good all-around locomotive, and the crew got a lot of work from it.

The company had two other Lima locomotives (gear driven), a two-spot and a three-spot. The three-spot was a fairly large locomotive geared up for slow speed and capable of pulling heavy loads over steep grades or rough land. It was used for building railroads and pulling car loads of forest products off branch railroads.

The main line was always kept up in good shape, as the rod engine would have to speed up at times in order to pull a full string of cars over some grades. It was impossible to get railroads into Gurney, Saxon, Rouse, Upson and Iron Belt, without some steep grades even on the main line.

The branch lines or spur tracks were something else. They were run into areas of heavy timber on as high ground as possible in order to have a good solid railroad bed without too much cost. The branch lines were only used for a short time, much the same as truck roads are now used in logging, but the timber was much larger and the stands were thicker. The branch lines would be used for summer logging. The timber would be cut and skidded to the tracks with horses, then loaded onto cars. The old No. 3 Lima locomotive came in handy on these branch lines. It could crawl across swamp or low lands where the railroad bed would be reinforced by blocking up with long cull logs. At times the rails were from six to twelve inches under water, but the old three-spot crawled right along with her one-, two-, or three-car load of logs. The cars were set out on a side track. Then the engine went back for more to make up a full train on the main line.

The two-spot was a little handy-Andy, a very small compact locomotive used mostly for spotting the tie and rail cars when laying steel or picking up rails and ties from branches already logged. It was also used for hauling gravel from gravel pits for ballast on the railroad grades.

One incident happened that summer of 1914 which comes to my mind whenever I drive over that fire lane road from Rouse to the Tyler Fork River or to Gurney. I drive it often, especially in the fall. It is a real wilderness. Not a person living in around a twelve-mile square area. There are many scenic spots and some good fishing and hunting.

On this particular day the two-spot crew, Charles Hawkinson and John Stoltz, had spotted three gravel cars on a sand or gravel pit where the steam shovel was making a cut for the railroad to go through. I had been out scaling logs on skidways on another branch and decided to go into camp for a lunch. While crossing the main line, railroad on a raise just east of Camp 29 Creek[1], I could see the two-spot taking water out of the 29 Creek. At about the same time I heard a rumbling noise up the track to the east. I was aware that there was no railroad engine up that way so it came to me at once that those gravel cars had gotten away from the steam shovel site. I waved my arms and hollered as both Charles and John were outside the engine. Luckily, they heard me and jumped on the engine and started it up. Those three gravel cars had traveled on a down grade for a mile by then and were really moving when they passed me. One gravel car was loaded, the second half loaded, and the third was empty. They caught up to that engine before it could get moving in high gear, but it did have some momentum so that when the cars hit it was not like hitting something solid. The half empty car and the empty jumped off the rails a full car length then back to the rails, but of course, not onto the rails. The crew members were not hurt, but the crash did bend the frame on the engine. It was lucky the crew got that engine moving or without a doubt, they would have been covered with gravel.

At noon time the two engine crews were talking about it when Fred Martin spoke up saying, "Oh, I've received worse kicks on the seat while growing up!"

One mile up the main line east from Camp 29, the company decided to have two main lines, one to the southeast for a few miles, then more directly east to get over in the Rouse, Upson Lake, Alder Creek, Upson, Weber Lake, and Iron Belt area. This main line followed the Potato River Valley fairly close and crossed the river three times, keeping north of the Penokee Range and south of Copper Peak, a part of White Cap Mountain. The railroad ended on the southeast shore of Weber Lake.

[1]Now known as Vought Creek; named after Wren Vought who, after the logging days were over, bought some land on the creek and farmed for a time.

The following logging camps were located and serviced by this main line or its branches: Camps 33, 34, 35, 36, 37, 38, 39 and 40. The boarding cars were used for railroad building in summer and winter sleigh haul or landing camps in the winter.

The forest area covered by this main line and its branches was very rough. It took good engineering in building the railroads and good logging know-how to get the timber products out and still show a profit.

The company decided to build this main line through the Town of Anderson, into the Town of Knight first rather than into Gurney and Saxon, because the assessors in the towns of Anderson and Knight, on orders from the town boards, were starting to boost the tax rate on timber lands much higher than in the towns of Gurney and Saxon. In addition, this area presented a much harder logging chance, due to the rough, hilly terrain and the heavy snow belt in these towns. The company did some serious thinking and decided to log the towns of Anderson and Knight first.

It was necessary for the company to take all those obstacles into consideration because before World War I there were no large profits in logging and milling hemlock and hardwood timber. Many companies which had been logging and milling pine found this out when they went into the hemlock and hardwood business.

This is the reason a few blocks of hardwood timber were left on the Copper Hill divide which runs on both sides of Weber Lake on east to the town road which runs north and south from Hoyt to Kimball.

It was almost a miracle that those blocks of timber missed the forest fires of the late '20's. In the fall of 1947, a forest fire did go through some of it, but with the better forest fire equipment, it was possible to contain the fire.

Where the main line left going southeast, there was a dip in the terrain with a steep grade on the south side for a railroad to go over. It was the only good chance to get a railroad into a heavy timber stand. It was decided that the steepest grade to be used was taking the empty cars in with the lighter grade going out with the loads. So the work on the fill and cutting the hill as much as possible without making the hill steeper was undertaken.

As the work progressed, a new long square timber had been placed to set the switch stand on where the switch was put in to make the turn off to the sag. About this time, a fine old-time kitchen hand by the name of Ed Casey, who had been working in the kitchen at Camp 31, above Foster Falls, decided to take a vacation and just before coming back to the camp had celebrated a little too much at Mellen. The train crew brought him up the next morning and left him off at this switch while they did some switching before going into Camp 31 for dinner. They thought Casey would walk into camp to sober up a little, but when the train got through switching and came back, there was Ed Casey stretched out on the switch stand face up to the sun -- sound asleep. That place has been known as Casey Switch and Casey Sag since that summer of 1914. I am going to ask the Iron County Board of Supervisors to put a marker at this spot. A fire lane road branches off here which follows the old main line railroad east across Highway 122 toward Kimball.

During June or July, 1914, there was a spectacular incident at Camp 7 on the Mellen Lumber Company Line.

This trestle crosses the Brunswieler River in a rough low area in the vicinity of the Louis and Martin Hanson estate on French Lake and Brunswieler River - 1920.

The camp was located on the Brunswieler River near the Walenek homestead. The crew at Camp 7 was peeling bark and summer logging. On a very hot day, a sudden thundershower moved in, just as the teams were coming in for the noon meal.

Pat Hickey, a midget teamster but a good one, who had been badly crippled in a sleigh log hauling accident a few years earlier, was driving a team skidding logs. As Pat was crippled so badly, the foreman would allow him to ride one of the horses to and from work. Ordinarily teamsters were not allowed to ride the horses. The water trough was on the riverbank, so when it was hot some of the teamsters would let the horses walk into the river to wash and cool off their legs. This day, Patty drove his team into the river just as the electric storm hit. A bolt of lightning hit the horse he was riding. The horse was killed instantly, but Patty was only shaken! His being so short paid off that time as people experienced with lightning say if one of his feet had touched the water, he, too, most likely would have been killed.

The bolt of lightning then traveled along the ground entering one open door of the men's camp, followed through the center of the room under the stove and out the other door, without doing any harm. I know it happened, as do many others around Mellen and Marengo, Wisconsin.

Patty Hickey was as game a little man as you could find. He had that extremely crippled leg, but still he drove team, skidding logs in the summer when he was covered with mud from head to foot. When the team hit a mudhole and he was unable to throw the lines and get out of the way, he held tight on the lines and let the team drag him through the mud puddle.

Some foremen tried to make a barn boss out of Patty, figuring it would be easier for him, but he was so grouchy and had such a nasty tongue he could never get along with the teamsters in the barn. He had to make his living the hard way, which goes to show that you cannot change human nature. I guess that is why we cannot stop wars.

One of the many extra jobs Aristo David was doing at that time was taking care of the company telephone line from the Mellen office to the camps. It was also connected for ringing the central telephone office at Mellen in case of accident, emergencies, or troubles of any kind. It was quite a chore taking care of the line, as very often trees or branches broke or crossed the wires.

One evening Aristo knew something was wrong with the lines so he jumped on the two-seat, bicycle-foot track-speeder he and I had for getting home on weekends or to attend some special event in Mellen. While he was gone, George Taylor, the camp foreman; Frank Simmonds, another Mellen man who was clerking at Camp 30; and myself fixed up a trap to catch Aristo on his return. A pail of water and some old stove pipes were fixed up and hung on the door so they would be tripped when the door opened.

Without knowing of the trap, Dan McDonald, the woods superintendent, had gotten off the train this particular night at one of the other camps where he stayed for supper, then decided to go on to Camp 29. We had just gone to bed when we heard footsteps. Naturally, we thought it was Aristo. When the door opened, down came the water and stove pipes and we heard a loud exclamation: "Cripers, what is going on here?" Of course, we were stuffing blankets in our mouths to keep from laughing. Then just in time Aristo showed up. Dan said, "Where have you been?" Aristo said, "I was out working on the telephone line." Dan knew then the trap had been set for Aristo. In the morning he joked about it with the rest of us.

There was one more incident at Camp 29 which amused me at first, then a short time later it was not so funny. The Foster-Latimer Company had a reputation for being one of the best when it came to boarding their crews. To do that it had to have good cooks most of the time. But in the spring of 1914, the good cook who had been there all winter decided to spend a summer out of the woods. The company got one replacement who was okay for a while, but left because he decided there was too much work for the salary he was paid. The company then heard of a cook in Ashland. This fellow could cook some but was extremely sloppy (no other description fits). To make matters worse, it was a hot summer, and that was always a bad time to change cooks. Dan McDonald was trying to get a good cook, but it took some time. Some of the crew started talking about a lynching party and were really getting the crew worked up to where I believe something would have happened, when a new cook arrived. If it had been a summer when it was easy to get a job, there would have been no problem as the crew would have quit before making trouble, but at that time there were two or three men for each job.

3

Move to New Camp

My next move was to Camp 31 on the Potato River after Camp 29 finished its cut in the spring of 1915. This was a dandy campsite, and I enjoyed my time in this camp as tops. The office and kitchen were built one on each side of the track on the riverbank near where the bridge crossed the river, with the balance of buildings back a short distance. The soil was a sandy loam with good drainage and was never very muddy. The water drifted by in the river over rocks at a medium speed before going over the falls just far enough away as not to make too much noise. The water rippling by along with the slight sound of water going over the falls made for excellent sleeping conditions.

Another thing, the Foster-Latimer camps were blessed with good drinking water as the Penokee Range country is noted for its famous spring water although some cities and towns still put up with terrible drinking water. The area from the Tyler Forks River, from east of Gurney one mile, covering the east half of T. 46N-RIW, all of T. 46N-RIE, T. 45N-RIE and T. 45N-RIW in the towns of Anderson, Gurney, Knight, Kimball and Saxon were especially blessed with excellent water. The people in that area should keep on the alert so those nice fresh water creeks, streams and lakes never become polluted.

There are two exceptionally fine flowing springs in the area. One is near the section line of Section 1 and Section 12, Township 45N-RIW, Town of Anderson in Iron County, near where a railroad bridge crossed the Potato River. At the time Foster-Latimer laid the steel, the spring was located seeping out of a solid rock ridge. They laid some pipe where the main stream was coming on the ridge to the railroad just high enough so the water could run into water tanks on flat cars if so desired or anyone could stop with a can, jug, pail and get some of that fine water. That was 59 years ago and while hunting in that area two years ago, I found some of the old pipe which had been separated from excessive water run-off and rust, but the water is still running. A scenic trail could well be made through that area.

The other flowing spring is on County E, just before arriving at the Iron County Park on Weber Lake shore, near the entrance to a marked walking trail running from Weber Lake to near Montreal north of Alder Creek and Hoyt. That one I know has been flowing at least 59 years. The waters south of the Iron Belt Mountains run into Alder Creek.

The years of 1914 and 1915 were bad years in the timber industry. They did not call them depression or recession years, just plain "hard times." Log, lumber and pulpwood markets were very slack which made it tough for the woods worker. When the mills were not running, more men went to the woods. There were no unemployment checks or relief stations, or widow pensions either. Workmen's compensation started around 1910 or 1911 with very small payments, however.

All the larger log and lumber companies were operating as much as possible as it was almost impossible to shut down entirely. There were so many men traveling looking for work that the companies were afraid the men walking around would set fires and burn out the camps and the timber. For this same reason the companies fed the job seekers.

It was not unusual to have a crew of 60 to 125 men and have that many meals extra in a day, most always for supper and breakfast. The camp cook would let the crew eat supper first and then let the extra men come in to a meal of soup, potatoes, vegetables and bread. For breakfast the cooks would give them pancakes and cooked cereal. No complaints, they were glad to get it. Some very good men were walking around who really preferred to work. Of course, they would have to sleep wherever they could find room. It was really rough and many times we all felt very sorry, especially in cold weather, but there were not as many traveling in the winter. They just could not take the chance and would jungle up near the cities or towns where they could sleep in saloons, jails, city or town halls. I hope we never see times like that again, but it was almost as bad in the 1931 to 1935 era, but they had free eating centers then.

One morning after the crew had gone out to work, a fine, well-built man stopped at the office and said to the foreman, "Are you able to use one man? I do not care what kind of a job." It had just so happened that the bull cook, or chore boy, had wished to go to town as he had been in camp fourteen months without leaving and sure deserved a vacation. The foreman told the new man, Frank Martinus, he could use a chore boy. Frank said that it was fine as he felt sure he could do the work. He surely did, as he was the best chore boy I had seen up until that time. But he was too good a man to keep at that job. It turned out that he had been a wire rope splicer in the mines out west. He was a good man wherever they placed him and ended up as a steam jammer engineer and worked for the company until they finished operations in 1933. He then worked at Marenisco for the Boniface Lumber Company and the Kimberly-Clark Corporation until his death a few years ago.

Another incident in summer of 1915 was very funny to me. The Mellen Cedar Company had a crew of men at the old Foster-Latimer Lumber Company Camp 23 near the Tyler Falls on the Tyler Fork River. The camp had broken up in March with only five or six men left at camp to peel cedar poles and posts and to load out some other forest products.

"Shorty" Baatz was camp foreman and was also doing some blacksmith and wood work while the crew was small. He was a short, stocky, well-muscled man; a little bow-legged, always pleasant, with a lot of humor.

He was a blacksmith by trade and did not care about being a foreman.

The Mellen Cedar Company did not need a full-time blacksmith so they pressed the foreman job onto him. With blacksmith jobs hard to get, Shorty took the combined job. It took a man like that to get along at the Mellen Cedar Company camps.

One of the cookees had stayed on to do the cooking for the small crew. In June, Oscar Anderson, the cedar company superintendent, decided to put on more men. He told Shorty, the foreman, to plan on about twenty additional men. "Okay," Shorty said, "but you better send some supplies and a cook first." Oscar said that a cook was on the way from Duluth and that he would see to the supplies at once. Oscar, being a little forgetful, didn't get the supplies up to camp at once, but the cook did show up the next day at noon so the cookee wished to go to town right away. Some of the new men also showed up making it worse.

The cook put out some supper with what kitchen supplies he had, then told Shorty that there was nothing to cook. Shorty said that he was sure the supplies would arrive by the next noon and that he should do his best with what he had. The next morning the cook went out to the barn, got a pail of oats, made coffee, put a little oats on each plate, set a pot of coffee on the table, put his coat on, blew the breakfast horn, and then took off out the back door down the track. The crew came in, took one look at the table and said, "Shorty, we cannot do much work on this meal." Shorty, being a humorous guy himself, took one mouthful of oats and said, "Gee, it's not so bad at that! No wonder horses can work so hard on hay and oats!"

Shorty did not turn the crew out that day. The supplies did arrive at noon the next day with a new cook too, so all was well again.

It was a great era to be working in logging camps as 90% of the crew were very capable men. Many were well qualified to handle better jobs, but it was a case of making a living or keep on the tramp.

During the summer of 1915, Camp 31 was used as a railroad logging operation. There were some rough logging chances along the Potato River, but there was always a way of entering the rough area with short branches up the ravines. Once in a while a kick-back branch was used in order to get away from the main line without wasting areas with branch spurs too close to each other. Much of the timber in that area was good mixed hardwood species which was what the company liked at that time, although, they did saw some of the good hemlock into lumber occasionally. Camp 31 turned out about 50,000 feet of logs per day on a six-day week with only a little loss of time when there was too much rain. It averaged about 1,000,000 feet per month during that summer with about 70% mixed hardwood and 30% hemlock.

The author, George A. Corrigan, 21 years old. Helping to load out logs with a Cody Steam Loader. This was in 1917 at Camp 34, 2 miles north of Rouse in Iron County for the Foster-Latimer Lumber Company of Mellen, Wisconsin.

The logs were all cut with cross-cut saws, and horses did all the skidding. A Cody steam loader was used for loading the Russell cars.[1] A Cody loader was built on car wheels with an extra track with inclines on each end of the loader with space enough for the empty cars spotted behind the loader to be pulled through with a cable on a drum and a tackle block. The engine and boiler room were in a room built over the empty space where cars were pulled through. The boom protruded out and up to forty-five to fifty feet in length in an A-shape with a good heavy block at the end of the boom. The Cody loader was built for speed and for loading cars without stakes, using corner binds and wrappers of chain or cable.

A crew on a Cody loader had to work together in a speedy, accurate manner with good foot and arm coordination in order to get

[1] A Russell car was a special car made by the logging companies with a frame of two 24' long stringers and two 8' long bunks so as to load one tier of logs up to 20' long with regular wheels as used by all railroad companies. The Russell cars used by the Foster-Latimer Co. were made to use only hand brakes with a ratchet wheel and a hammer-like piece of good steel, with a head to fit the ratchet so brakemen could tighten. It helped some but was not real effective.

good results. The engineer or hoister had to be very alert as those long booms and the engine room up high, the engineer would have to watch when traveling in gear so the booms would not catch tree limbs up high or hit an uneven spot suddenly on the rail bed. There were many such spots, especially on the railroad branches where they crossed swamps and rough terrain. A large log, if not handled properly, could tip the loader. The top-loader also had to be a man of skill, especially when the engineer was not an expert, as he had to build those loads up three or four tiers high before putting the first wrapper around the center of the load. He would then build up another tier or two before putting on two more wrappers, one on each end of the load, then put enough logs on top of the wrappers to keep those wrappers tight. Some top loaders used gin poles.[1]

The crew on summer loading or railroad loading where the machine moved from skidway to skidway would be made up as follows: engineer, top loader, bull cook and two hookers. The cable would have a crotch on the loading end where two separate pieces of cable about 10' long would be attached to a swivel hook with loading hooks attached separately. These hooks had sharpened points to grab and hold when placed on the end of each log. The loading on unstaked cars was done with one log hooked at a time and only when a lot of small logs were being loaded would the hookers sometimes wrap the cable around two or three small logs.

A crew of this size, traveling to 12 - 15 different skidways in a day, would load from 12 - 15 carloads of logs, running from 3,500 feet to 4,500 feet on each car. This would run 40,000 feet to 50,000 feet per day which was considered a day's run for one shift at the mill sawing mostly hardwood. If sawing hemlock or pine, they would load the cars heavier and load up to 75,000 feet in one day. When loading that heavy, an extra man would be added to help keep up the loading pace, as that would be a lot of logs for two men to hook in a day. The extra man, called bull cook[2] would change off with the two hookers.

The bull cook was a busy man on a loading crew also as he had to see the empty cars all had the proper corner binds and wrappers with tightener, place the cable on empty cars to "sluice" the empties through the loader, see that the brakes were set on the loaded cars and sometimes block the wheels when the crew was loading on an incline.

The Foster-Latimer Lumber Company was fortunate in having some very good loading crews. All the foremen knew that it was necessary to have a successful logging crew as there would be no use to have a

[1]A gin pole would be a good strong hardwood stake 12' to 15' high placed upright on side of car opposite the skidway side. Generally used in loading large loads onto sleighs.

[2]The word, bull cook, was used for a helper around a steam loader crew. He performed the same work as a chore boy did around a cook camp kitchen.

real good cutting and skidding crew, then not get the logs loaded. It was necessary to get the skidways cleared on time so the skidding crews could produce their quota of logs.

There was no "monkey business" on a woods logging crew in those days. It was all business and if a foreman didn't produce to the woods superintendent's demands, he wouldn't be there long.

One of the best loading crews I was ever around consisted of the following men: John (Shorty) Pollock, engineer; Paul Pemper, top loader; George (Casey) Mataya, bull cook; Pete Padjen, hooker; and Tony Pemper, hooker.

The reason this crew was outstanding was that these men worked together so much that it was like one unit. Each man knew what to expect from the other at all times.

Shorty was a great hoister and a really fine top loader so Paul Pemper and Shorty worked as one man. Casey Mataya would always have the empty cars ready. Pete Padjen and Tony Pemper were strong, active men and could really handle that rope and hook. A log would no more than touch the load when those hooks would be back for the next log. They kept this up all day. They were so good that when the skidways were filled before the loader arrived, they would get the cars loaded and have two or three hours to spare before the train crew would spot empties the next day.

One winter at Camp 16 landing, there were many days I saw this crew load from 100,000 feet to 125,000 feet. It was a big landing with many skidways. The logs were hauled in on an ice road with teams pulling sleighs with a car load on each sleigh. The steam loader didn't have to move around much. Shorty would be out before breakfast to steam up the loader so it would be ready to load when the crew turned out. It all went like clockwork.

During the summer of 1915, there was a bad wreck on one of the logging railroad branches.

A branch line ran almost directly south from Casey Sag over a long hill. There was about three-fourths of a mile upgrade going in with empty cars, then another three-fourths mile downgrade into a ravine where Section 10 Creek runs through to the Tyler Fork River. It was upgrade again toward old Section 10 mine, T. 45N-RIW, Town of Anderson. Many carloads of logs had to be hauled over this grade as it was through some really good timber. There was a short branch run off to one side after crossing Section 10 Creek which was used to set out the Cody steam loader while the train was switching.

When loading on the heavy grades, besides setting the brakes on the loaded cars, the crew would use a gill poke, a stick of timber six or eight feet long, braced against the end of the car on the downhill side and into ground on the other end, making it fairly safe for train crew to couple onto the car. One day the train crew started to take three car loads at a time as usual. The steam loader was loading cars near the bottom of this three-fourths mile grade. The train crew took the first three cars out okay, then came back, coupled up two cars, and backed up for the third car, with six more loaded ahead of the steam loader. They hooked up the third car and started up the hill when the cars uncoupled between the first and second car. With a little momentum the two loaded cars hit the next loaded car hard, knocking the gill poke, or brace, loose. The cars kept gaining momentum as there was generally about 300 feet space between each car. You can imagine what was happening on the chain reaction of eight carloads of logs. The wreck would have been a lot worse except for the reflexes of John (Shorty) Pollock, the steam loader engineer and his loading crew.

The train crew engineer gave the trouble signal of short whistle toots. Shorty knew at once what had happened. He gave orders to his crew to get in the clear. He put the loader in running gear and started moving the loader back, with all the speed he could muster, up a little grade. Luckily there were no empty cars behind the loader. Even with the quickness that Shorty reacted, the loaded cars caught up to him and ran up onto the rail inclines of the loader, hitting the beam holding the 45 foot spruce loading booms breaking them off, cracking the beam, breaking the rail inclines off and dumping about six cars of logs in a pile. This put the loader off the track. It didn't tip over so no one was injured. Shorty was in the loader all the time. It did take a few days to get the loader back in working order. Another loader was brought in and by the next morning we were loading logs again. The loading crew loaded up one carload of logs from the wreck each day in addition to their regular quota until all the logs were picked up.

Some modern people will ask, "What happened to the air brakes?" A good question, but those cars had no air brakes, just hand brakes with a ratchet gear. The hand brake could only be used, with any success, for empty cars.

In spite of all the heavy railroad grades in the area the company was logging, they didn't have too many bad wrecks as they kept the railroad in good condition with track crews.

One time at Camp 29, Dan McDonald got off the train at a switch and happened to see a teamster driving a team on the track from one skidway to another. He stopped the teamster and said, "Don't you know you aren't supposed to drive the team on the railroad track?" The teamster said, "No, and you do not look like the man who hired me this morning." McDonald said, "But I may be the man to have you fired this noon."

The foreman, George Taylor, took the blame. He told the man to keep on working and the fellow turned out to be a very good, steady teamster, working at the Foster-Latimer camps for several years.

During the summer of 1915, I began to be more useful in the logging end of the business. By working with those good loading crews, I tried to emulate them. I offered to spell them off one at a time and they were willing, as they knew I wasn't looking to take over their job. Being on the spot with four good men against me, I tried harder to keep up my end. Later in the summer when one of those good men wanted a day or two off, the foreman called on me to take over. The foreman then helped me with my work. It worked out fine as no job became monotonous. I didn't try top loading that summer as it was too dangerous, but the engineer let me try hoisting and he top loaded. He kept on the safe side and at the same time, coached me. When it came winter and they decked logs with the steam loader, he gave me more chance as the engineer hoister.

With World War I, business conditions began to pick up in the United States and the labor surplus began to fade. The winter of 1915-1916 was a winter of deep snow as it so often is in northern Iron County. Consequently some men, especially teamsters, left for areas of less snow, so that teamsters were at a premium at Camp 31 that winter. The net result was that I was driving team more than I was scaling logs.

During the summer of 1915, J. A. (Hans) Wagner who had been a manual training teacher in the Mellen School decided he wanted to learn the logging occupation and took a job at Camp 31 where I was working. George Taylor, the foreman, took him in tow and when he had time, he showed Hans how to use an axe and cant hook. He also tried to show him how to drive team but Hans never took to that, as he didn't like it. By the time the winter season rolled around, the foreman used Hans to the best advantage. During the fall season I showed Hans how to scale logs and clerk so when an opening would show up, he would be ready. It paid off for him and the foreman in 1916.

Hans has furnished some information on the Mellen Lumber Co. camps where he worked for a few years after the winter with us.

After working in the woods a few years, he went back to school. He worked many years in the engineering department of the Northern Power Co.

He retired several years ago and is now living in Green Bay.

Wagner scaled and helped me with the clerking. I never liked scaling for a decking crew anyway. The logs were decked up for loading out during the spring breakup. Standing at a log deck all day in the cold didn't appeal to me so I would willingly drive team. With this changing around, it turned out to be a very interesting winter for me.

In the late fall of 1915, I was scaling and Wagner was helping the top loader, Victor Nurmi, a big strong Finnish man, pull the slack back after the logs in bunches had been pulled to the top of the deck. All was going along smoothly when a bunch of logs was pulled up and Victor placed them and was unhooking the other chain when one small log moved a little, pinching two of Wagner's toes. It hurt alright -- Wagner started hopping around on one foot holding the toes and Victor said in a very sober tone, "Ach, that's nothing. I knew a Finlander one time who had his head cut off between two logs and never said a word."

During that same fall of 1915, while they were still skidding logs to the railroad track to be loaded on cars, George Taylor, the foreman, was short of room on a spur to spot empty cars while the loads were switched out. Since the ground was frozen, he decided to lengthen the spur with maple saplings spiked to the ties to keep from rolling and it worked fine for a long period. Then one day, one of the poles loosened while the crew was spotting the empties, putting several empty cars off the track. Arvid Anderson, the brakeman, stopped where the foreman was and said, "There you are, Mr. Taylor, you and your Abraham Lincoln Railroad!" It was not serious since the empty cars came back on easily.

Another time Arvid listened intently while George Taylor told him where to take out some loads and put in some empty cars. Turning to Taylor, Arvid said, "Esoph-sophically speaking of the sentimental ideas at large, it will be utterly impossible for me to alter the situation of those cars, Mr. Taylor!" Many of the old timers in Mellen and vicinity will remember Arvid, as he was really a talented character.

The winter of 1915-1916 was very eventful for me in many ways, in that I picked up so many pointers. It was an extremely hard winter on skidding horses. The swampers had to have shovels at all times in order to find all the logs. Some logs would be buried and both the horses and the teamsters would get leg-weary.

One day during the latter part of February, George Taylor, the foreman, said, "I'm going to take you with me today to lay out a dray road to another block of timber I believe we can get out yet this winter."

We took our snowshoes and axes. The pet dog at the camp followed us. We got out in the area where we were to mark out the road and just got nicely started when we heard the dog barking in an unfriendly manner. We figured right away the dog had located a deer in trouble in the deep snow. The foreman told me to check. I hurried all I could on snowshoes and sure enough, the dog had a yearling deer down in the snow but no serious damage had been done. I chased the dog off, then helped the deer onto its feet. No kidding -- big tears were shed by that deer. After I got back to the foreman, we worked awhile when we heard the dog again, so once more I made the run on snowshoes. (Try it sometime if you haven't already!) The dog didn't have it so easy this time, as he had tackled a big buck, backed up to a large elm tree. When the dog tried to attack, the buck lifted up his front feet and struck at the dog and came very near getting him. I was wishing he would at the time. We took the dog home and had to do away with him as a camp was no place to have a dog that chased deer.

The deer could have been in trouble that year but fared okay with plenty to eat as there was so much logging going on. A new market was being opened for cedar posts and poles.

There was another amusing incident during February, 1916, which got a good laugh out of the crew at my expense.

Sometime during 1915, Joe Stecher had become the World Heavy Weight Wrestling Champion and was making a tour through the midwest taking on all comers. He was a great wrestler back when wrestling was really an art, not like what we have now. Walter Willoughby, who had been a great middle weight champion and was still a very good wrestler although up in age, had settled in Mellen where he owned a garage. He also helped put the Mellen area on the map as a good sports location, as many good wrestlers appeared at Mellen and Ashland. In fact, for five or six years there were matches nearly every weekend at Mellen, Ashland, Hurley, or Park Falls.

On Saturday night, February 19, 1916, Joe Stecher had a match scheduled at Ashland, so the Mellen promoters, with Willoughby's help, got Stecher to stop over at Mellen for a handicap match on Tuesday evening, February 22, 1916. Stecher agreed to throw Willoughby twice in an hour; Stecher weighed 220 pounds to Willoughby's 160 pounds. The match was to start at 8:00 p.m.

I came in from work at the camp, changed clothes and jumped on the bicycle-type track speeder; the only difference between pumping the speeder and walking was that the speeder would make a little better time. It was sixteen miles from camp to Mellen, a very cold night -- 30 below zero. Luckily we had no snow for a few days so the rails were clear. I got to Mellen just in time for the match. It was a good thing I got there on time as Stecher took the two falls in about five minutes. I had to pump the speeder back those sixteen miles, much of it uphill. Every once in a while I would think to myself, "What a nut!" The crew really put the needle to me the next day, but no matter, I was ready again the next time. Dan McDonald said he went to the match but by the time he got his fur coat off it was all over.

4

Another Camp Move

About the middle of March, Dan McDonald stopped one night to tell the foreman he wanted to take me over to Camp 16 landing to scale some logs and take care of the loading crew and a few other men peeling cedar poles and posts. He told George Taylor to put Hans Wagner in my place.

I moved to Camp 16 landing, and what an interesting spring it proved to be. We even had a log drive on the Tyler Forks of about 500,000 feet of peeled hemlock logs. Aristo David, who had been running Camp 32, located near Highway 77, had dumped the logs into the river between where Highway 77 bridge crosses the river and Camp 16 landing.

We had the fastest loading crew I have ever been around. The train crew would spot the empties around ten in the morning. Shorty Pollock was the hoister and leader of the crew. It was sure a pleasure to work around a crew like that. The landing was about three miles from the village of Moore. The Moore family had care of the station, short order meals, and a few rooms to let out.

The Wisconsin Central, now the Soo Line, had a three-car passenger train, called the Scoot, running three times a day, over and back from Mellen to Bessemer, with stops at Ballou, Moore, Upson, Iron Belt, Pence, Montreal, Hurley, and Ironwood. They tied up at Mellen overnight. There was a good walking trail from Moore to Camp 16 Landing, about three miles, but it crossed Wilkinson Creek at least a dozen times between Moore and the landing. This was okay in the winter, but not so good in a spring break-up as John (Shorty) Pollock, the hoister and I found out one Sunday night the latter part of March.

John and I, after the crew had loaded the cars on Saturday, walked out to Moore, caught the Scoot into Mellen. We stayed at Mellen until the late Scoot left on Sunday night. It had rained all day, then turned to a heavy wet snow with snow flakes the size of quarters.

On Saturday night, we had presence of mind enough to take a lantern from the camp, which we left at Moore. We got off the Scoot at

Moore Sunday night, picked up our lantern, lit it, and started on the trail to camp. When we hit where the trail crossed the creek the first time we got a surprise. The water had raised so much, we could not tell where the trail was. It didn't take long for us to decide not to go that way, or we might break some bones in the attempt. We turned back to Moore and walked toward Upson about one-quarter of a mile to a clearing where fishermen still park cars in the summertime. Then we followed the ridge to one of the Camp 32 winter log roads. By that time, we were soaking wet from head to toe. Our lantern chimney was all black, but we said at least we are on some kind of a road that leads to camp. The road was also covered with water in spots, but we could follow it. When we came to the river, the bridge had gone out! Here we were, just across the river from the camp, but with a lake filled with debris in place of a river.

Again we had to turn back to high ground. By that time we were pooped out and weighed down with wool clothing, so we decided to build a fire, if we could find enough dry wood, stay there until daylight, and then make a decision as to what to do next. Again the good Lord was with us. We found two good sized pine stumps, rather close together, and after a few attempts, we got a dandy fire started, as those two pine stumps along with some old cedar branches burned until morning.

After we got the fire going well, we wrung out our clothes and socks, emptied the water out of our boots, and even snoozed a little. At 4:00 a.m., we followed the ridge around to the company railroad bridge and got into camp at 6:30 a.m. Monday morning. We had a good warm meal, then slept a couple of hours until the train arrived with the empty cars.

Needless to say, it was not much trouble to get to sleep that night. We were both young and by the next day it was just a memory. In later years, when Shorty and I would meet, that trip was always brought up. In fact, the last time I talked to Shorty, before his death, he had driven over to Mellen from Ontonagon to see a wrestling match sponsored by the present Mellen Lions Club to which I belong. Shorty said, "I was thinking about you when I passed Moore this afternoon." I told him I was thinking about him also.

Everything was fine at Camp 16 landing that spring, except the food. It wasn't too bad right at that time, as the crew was small, so the cook did put out a little better for the loading crew; but according to the foreman and some of the men who had worked there during the winter, it had been pretty bad.

It seems they had a French cook named O'Mack. He could cook, but the woods superintendent had impressed on him so much during the winter the importance of no waste of food and of keeping the meal costs down, that the cook over did it. One of the economy dishes he served, oatmeal pie, was never served by any other cook to my knowledge. He would have oatmeal for breakfast, mix a little extra, then add some raisins or currants, cinnamon and sugar, put a good pie crust on top, and it was a pleasing dish, except for the name.

The foreman had tried all winter to change cooks, but Dan had decided to keep him until after the loading-out was complete. Then the cook decided he wanted to go back home to lower Michigan where he had a small farm. Tom Padjen, who became a very good cook later, was a cookee for O'Mack that winter. Arvid O'Mack took a liking to Tom, so he asked Tom to go home with him to his farm in lower Michigan for a vacation. Tom made the trip as he wanted to see some of that state.

Tom had come over from Austria during the summer of 1913 and had spent all the time in the camps working, except for a few visits in Mellen. Tom wondered why O'Mack wanted him to go so bad, but didn't find out why until they arrived at his home. It seemed O'Mack had a daughter around Tom's age and was hoping they would take a liking to each other. But it was no go as far as Tom was concerned.

One morning after this cook had left, I was riding up to the camp in the engine with Dan McDonald, the superintendent, when Dan and Fred Martin the log train conductor started talking about camp cooks. Dan said to Fred, "You were one of the men who kicked on our cook at Camp 16 Landing last winter." "No," Fred said, "You are mistaken!" "No by cripes," which was Dan's cuss word, "you did." "No," Fred said, "I didn't. You simply had no cook at that camp!" Needless to say, that ended the argument.

In addition to an unusual cook, we had another unusual activity at Camp 16 that spring .. a log drive on the Tyler Forks River. It wasn't a very good comparison to the big drives of pine logs of the past. In those days, dams on the rivers, used for floating great quantities of logs controlled the water to some extent, whereas the drive on the Tyler Forks was made while the water was at the high spring-time stage.

George Taylor, one of the camp foremen, was the most experienced man on the drive and did a good job with inexperienced, although very willing, help. It turned out to be more hard work than fun as the water didn't get up to the high rocks along the river bank, which let the logs get hung up on the rocks. This made a lot of hard work with pike poles and peaveys to keep the logs floating. We had nice weather at least and finished the drive on time without loss of logs or men. Although it was hard work, the crew enjoyed it, as it was something different.

The log drive on the Tyler Forks river was made for economic reasons. A decision reached by Log Superintendent, Dan McDonald, who had a lot of experience in log drives of white pine.

The Foster-Latimer Lumber Company had a few forties of good hemlock on the two sides of the Tyler Forks River on Section 21, T. 45N-RIW in the Town of Anderson, Iron County.

The company had cut and peeled the logs during the summer of 1915 to get the bark for shipment to tanneries. They skidded the logs direct from the woods to the river bank in the fall of 1915. As they were peeled logs, they dried out well and were in good shape for the drive;

being dry, they would float.

The exact location where the drive started was between the bridge on State Highway 77 on Section 28, T. 45N-RIW Town of Anderson and Camp 16 Landing on Section 16, T. 45N-RIW where the Foster-Latimer Lumber Company railroad bridge crossed the river to Camp 16 Landing. The logs were piled on the river bank at a distance of from one to two miles from the landing.

The log drive crew worked out of the Camp 16 Landing camp. The company kept a cost accounting of the job. It cost less to drive the logs and load out than it would have cost to haul on sleighs and load out. The logs were loaded onto cars directly from the river.

The drive consisted of about 6,000 logs, which scaled out to very near 500,000 board feet. Not a large drive.

I believe it is safe to say that it was the only drive ever attempted on the Tyler Forks River. At least, I have never heard of another one.

Just after we finished the log drive on the Tyler Forks River and loaded out the logs from Camp 16 landing, we had a big flood on the Bad River. This wasn't caused by the snow melting, as that period had helped the log drive, but by a heavy three-day rain coming on top of ground already soaked from the spring thaw after a winter of heavy snow. This made a dilly of a flood, closing the Foster-Latimer Lumber Company Sawmill, planer, and flooring factory, the Mellen Cedar Company Shingle Mill, the Tannery Company and part of the Kiel-Woodenware Plant located where the Calumet-Hecla Veneer Mill now is located.

I rode in on the Foster-Latimer log train the second day of the rain. The train ran through twelve to fifteen inches of water from west of Loon Lake, past the John Mesko farm and Mellen Cedar Company Shingle Mill located on what is known as the Louie Unger farm (Butler farm at that time) on into the Foster-Latimer Lumber Company yards where the train was tied up almost a week. This happened the week of April 20, 1916.

After the third consecutive day of rain, the houses on "red row" across the tracks and bridge going east, after passing where the old Atchenson Hotel, now a nursing home stands, were partly submerged. Men could go through the house doors and windows with row boats, although the houses were built up on timbers and heavy posts a couple of feet from the ground level. The houses were saved, but there was a terrific clean-up job after the flood.

While the tannery was running at Mellen from 1896 to 1921, hemlock bark was piled from east of Highway 77 near Christie or the Shell Oil storage tanks, all along the road between the highway and the sand pit, up to where Highway 77 swings to the east. The bark piles were about twelve feet wide and eight feet high, capped into a rounded top so as to shed the rain. There was water from that point to near Loon Lake, making it look more like a lake when in a flood stage.

The Mellen area on Bad River in the heavy snow belt, has always lived in fear of floods. With a fast spring breakup and some rain, the water flows off the hills so fast that the streams at the foot of the hills cannot take care of it.

It was often subjected to flood disasters of this kind, as it is located at the foot of the Penokee Range with other high hills all around it. The Indians realized the treacherous water basin and that is how Bad River and Devil's Creek got their names. It would be worse except that the Penokee Range makes a water divide called "The Great Divide" located near Gordon Lake between Mellen and Glidden on Highway 13 and between Hurley and Mercer on Highway 51 where appropriate markers are set up. The water north of the Great Divide, flows north to Lake Superior and South to the tributaries of the Mississippi River.

The year of 1916 had many things happening. For one, World War I was spreading, eventually including the United States. People were getting more restless, especially the younger men. We were practically in an undeclared war. Business conditions were getting better, so naturally there were more employment opportunities for the men and they began to be more independent, especially the better men, and that was good. The woods workers in those days were always the last men to get wage increases when times were improving and they were always very small increases. It seems the top management in the logging and lumber industry figured there were so many lumberjacks who would spend their money on liquor and women that there wasn't much use in paying out more wages than was absolutely necessary. It seemed a very unfair judgment to me as about 75% of the men were using the money in a sensible way. Some were men who were making starts toward buying a small piece of farm land so they could marry and raise a family. Some wanted their children to have a better education, others wanted to start a little business. Some were immigrants, who had left their families back in the countries they came from, and wanted to bring them over here. A lot of men would spend from four to six months in a camp without going to town so they would get a larger check at one time.

The word "lumberjack" is considered by many to mean that he was an illiterate and shiftless man, but nothing is further from the truth. The true definition of a "lumberjack" is a man handy at most all woods work, (a jack-of-all trades in the woods) and didn't depend on certain job classification.

In the spring of 1916, we began to have labor agitators. With more demand for labor, there was increasing unrest among the labor force; as wages had been terribly low for about two years and the men listened intently, especially when someone with a better vocabulary talked to them.

I was always under the impression that industry was partly to blame for the unrest at that time as the companies didn't recognize the trend soon enough to do something about it. There had been such a labor surplus so long that employers had become smug and were of the belief it would always be like that. We noticed it more readily in the camps.

The old camp foremen had been indoctrinated·so long in paying wages for each job classification at one level, regardless of the abilities of the workers, that there was no incentive for the men to be better workers, other than their pride. Many did show they had pride, although in time some lost that also.

I was close to the restlessness of the crews all the time, as by this time, I was called on to do many jobs and was considered one of them. I always tried to keep their confidence by being honest with them and helping them when their complaints or grievances were justified.

Many times, the old time foremen would not listen to reason and, while not intending to do so, caused resentment in the crew. The newer and younger foremen were beginning to see that if they were able to get the good will of the crew, they would get much more work done without driving the men.

Up to this time, there had been no attempts to get the woods workers organized in Minnesota, Michigan, or Wisconsin, but the Industrial Workers of the World (I.W.W.) had started organizing the woods workers on the Western Coast and had started working this way. When one of their agents, Arthur Thorn, showed up in Mellen around April 20, 1916, he attracted a lot of attention and it seemed to go to his head. He expected the men to join right away without explaining what it was all about. If they did not join, he became abusive, which never makes matters better. He was finally arrested in Mellen, and given a short time to get out of town, but more trouble popped up later.

By this time, I had been working for the company a little over two years without a raise and I also had begun to get restless. I must say I never heard of anyone getting a raise during those two years, but many cuts had been made in wages.

Since my oldest sister, Ida, had gone to Alaska in 1904 to work in a hardware store in Valdez, for our Uncle Charles Rudolf, I was thinking some of making a try in Alaska. It was looking more right along that the United States would be unable to keep out of the War. I figured that was probably where I would end up.

I never did have to make that big decision though as one day, George Taylor, the foreman, was talking about logging plans for the summer with the walking boss, Dan McDonald, and mentioned that he thought I should have a raise. The walker said he guessed that was right and he would see about it at once. The result was a $5.00 a month raise, which doesn't sound like much now, but would be about the same as a $50.00 a month raise now. At least it was a raise, and not a cut, which I appreciated, and I stayed on. I was paid $35.00 per month plus room and board before the raise.

While there was no crew of men in the woods during the early part of May, 1916, I received some more expert knowledge. Aristo David asked if I could help him run out some railroad right-of-way in the Rouse-Upson Lake area leading to the Alder Creek-Weber Lake area. In fact, we ended up going through where White Cap Mountain ski area is now located and going along the shore at the foot of White Cap Mountain, where one may still see part of the old railroad right-of-way now used as an emergency road for the ski tow.

After bark peeling started around the middle of May, with the increased demand for more hemlock bark for the tannery, more hemlock logs for the pulp mills, and more building lumber for the army build-up now getting in full swing, Dan McDonald put Aristo David in charge of laying out the railroads and supervising their building. Today it would be a civil engineering job.

In the previous summer, Aristo did all the bark scaling, so this now left an opening for that job and I got my first real promotion along with a $20.00 per month wage increase. It was a very busy summer. When the bark scaling was caught up or during wet weather, when bark was unable to be piled, I would help stake out railroad right-of-way. This was a job I always liked, because completing a railroad through that extremely rough country produced a feeling of real accomplishment.

During that summer I began to realize what a true group of workers was really like.

Many of the railroad beds were made by men with hand tools, with most of the men working on a contractual basis. That is, they would be paid so many dollars for every 100 feet of railroad graded, called a station, with an extra price for logs cut out of the right-of-way. The men blasted the large stumps or rocks with dynamite so they could be handled. They leveled the ground with picks, grub hoes, crow bars and shovels, making ditches, culverts, and even small cuts using wheelbarrows. What a wonderful job they did.

Some of those old railroad beds made fifty to sixty years ago are still usable for fire lanes and truck roads with a little ditching and graveling.

Up until this time, when my work had been with loading and skidding crews mostly, I had realized how good the men were in handling horses and using a cant hook, but hadn't considered the skill of the railroad crews. Now I could see many men had other talents.

Camp 31, on the west side of the Potato River, just upstream from Foster Falls, had much timber to be logged on the east side of the river, so we had to have a bridge for horse teams to cross. Ordinarily the water wasn't very high. Since the bridge would only be used that one summer, the boss didn't spend much money on it.

He put three log timbers for stringers up a couple of feet from the water at average water level, then covered the structure cross-wise with 9 or 10 foot poles, with a stringer on each side on top of the poles for weight.

This left just enough room for a team to walk on. It was good for a couple of months, when all of a sudden we got one of those flash floods so common on the Gogebic and Penokee Range, where the steep hills, mountains, river gorges, and ravines make for high water in a hurry.

This time it had rained very hard for about twenty-four hours, then tapered off and the Potato River raised fast on the second day. The teams were all out, but were not far from the camp, so the crews would dinner in. By dinner time, the water was starting to flow over the bridge with some speed. The water was gaining momentum and it was only a short distance to the falls.

As the teams arrived, some of us were already steering small pieces of debris under and over the bridge. The first few teams, with real good teamsters, took it easy and made it okay. Then a team of two high-spirited horses, mated only a short time, started to crowd. This naturally aroused the teamster, who tried to drive them across and that made matters worse. The results were that one horse crowded the other, which toppled over the lower side of the bridge into the river. Luckily the bridle broke on that one horse, the other one ran free. The one in the water couldn't get to its feet, as water was swift enough to float the draft horse weighing around 1,700 pounds. Luckily the flow of water at that point took a little turn toward shore, just enough to take the horse that way. Two or three men of the crew were able to grab the harness. Others grabbed whatever they could and were able to hold the horse until a chain was put on his collar.

Since the horse wasn't injured, he was able to help himself to get up out of the water at a point not over one-hundred feet from the top of the falls. If the horse hadn't been pulled out at that point, it would surely have gone over the falls.

The bridge didn't go out . . it just happened that the water had crested at that particular time.

This was enough excitement for the crew for one day, however, and it was a good lesson to me and a lot of other young men in the crew on driving a team.

When driving a team without a load with a narrow, tight spot to go through, you must let the lines slack and not try to drive the horses, as they will then generally make it without trouble. I have seen it work many times, as most horses, when trained properly are smarter than one thinks.

Other incidents happened at this time to indicate the kind of teamsters we often had.

There were two young teamsters working at camp in one gang, one a young Irishman and one a young Austrian. The Irish lad had a real good big team, the Austrian lad had a very good small team. One day the lad with the big team was skidding a big log when he pulled into a large root in the ground which wasn't showing. The lad thought the team should pull the log straight ahead, but the team knew more than he did and wouldn't try hard. The Austrian lad realized what had happened, so when the Irish lad asked him for a pull, he said, "Unhook those big counterfeiters. My team can pull that log." The Irish lad said, "How can that small team pull it when this big team cannot?" The other fellow replied, "Just unhook and I will show you." So the lad unhooked the big team, and the other hooked on with the small team. He then turned the team on an angle, pulled to one side a little, and away he went with the log to the skidway. The Irish lad had a classic answer. "Well, I bet your team couldn't pull that log the way I was pulling on it."

Another time, a real old time teamster was driving a nicely matched team of Clydesdale horses named Baldy and Dave near where I was scaling logs. I heard him talking to what I thought was his swamper, but I couldn't see any man around. I listened and heard the teamster say, "Now Dave, I'm hooking on to this log with the tongs and I'm going to hang this skidding chain on this tree until we come back this way. Now don't let me forget where I left this chain. If I forget, I want you, Baldy, to tell me."

I laughed to myself, then went by the skidway man shortly after and told him about it. He said, "Oh, he does that continually all day. I'm beginning to believe the horses understand him." When some people say it must have been dull times in the woods in the old days, I recall these characters and remember why it never was dull for me.

The summer of 1916 was a very pleasant one for me, as I was gaining in knowledge and experience in all phases of the logging industry. Camp 31 was located in an ideal location, on the bank of the Potato River, with good sandy soil and nice spring water bubbling out of the ground. That spring is still furnishing water to the Potato River.

During the summer of 1916, Fred Martin, one of the all around train crew men, was sent out to Aristo with the two-spot Lima locomotive to lay and pick up steel, haul gravel, etc. Fred was one of the most likeable men you could ever meet and was always like ray of sunshine, . . . very witty, but never sarcastic, unless with a laugh.

When the crew was laying steel, the train crew wasn't busy and since they weren't too far distant from Camp 31, they went to camp where the office was scenically located on the river bank in the shade where it was cool most of the time. Fred would sit in the rocking chair with his feet up on the box heating stove and go to sleep. One day, Aristo happened along when Fred was in that position having a short nap. Aristo had a camera back of the counter, took a picture of Fred sleeping and had it developed without saying a word to Fred about it. One day the following week, Fred said, "Aristo, I don't mind doing a good day's work, but this job is just getting too tough for one man to handle. I think you should tell Dan I need help." Aristo didn't say a word, just walked over to his desk, pulled out the picture and said, "This sure looks like you need help." Fred always laughed about that one.

Logging was carried on heavily at Camp 31 the summer of 1916 with all logging completed by September. The crew was then moved to

Camp 34, located about one and one half miles north of Rouse on what is now the Rouse Fire Lane, which runs from Rouse on Highway 77 north to about four miles out of Gurney on State Highway 169.

The Town of Anderson has a gravel pit there now. There is good spring water and it was a very good camp ground as it was all gravel ground. It was very rough country for logging, but they were able to get a railroad up to the camp location and had plenty of room for a good landing. Most of the logging was done by sleigh, hauled to the Camp 34 landing and the Camp 16 landing on the Tyler Forks River. The logs were cut, skidded and decked on log roads in the fall, then hauled on sleighs by horse teams on ice roads.

George Taylor, the foreman at Camp 31, moved to Camp 34 with his crew in the early fall and I was left with a crew of fifteen men and two teams to dray out and load hemlock bark onto cars to be shipped to the Mellen Tannery. The tannery was running steady at that time on a three shift crew, employing around three hundred men.

When the logging crew moved out of Camp 31 to Camp 34, the boarding cars were moved to the Camp 31 location as there was some railroad work to be finished. Then the cars were moved to Camp 16 landing for the winter again. The bark crew I was handling ate their meals in the cars so it saved the company one kitchen crew.

A funny little incident happened while the cars were set up at Camp 31. William Richardson, the assistant woods superintendent, had been to town on the weekend and had come back to camp on the Lima two-spot locomotive early Monday morning. The train crew left Mellen at 4:00 a.m. Evidently, Bill had not slept much on Sunday night, as immediately after breakfast, he went into one of the empty boarding cars for a little snooze but forgot to set an alarm clock or to let anyone know where he was.

At noon, Dan McDonald, the woods superintendent arrived on the main line log train, had his dinner, then took off for the steam shovel crew, as he thought possibly Bill would show up there and he wanted to talk to him. After Dan had spent a little time at the steam shovel, he asked Ed Pray (Chicago Pete) if he had seen Bill. Ed said, "Yes, he was going out the branch where Corrigan's crew is skidding bark." So Dan came out where I was and after visiting awhile said, "Have you seen Bill?" I said, "Yes, he was going out toward the steam shovel crew." He didn't say a word, but started off mumbling, "By cripers, someone is lying around here." I really think he gave us credit for it, but Ed and I hadn't made up what we were going to say. Anyway, he didn't locate Bill, who was o.k., until the next day. He had slept 24 hours. Dan caught up to him at noon Tuesday, and we heard no more of the fib.

It was an interesting few months. It was the first crew placed in my charge where I was completely on my own with all the responsibility. Naturally, I didn't wish to muff it and it all turned out okay. I had no trouble. We had fairly good weather that fall which helped a lot when draying out bark and completed the job on time.

5

Camp Move and New Job

I was then sent over to Camp 33, located on the high ridge south of Upson Lake and about one mile north of Camp 34, to look after log cutters for both camps.

Looking after sawyers was an entirely new experience and a new challenge, as sawyers in those days were a hardy lot and of all different nationalities. About 50% worked as piece workers and about 50% by the day. You must remember that we had ethnic tension in those days also, which has been a help to me in surveying the tensions of today. Some foremen favored one nationality or another and once in a while a foreman would say, "I don't care what nationality my crew is made up with as long as they do their work," which I found out later was the ideal setup. Henry Cronk at Camp 33, and George Taylor at Camp 34, were foremen who favored certain nationalities more than others. They had more turn-over of men in their crews as a result, so were often short of men. I had good luck with the sawyers, with only a little minor trouble at times. Most of the logs were out by January 1, 1917, which were to be sleigh-hauled that winter.

At about that time, Bob Newman, who was clerking and scaling at Camp 34, was called to take an office job in town. He later married Frances Latimer, daughter of the Harry Latimer, Vice President and Manager of the Foster-Latimer Lumber Company. With only a few log cutters to look after, the company had me do the clerking for Camp 34; the logs being scaled at Camp 16 landing. I spent the days at Camp 33 and the nights at Camp 34 which helped break the monotony of a long hard winter. During the days I helped around the loading crews as the work always fascinated me. The steam log hoisters were John Pollock and John (Snowball) Ferkovich. John (Snowball) Ferkovich was of Austrian descent, with a very dark skin. He always worked around loading crews or steam locomotives. He worked up to be a steam loader engineer. Snowball was a loyal and faithful employee, wherever he worked.

With so much outside work and natural dark skin, he was really dark. Along with it, he had a lot of dry humor and wit which he used with pronounced accent.

One day a member of his loading crew needed a wrench, and hollered, "Snowball, let me use one of your wrenches for a short time." The nickname "Snowball" stuck from then on.

By the time Snowball died, several years ago at Hurley, Wisconsin, he was very well known in Ashland and Bayfield Counties in Wisconsin and Gogebic County, Michigan, but very few people knew him by any other first name.

They let me hoist logs at times while they helped on the ground just for a little change. It was good for me and for them, too. It wasn't long before they could trust me to hoist a few hours a day so that they could get into town once in awhile on a Saturday afternoon without losing time. At one stretch they each had bad colds and I filled in for them. It was good experience for me.

The cook at Camp 33 in the early summer was Max Makoske, a very good, reliable all-around cook who was married and living at Upson at the time. About the middle of summer, Max was laid up with a rheumatism attack for a few months.

Tom Padjen, a cookee for Max, with only a few years' experience, was asked to take over by Dan McDonald, the woods superintendent who had taken a liking to Tom. Coming over to this country from Austria in the fall of 1913 at the age of sixteen years, Tom was ambitious from the start. Tom wanted to be a cook, so naturally started work as a cookee the first time there was a job available. He could speak no English, but worked hard at learning and paid attention to his work at all times.

At this time Dan told Tom, "If you do all right while Max is laid up, I will give you a chance at one of the other camps, when we have a vacancy and when Max returns." The first couple of days he had no trouble as Max had some bread on hand. This is the way Tom tells the story. "I mixed up a good sized batch of sour-dough and when I thought it was ready for the pans, I rolled it out and baked it; but when I tasted it, the bread which looked good, tasted awful, so I threw it to the pigs. The next morning the chore boy told me he found a 400 pound pig 'deader than hell' and I was then very thankful I hadn't fed it to the crew."

The next batch of bread was okay, as was his other pastry, meats, vegetables and other foods. He held the job until Max returned and in a short time, early in 1917, he was sent to one of the other camps as cook. He was a steady cook from that time on.

During the fall of 1916, when woods workers were getting more in demand and the more talented workers were asking for salary increases, with a better chance of getting it because of World War I, two men showed up from the Newberry, Michigan area. They were regular farmers but usually worked in camps during the winter months. Their first names were George and Herb, with Herb having some experience as a steam jammer engineer and George, while not a good top loader, was able to get by with Herb's help.

George Taylor, camp foreman, had just been informed by his steam-jammer man that he was going to leave at the end of the week, so George put the two men to work at odd jobs until then. It happened that the top loader left with the engineer, which generally was the case in like situations.

On Monday monring, Taylor put Herb on as engineer and George as top loader. All went well except it was like a circus most of the time, as George was one of those kind of fellows who was called Rube by the crew. He was always talking, but never saying much.

One day, George was pinching the logs on the car with his peavey, cursing and mumbling all the time. Finally Herb hollered, "George if you would keep your mouth shut, no one would know what a damned fool you are." George looked up, then said, "Tit for tat, Herb." It was little incidents such as that which helped keep men in good humor around a camp.

To indicate how the First World War was beginning to have its effect on men at that time, I recall an incident which happened at the Mellen Lumber Company Camp Cars during the week of October 5, 1916.

Edward Bouge, a Frenchman, and an Ole Olson, a Scandinavian, argued over the war. When Olson backed Germany, they had a free for all fight. As a result, Olson died of a broken neck. No charges were filed against Bouge.

One day in the late fall of 1916, I was checking over the men at Camp 34, when I heard a lot of noise in a log decking crew so I stopped to investigate. Three young men had made their way into Camp 34 a day or two before this. They had some experience in woods work, so when three members of George Taylor's decking crew left that morning, he put the three new men in the decking crew.

One, a red-headed, swashbuckling young man, who would try any job, unless he had a dislike for it, took the top loader job and the other two, the hooking job. The man who took the top loading job was Frank Banke, a hardworking man with a good keen mind and reflexes, but had a terrible habit of cussing while working, and in any lull of the work would be the leader in most discussions. When I happened along, Frank was in a cursing mood about the tools and equipment of the company being all hay-wire, a term used frequently by the lumberjacks of that era. I listened for a while, then went on about my work, saying to myself that he probably won't be around long. In about a week, I had to make a call on that decking crew again to get a count of logs decked which had increased by about 25% over the previous crew.

I casually mentioned it to George Taylor, the foreman, who informed me that Frank was cussing and cursing all the time but was also

working all the time and the other members of the crew, including the
teamsters, would rather work than listen to him.

Frank was also very good about seeing the logs decked properly
with all tools in good shape. The result was that the crew worked
steadily all winter until the spring break-up, with George Taylor finding out that Frank Banke was a very handy man. Frank left in the
spring of 1917 and didn't show up again until about 1919. You would
find many men like that in woods work; it was a way of life for them and
most of the time their cussing didn't mean a thing.

During the early part of 1917, the war clouds were getting darker
with the threat of the U.S. entry into a full scale war. To show how World
War I was starting to have its effects on people at this time, I am
entering a few headlines of news items of that period taken from the
Mellen Weekly files:

January 18. 1917 . . . The I.W.W. (Industrial Woods Workers of
the World) men active in Mellen area. Jack Beaton, the Timber Beast,
was banished from Virginia, Minnesota on account of his I.W.W. activities, was arrested at Park Falls, Wisconsin , for carrying concealed
weapons, sent for his gang of men to come and rescue him. He was moved
to Phillips for safekeeping.

January 1, 1917 . . . Employment picking up latter part of 1916.
War news helps foreign trade.

February 15, 1917 . . . Northern Products Company, Glidden,
Wisconsin, began operations. The output of local factory will be handled
by the Leedbroom & Brush Handle Company, a million dollar corporation.

February 22, 1917 . . . New shingle mill rebuilt of Mellen Cedar
Company to replace mill burned July 20, 1916. Started operations with
two machines running. Cut 70,000 shingles one day. George Schuler,
manager. War clouds more ominous.

April 4, 1917 . . . Senate passes war resolution.

April 16, 1917 . . . House passes war resolution.

Military registration day, under selective draft law in the United
States set for June 5, 1917. Approximately 10,000,000 men will register.
It made all men twenty-one years and older think more of their respon-
sibilities.

Work had been getting more plentiful during late 1916 and early
1917, so this made more unrest in all industries, with the woods no
exception.

When George Taylor left, I was put in charge of the skeleton crew
at Camp 34, which consisted of a loading crew, a blacksmith who could
do some wood work and a couple of men taking care of horses, etc. I was
to be in charge of bark peelers and scale bark when the season opened in
May. As soon as the snow was out of the woods, I started surveying out
section lines and bark strips at the camps which were going to peel bark.

I received another raise in pay to $75.00 a month and board, which was not hard to take.

Around the first of May, Dan McDonald brought the new foreman for Camp 34 for me to show around. He was John Broadwell, a very interesting fellow as I was to find out as time went by. John had been a logging camp foreman for many years, with some of the larger companies of that era, but had no experience with bark peelers. McDonald knew I was to scale bark for all the camps that summer. He told me to take John with me while running lines, then when we started to put peelers on about the middle of May to work with him and show him how bark should be peeled, cured, and piled.

John and I got along fine, and we got a lot of bark peeled that spring and summer, even if the men were getting more independent and particular about jobs, as jobs were getting easier to get with the war on.

John was part Mexican, Indian and Irish, and was a very hot-tempered man at times, especially if he happened to have too much fire-water, which was only occasionally. He had a rather unusual build, rather short, with a medium chest and shoulders, with very small legs, but he was a very active man.

There was one place he stood out from most other foremen of that era . . he expected a good day's work from his crew, but he also wanted them to have the right chance to do the work. He was a crank about having as good camp conditions as possible. He expected the cook to put up good meals, the chore boy to keep the shanties clean and warm, with warm water ready when the crew came in from work. He also expected excellent conditions in the horse barn and blacksmith shop, which were so important. He furnished good tools and expected the men to take care of them. Of course, all foremen took some interest, but not to the extent John did.

I liked the idea very much, so later on when I became a more steady foreman and later a logging contractor, I copied some of his ways. Another thing, if the chore boy was rushed too much some day and would have to neglect some work, Broadwell wanted him to neglect the office and not the men's camp. It was the other way around with some foremen who were not so competent.

He also had some humor but used it very seldom; but one little incident stands out. One day, while running bark strips, we were running lines between Upson Lake south toward Highway 77. There are steep hills in that area. One day while on the steepest hill, we had a dog with us and the dog was trotting up the hill on one of the trails.

I was walking next and John in the rear. I was always fortunate in having very good wind and being a good walker, so I wasn't paying much attention to John. When I happened to look back, there was John about three-hundred feet back, standing in the trail with his watch in his hand. I said, "What's the matter?" He answered, "Oh, nothing. I just wanted to see how long it would take you to catch that dog."

After we were in a declared war in 1917 and many men entering the war daily with others going to work in essential war industries, there started to be a shortage of woods workers.

6

First Trip to Hurley to Hire Men

Once in a while, I would be sent to Hurley to hire men, which was quite an experience. I wasn't acquainted in Hurley at all, as I had only been there a few times when the Mellen Baseball team happened to play there.

I would walk from the camp to Upson, catch the morning Scoot run, Mellen to Hurley, try to hire the men needed, then take the afternoon Scoot back to Upson with the men. I would then walk them to the camps, two to three miles away. By this time I had about five years experience in the woods, so knew a large number of lumberjacks. This helped as some of them would put in a good word for the company and I would generally get my share of men.

Once in a while, a man catcher would ask a group of men, "Do you want to go out to a logging camp?" One of them might say, "What kind of a job do you have?" After you told them, he would say, "You'd better bring the job in so we can take a look at it first."

One day I walked up to a good-appearing man and said, "Are you looking for a job?" He said, "No, are you?" It was Charles Parker of Saxon, Wisconsin a man catcher for Scott and Howe Camps near Hurley. I got to know Parker real well in later years. Other man catchers of that era were Oscar Auley and Phil Boissoneau of Mellen for the Foster-Latimer Lumber Company.

Some of the men would be taken on the C. & N. W. to camps in Michigan or Northeastern Wisconsin, others would be taken on the Scoot run to Mellen then change cars to the Ashland to Chicago, Wisconsin Central passenger train, where they would be taken south to Morse, Glidden, Butternut, Park Falls, Phillips, and Rib Lake. There were large logging and lumbering companies all over the northern part of Minnesota, Michigan and Wisconsin.

When the man-catchers put the men onto the train, they knew

how many they paid for, but that isn't saying how many they would have on arrival at destination. Sometimes they would have more, sometimes less, but over a period of time, it would probably average out about even. At least the man-catchers kept the men in circulation.

Foster-Latimer was situated pretty well for keeping men as there were many logging camps on all sides of them and their camps were fairly close to Hurley and Mellen where many men were traveling back and forth to the different companies.

It was on one of those man-catching jobs that I began to wonder what so many women of all ages were doing in the saloons at Hurley.

One evening when taking men to camp, I asked a man who had worked for the company previously that question. He said, "Are you serious?" I said, "I sure am."

He said, some of them are wives of the saloon keepers, some are hired house workers, but most of them are prostitutes.

I informed him that I knew what prostitutes were, but at Bibon and Mellen they were inmates in a building more like a hotel or club of some kind located out of the city or town. You did not see a woman in a saloon very often in those days.

With this experience gained, I began to wonder if all the cities or towns in the area had prostitutes to contend with. I found out that most cities or towns did have some.

In each city or town the problem was handled in different ways.

Wherever a saloon and a restaurant or rooming house were combined, a prostitute could be hired as a house worker. Then she could ply her trade on the side.

I found out that some small saloons started to locate in small villages or towns where many logging camps were located in a central location. They would keep a prostitute or two when they could get by with it.

I heard of such operations in different parts of Ashland, Bayfield and Iron Counties, but I am unable to say it was true.

As a youngster living at Bibon in Bayfield County, I was a friend of the Whelihan boys whose parents were running the company hotel and my mother was running the restaurant. We began to notice when us boys were around the lobby, the men and women would talk in undertones to each other. It seems when you hush-hush youngsters, they seem to get more inquisitive. It seems to be natural.

One day, Nick Whelilan and I were fooling around the hotel lobby when we heard a few of the young men who were working on the night shift at the mill talking with the kitchen help and waitresses, when one of the girls said to the men "I suppose you have all been out to the Sporting House to inspect the new girls who arrived last week." One of the men said, "Of course, why not?" There is no other place to go around here, only the saloons." Then he added, "You know there were a few nice looking girls that came in last week." Of course, Nick and I let it go in one ear and out the other, but the waitress did not let the matter drop. She said, "Oh! What trash!" Then one of the other girls put her finger up to her lip for the one who was getting riled up to be quiet, which made Nick and I more interested.

By this time a couple of more men had come down from their rooms and one asked, "What's going on down here?" One of the men who had been in on the argument began to tell him all about it. It was evident that the one man was a newcomer at Bibon, because he then asked, "Where is this Sporting House?" The other fellow answered that it was about three miles away toward Grandview on the road which is now Highway 63. The newcomer said, "Who is the Madam?" The other man answered, "Molly Cooper." This instantly rang a bell with the newcomer. It was not long after this session that we heard that name often as all the sawmill towns were made up of lumberjacks or woodsmen and mill workers with about twenty-five or thirty percent married men and the balance single men or boys in the sixteen to eighteen year old class. Some even worked at a younger age. Of course, Nick and I did not think any more about it as we imagined the place was another saloon with a dance hall attached, but we could not understand why the girls in the hotel were so riled up about it.

At this time, there was a mill crew at Bibon of around sixty men and another mill crew of at least one hundred fifty men at Mason, only about a mile and a half away. The Mason Mill was one of the largest in the North Central area having three carriages sawing lumber at one time and running two ten-hour shifts with a lot of pine lumber being sawed.

There were at least another three hundred men in the logging camps to supply the logs, so there were probably times when the Molly Cooper entertainment center was very busy.

Another incident happened at Bibon which will show that people were no different morally then than they are now. The Hines Lumber Company had prepared a swimming hole on the White River for the employees and their children. The employees to use it evenings, the children to use it days. One day, Ed Whelihan who was an older boy, noticed a man clerk employed by the company in the general store trying to entice some of the younger boys to take a walk with him by giving them candy. Ed immediately told his parents, who in turn notified the right authorities, and the man was sentenced for five years, which was what he deserved. It was a good lesson to us boys as the man was a neat-appearing fellow who would be the least suspected of such a crime.

After moving from Bibon to Mineral Lake in May, 1905, the sex question or the entertainment houses were never thought of. There were only eight or ten families in an area of about twenty square miles and these people were all busy trying to make a living by the men working out wherever they could find jobs, with the women and children doing the chores.

In my early days around Mellen, which was a logging, sawmill and tannery town, there were a lot of men living with families and many single men boarding and rooming in hotels with a lot of transients also passing through.

Here again you would hear of entertainment houses and with our family losing a father and step-father while still very young, my brother and I did not have any men close to us to give us good advice on such matters. Our mother was very busy making a living but, my sisters said, she did talk to them a lot. As a result, I did not know much more about an entertainment or sporting house than I did at Bibon in my childhood until I started working at the bowling alley setting up pins. Then I heard men talking about a couple of those houses around Mellen, one of which was in the city limits and was regulated by the city council.

The Madam, Mabel Kingsley, had her orders to keep a good, clean establishment, with no rough house tactics and no minors allowed. The call girls were to be examined whenever a new girl arrived, by a licensed physician and I always heard that Mabel Kingsley followed the rules to the letter. As she was allowed to run that house for many years, it must have been so. The merchants and other businessmen always said that Mabel Kingsley would never recognize one of her visitors when she was in town.

I am not saying what is right or wrong, but I believe a house of that kind is better than one without any regulations, and the facts speak for themselves as in all my years around Mellen I have heard very little criticism about how this entertainment house was run. Some of the girls from that house married and lived in Mellen for years and made good wives. One of the men who married one worked for me and she made a good wife for him. She said it was a man who let her down, then broke and hungry, she fell into that way of life for a living. She said she was glad to get out of it.

Another report, never confirmed, but which my knowledge of logging companies persuades me to accept, is that where the regulated houses were allowed to run, the cities or towns had the support of the companies. It was a way the companies had to keep more steady employees.

What gets my anger up at times is to hear some "goody-goodies" talk as though they never heard of those houses or the entertainers. I dare say there is not a family, or a boy or girl over the age of twelve years, then or now, who has not heard about sex. A lot of families would have been better off if they had explained sex to their children in the right way. I believe the present generation are getting a better education on sex, which is all to the good.

Now that is off my mind. I will go on with my logging history and to Hurley to hire men on famous Silver Street. This was an education in itself, not that Hurley was any worse than any other town, but the houses and saloons were more wide open, which made Silver Street and Hurley famous all over the north central states. This also brought much revenue to Hurley, as well as much notoriety, some of which Hurley takes too seriously. I have heard it said many times: Hurley should change its name and also re-name Silver Street. Why? I have lived in Hurley two periods of eight years each time, and found as many fine people as any other city its size. My three children graduated from the Hurley High School and were able to go on without trouble. I not only lived in Hurley, but worked in and out of there during many other years, and I have many people I call my friends in Hurley.

Instead of playing down Hurley, Mellen or any other town or city in this north central region of the United States, where mining and forest products were the main industries, we should pay tribute to those hearty pioneers, including the entertainers.

When I started hiring men in Hurley, in 1918, there were lumberjacks and miners coming and going steady with the saloons crowded most all the time. I wondered why there were so many young women going and coming out of the back room as they were not allowed to be hired as bartenders at that time. I was soon informed what they were there for, but I will also say I never saw one of them drag a man into the back room or upstairs, and just about every saloon had at least one or more. It was none of my business, so I let it go at that. I was looking for lumberjacks, not women, but I did have an opinion that the regulated system of entertainers, as provided at Bibon or Grandview and Mellen as much the best system. I will close this section with remarks made by Molly Cooper at Bibon and Mabel Kingsley at Mellen.

A merchant at Ashland asked Molly, "What do the lumberjacks talk about at your entertainment house?" She answered, "They talk logging in town and women in camp."

I do not know what the answer was in Hurley, but Hurley is still cashing in on its name of the past and may as well cash in on it as long as visitors keep coming. Many tourists make it a point to go through Hurley, thinking they will see some of the past, but are disappointed and will never see that again.

7

Danger in the Woods

One of the real dangers in the logging industry up to the middle 1930's was forest fires. There was no fire protection except that provided by the owners. There were only very poor town roads with only rough tote roads into the camps. Where a company was railroad logging, it helped some, but didn't eradicate all danger.

The forest fire danger was always there except in the winter season with snow on the ground, but the spring and fall seasons were the most dangerous. With all the slash from peeling bark and logging, I have often wondered that conditions were not worse. Of course, it couldn't have been much worse, as most all of the area did burn over. You can easily tell where the really bad fires did burn by the forest growth which came after.

Many times with the winds turning as to be a threat to camps or growing timber lands, it would be necessary to back fire in order to save life, horses and camps. I remember one fire when the main line train crew had to run through a forest fire with the crew on a flat car in order to keep from getting surrounded by the fire. Luckily the fire wasn't burning extremely hard when the train passed through. The hemlock limbs, with a few bark piles mixed in, made a really hot fire, as did cordwood.

I witnessed some bad fires in the spring of 1917 as I spent a few weeks just ranging the high hills and points to see how close the fires were to the Foster-Latimer Lumber Company holdings.

Aristo David and I talked many times of the huge waste from forest fires and did agree that some day something would be done about it. There was more talk by a few of the larger companies even that early, that reforestation was a possibility for the future. Up until this time, the majority figured it was a waste of time to try to save the forests after major logging operations. If forestry had been practiced then, as it is today, we would have more beautiful forests now.

An incident happened at Casey Sag in the summer of 1917, which could have been very serious. The Industrial Woods Workers of the World (I.W.W.) were getting very active in attempting to get the woods workers to join up. As it was all new to the workers in this area, the men were not rushing to join.

But, every once in a while, one of the organizers would get into the crew as a worker. One agent, Neck Ellison, got into the railroad crew at the Car camps and after four days of work began complaining to the other men how hard they were working for such small wages, $40.00 per month and board. He wasn't making much headway in signing up members for the I.W.W.'s when one day he complained to the foreman, Sam Johnson, about how hard they were working. Sam told him very nicely if he wasn't satisfied he'd better settle up at noon, which he did.

The timekeeper made out his time check and he started walking down the track toward Mellen. Luckily the Two-Spot Lima Engine had to go that way about a half-hour later, with Dan McDonald, the woods superintendent riding with them to Casey Sag where he had left his gasoline track speeder at the Y. When they got to the top of Casey Sag, they noticed a man with a spike pulling bar moving around the rails on the curve at the bottom.

They hurried to the foot of the sag to take a look, and sure enough, he had been pulling some of the spikes in the curve. By this time the man had dropped the spike puller and was walking down the track again. The engine crew jumped on the Lima engine and moved slowly over the tampered rails. Then, caught up to the man Ellison who had just quit at the camp.

The train crew and McDonald grabbed the man, throwing him on the ground. McDonald was going to jump on his face with calked boots, but the engine crew stopped him. They tied his hands and feet to hold him until the main line log train arrived. The engine crew then went back to Casey Sag and nailed the spikes back into the ties.

The log train with ten or twelve car loads of logs had to go through the sag where the spikes were pulled. If the small Lima hadn't gone ahead, there surely would have been a real wreck with at least two or three men killed, as that train load of logs would surely have turned those rails over.

The train crew members on the log train were Joe Taylor, engineer; Ray Sorrell, Sr., fireman; with Ray Scribner and Oscar Anderson, conductor and brakeman; with John Stoltz and Charles Hawkinson, the engineer and fireman on the Two Spot Lima Engine. When tried in Iron County Court, Ellison got a prison term of five years.

During the World War I period of the United States' involvement, from April, 1917 to November, 1918, there were many other war related incidents, some very serious and some not so serious.

I can verify this following story and where it happened, but do not remember the name of the man involved. He was a young cook, and a very good one, but he didn't care about going to war. He had signed up for the draft in 1917, then got married, thinking he might be deferred, but his draft board did not change his classification.

About the middle of the summer, he had hired out at Duluth to cook at the Foster-Latimer Lumber Company R.R. Cars. It was on what is now the Rouse to Gurney Fire Lane about four miles north of Rouse, where the railroad then, and the fire lane now runs close to the Potato River.

It is a good parking place for fishermen as there is a fine spring of drinking water between the river and the fire lane.

The boarding cars had a crew of fifty or sixty men building railroads. The cook asked the superintendent if the company could furnish a railroad car so he could move his wife in to camp if he filled the bill as a cook. Of course, McDonald knew he most likely wouldn't be deferred as it seemed cooks were in demand for the army camps. He informed the cook that if he was deferred, the company would consider fixing up a place for him to live at the camp.

Not long after this conversation, the cook received notice that he was still in Class 1 for the draft, but no date was set for induction. The fellow was despondent and took drastic action. He had a 22 gauge pump rifle which he often took out to a gravel pit near the camp and practiced marksmanship. One day he came back to camp with the tip of one finger shot off, hoping to gain deferment. It didn't help him avoid the draft, as they took him anyway. I've never heard of him since.

Many men were trying different methods of evading the draft and by moving often, many did evade the war.

When bark peeling finished around the latter part of July, 1917, we had a cook, Alphonse Cormier, who had a restaurant in Mellen previous to hiring out as a cook. The camp where Cormier was cooking had just set up for bark peeling during the summer of 1917. It was known as Camp 36 and was located a mile west of Highway 122, in from the southside of Copper Hill where Highway 122 swings east to where Highway E leaves for White Cap Mountain and Iron Belt. Logging wouldn't be carried on at Camp 36 until the summer of 1918.

There were ten or twelve station workers boarding at Camp 36 who wouldn't have their work completed grading railroad beds for another three weeks, but they needed a cook at Camp 35 where logging was being carried on.

McDonald, the woods walker, stopped me one day and said, "You're going to have to do the cooking at Camp 36 until the station workers get through, as I have to take Cormier to Camp 35 at once." I said, "Who me? Why, I'm no cook - the only thing I know about cooking I've learned by watching the cooks as I was a growing youngster the first few years in camp and was eating every time I got near the kitchen." He said, "I know different - I understand you have helped out on several occasions when we've been forced to change cooks or when short of kitchen help." This was so. He said I wouldn't have to do any baking of bread or pastry until I wanted to; that I should just send word to Camp 35 with the train crew and Cormier would send what bread and pastry I needed.

McDonald told me, "You're caught up on bark scaling and this will keep you busy for a few weeks until we start sawing logs when you'll have to look after sawyers again." I said, "Okay, but don't blame me if we have some fatalities, either men or pigs."

It was a great experience; I was lucky in having a good crew of men to cook for, and I always managed to have enough for them to eat. If it had been a week earlier, it would have been much harder, as for nearly three months that summer we had no potatoes in camp, due to a shortage of potatoes caused by the heavy demand for the army camps and the high price of new potatoes.

But, by the time I took over the kitchen we had new potatoes. With the men having been out of potatoes for so long, they really appreciated them. The substitute for potatoes was soy beans, and believe me, I have never eaten soy beans since that summer.

That was the year of substitute flour also, and many good cooks had trouble with the flour, so I decided if I was going to cook, I might as well try baking some pastry and pies at least. The newspapers were all publishing recipes for the substitute flour so I would watch each day for something which looked tasty and would try it. On one of the first tries, I was going to make drop cakes. I mixed up a batch, got the oven heated up, started to drop the batter in the pan, but the batter was a little light and started to run together. I just poured all the batter in the pan and made a cake out of it. To my surprise, it turned out not bad, so I mixed up a frosting and the crew made short work of it at supper time. I kept on trying out new recipes and only had bread sent from Camp 35 after that.

One day Aristo David, the assistant woods superintendent, was helping repair one of the Lima engines. They were packing the gear boxes, so his gloves were all grease when he stopped in for lunch. Just when I was rolling out the pie crust, he said, "Let me roll that out for you." Before I could stop him, he grabbed the rolling pin. You should have seen that crust and rolling pin. All I got out of that deal was a chance to get the grease washed off the rolling pin. It had to be scraped off.

But that is the way we got our enjoyment in the woods in those days. Without some of that, it would have been rather dull. Bill Richardson, Aristo David, George Taylor and Fred Martin, were very original on jokes as were many of the cooks who worked with us.

With the shortage of potatoes that spring, the company decided to plow up some ground at Camps 33 and 34 and plant some potatoes. Although the new ground was hard to work, they had very good crops, especially at Camp 33. It was up on one of the mountains near Upson Lake and escaped the early frost which hit thirty days earlier in the low land at Camp 34.

The Foster-Latimer Lumber Company boarding cars were located that summer on the Potato River on railroad which extended later on across what is now State Highway 122 on to Weber Lake and along the south side of the lake to where one of Dave Lundberg's White Cap Mountain ski hoists is located. Camp 38 was built later closer to the site of the present White Cap Chalet.

The railroad building was under the direction of Aristo David, with a steel laying foreman named Sam Johnson, a very capable man in his line. He could neither read nor write in English, but could lay out a switch perfectly. In that rough, hilly country, they couldn't help but have some sharp curves and near the boarding cars was one of those sharp curves.

The spur left the main line here to go on the west side of Upson Lake alongside of one of the Iron County Mountains, then turned west along the south side of the mountain to Camp 34. The spur crossed Potato River on a curve at this point.

One day the main line train crew, consisting at that time of Joe Taylor, engineer; William Niebauer, fireman; and Henry Hawkinson, the conductor, brought up a long box car to load bark in.

When the train crew left the boarding cars after lunch, Henry Hawkinson was riding on top of the box car when it hit the sharpest part of the curve, jumped the track, tipping over on its side. For a moment, I was afraid that Henry might be under the car when I heard him holler, "I'm okay." He had been very alert and when the car started to tip, he stepped the opposite way and ended up standing on the side of the overturned car with the car clearing the track enough so an engine could get by. It was a near-miraculous escape for Henry.

The steam skidder was brought in and put the car back on the track with only minor damage to the car.

Around the middle of September, I went back looking after sawyers and clerking at Camp 34. There was some railroad logging to do there for about six weeks, then a lot of skidding and decking of logs on log roads for the winter haul.

It was important to get all the peeled hemlock logs decked and get the hardwood from the roughest ground as there were real steep hills to be worked on. The skidding was all done with horses and much more could be accomplished skidding on bare ground than after the deep snows came. In logging mixed hardwood species and hemlock, the cost of logging had to be watched closely for the company to compete in price with other companies.

The mills in most of Ashland County, all of Iron County, and Gogebic County in Michigan were in the heavy snow belt and in rough country, so companies had to take every advantage they could to get out the majority of their logs in the summer and fall season and have the rest of the logs decked on sleigh roads.

Some may wonder how ice roads were made in those days. The road beds were cut and graded by hand. The snow plows were pulled by two or more teams of horses, depending on the amount of snowfall. A handmade rutter cut furrows a little larger than the width of the sleigh runners after the ice bottom was started.

The ice road bottom was made by using a water tank made from heavy lumber, tongue-and-grooved, bolted with iron rods. It had an opening at the top the size of a fifty-gallon barrel with an A-frame to hold a large block, and sheave, with one end hooked to the block and the other end hooked to a team evener. There would be a long stout stick attached with a short chain at the bottom of the block. A ladder would be made of stout poles, 18' to 20' long between which a barrel could slide on, and hooked on the side of the water tank at the top of the tank.

A man would pull the barrel down the slide with the pole, see that the barrel filled with water, then the team would pull it to the top of the tank where the barrel would dump water into the tank. The man would pull back for another barrel full and keep this up until the water tank was filled. A four horse team pulled the tank on the road. There would be one to two inch holes over the runners with wooden plugs to hold water until the crew would pull the plugs to let the water out. The man operating the barrel and taking care of the plugs had a very dignified name. He was called the water tank conductor.

You would be surprised how much water could be put out in one night by a good crew. This method prevailed up until about 1946 when horses no longer were used on sleigh hauls. Trucks and tractors were taking over to do the hauling.

At Camp 34, John Broadwell and I got along fine until about the time cold weather was setting in. Since Camp 34 was a little handy to get liquor at Moore or Upson, John began nipping a little more each week and at times would show the effects, especially on Monday mornings. Of course, you couldn't expect a hot-tempered Mexican-Irishman and a hot-tempered Irishman and stubborn German mixed to not have some clashes, but they were minor clashes which only helped to break the monotony, then would be laughed off.

One day in early December, 1917, the cook, Frank Gilcrist quit and Broadwell was going to send me to Hurley or Mellen to get a cook. I informed John that I was told by one of the log sawyers that he had a good cook swamping by the name of Ernest Smith. He had cooked on the boats all summer. He had gone broke in Duluth and shipped out with a bunch of men going to the Foster-Latimer Lumber Company camps out of Mellen.

He had heard it was a good company to cook for as they furnished well, but he wanted to work outside a while to get sobered up. John talked to him and he took the cook job. He was a very good cook but hadn't cooked much in logging camps with large crews.

He had followed the lakes in the summer and looked for small camp crews in the winter. Camp 34 was considered an average crew of from 75 to 100 men with a cook, second cook and two cookees. When down to 75 men, one cookee or the second cook would be laid off.

At the time Smith took over there were two cookees only, Wilson White and Ernest Anderson of Upson, both sixteen years old. In those days you could work anywhere they would hire you at sixteen years of age and were allowed to quit school at sixteen without a permit.

Ernest followed the forest industry, whereas Wilson was more mechanically inclined and after a few years of some woods work and some work for Town of Anderson in the summer, got on for Iron County where he retired from active work as Assistant County Highway Commissioner.

At Camp 34 the office crew and kitchen crew used the same outdoor toilet. Ernest and Wilson, being young, often were a little careless about closing the door on the toilet. One day when John went out to use the toilet, the door had been left open and a lot of snow had blown in.

John did his duty, then grabbed a snow shovel and shoveled the toilet half full of snow and then made the two boys clean it out. The two boys, being good sports, cleaned it out and laughed about it many times.

Not long after this incident, John brought in a tool to be repaired by the blacksmith and found the blacksmith, wood butcher, filer, barn boss and chore boy in the kitchen for lunch. He walked to the kitchen, pulled his hat to one side and said to the cook, "From now on, no one gets a lunch between meals. When you want something at this camp, you have to go to the kitchen first to get it. That order means me too," he told the cook.

I happened to come in about a half-hour later, and not knowing what had happened, I walked into the kitchen, picked up a cup, stepped over to the coffee boiler when I noticed the cook and cookees with curious grins on their faces.

The cook said, "I guess you haven't heard the new orders." I said, "What new orders?" He then told me and I said, more in fun, "You're not giving it to me, I'm taking it," when the door opened and in walked John. He put that hat to one side again, turned to the cook and said, "I told you not to give a lunch to anyone." I said, "John, he isn't giving me this cup of coffee, I'm taking it."

He turned, walked out over to the office, and when I got to the office, he was packing his knap-sack. I said, "What are your intentions?" He said, "I'm pulling out." I said, in a soft voice, "John, you don't need to quit over me, I can get out of here as quick as you can." He started to smile and said, "Oh! We better both stay." I informed him if he had told me what orders he had given the cook when I arrived at the office, I would have obeyed the orders, as it is no problem to get along without a lunch or coffee between meals.

The winter of 1917 - 1918 was one of those heavy snow winters we have so often in northeast Wisconsin, especially north of the water divide, where the water flows north into Lake Superior while south of the divide it flows into rivers emptying into the Mississippi River.

John had never been foreman in a camp where they had so much snow and by Christmas and New Year's was getting discouraged. He was drinking a little heavier all the time.

About the middle of January, 1918, I wanted to take a trip to Ashland to spend a Sunday with relatives and friends and would have to travel by rail. We took a passenger train in the morning to Ashland then back to Mellen in the evening, we could change from the Ashland passenger train to the Scoot which ran between Mellen and Bessemer, Michigan.

The Scoot performed a great service in those early days, not only for the lumberjacks, but for special shopping or medical service of the Mellen residents as well. They could get over to Hurley or Ironwood and back three times a day.

The Scoot consisted of a half baggage and a half men's car and a full passenger car, with addition of another car at busy periods. The fare, I'm sure, was one and a half cents per mile up until after World War I when it was raised to two cents per mile.

Many times in baseball season, when rivalry was always tense between teams on the range, and many teams such as Ashland, Mellen, and Washburn, a special train would be run on Sundays or holidays which would be packed with fans.

There were no automobile services between Mellen and Hurley, although in September 1917, plans were begun for an Ashland to Mellen to Hurley highway route. Automobiles were still few at that time, but more were showing up even though the roads were hardly fit for horse and buggy, many being just walking trails. When I hear people complain now of the bad highways, I get a real bang out of it.

I got off the Ashland passenger train that evening, stopped at my home in Mellen overnight, then took the log train out Monday morning, arriving at Camp 34 at noon. All looked well, but John Broadwell was not in very good humor. I noticed he had tape over a badly cut lower lip. He said his razor slipped yesterday and cut his lip. I didn't say anything, but I could tell it was not a razor cut.

When I went down to the log landing to pick up the count of logs loaded out on the previous Saturday, I heard the loading crew talking about the fight at the Mike White Saloon in Upson on Sunday. Broadwell had walked to Rouse, only a couple of miles from Camp 34, and caught the Scoot into Upson where he spent the day.

During the day, Max Makoske, the cook at Camp 33, who lived in Upson, stopped into the saloon, had a few beers with John, and was going back home, as Max wasn't a drinking man. But John had a fairly good start and asked Max, "How is it that you never cook at my camp?" Max answered, "I have no say of what camp I cook at; the woods superintendent, McDonald takes care of that." John then started to become abusive.

Max didn't want to quarrel, so he made another start to go home when John threw a punch at him, but only a glancing blow. Max, being much younger and stronger, grabbed John, then threw him on the card table, holding his hands. John got one hand loose, reached in his pocket for his knife which was always sharp. He couldn't get his other hand free to open it, so he put the knife to his lips to open it with his lips. He almost made it, but his teeth slipped off when the knife was partly open with the blade snapping shut onto his lip, cutting it badly. Max took the knife away from him but pressed no charges, which was very fair of him. It could have been serious.

I didn't mention what I heard to John, but all that Monday evening, he was very quiet. I was busy catching up on the book work so paid no attention to him.

That evening I went to bed at bedtime, thinking John would be okay the next morning. But when the horn blew to get up at 5:00 a.m. the next morning, I was lying in my top bunk relaxing for a few minutes when Ed Pray, engineer on the steam loader, hollered "George, are you going to sleep all day!" I said, "A fat chance of sleeping all day around here when everyone is so log hungry!"

He didn't say anything but nodded his head towards John's bunk. I looked that way where John was packing his knapsack. I said, "What's the idea, John?" He answered, "I'm going to pull out." I said, "Why don't you wait to tell the woods superintendent, as long as you don't have a good reason for leaving in this way. Right now you don't care, but possibly you may wish to come back for this company some day." He answered me, "I'm going now," picked up his knapsack and started down the trail to Rouse.

Being sawboss, I dressed for the outside, turned the crew out to work, then called the assistant woods superintendent (walking boss in those days) Aristo David, at the car camps, who informed Dan McDonald at Mellen.

McDonald had no foreman applications on file, but took the log train up to the woods, stopped at the car camps where he talked the situation over with Aristo, then came on over to Camp 34 late in the afternoon.

The crew was in when he arrived, but I had gone down to the landing to pick up the log count on logs loaded that day, as we had to have a scale or count on all logs each day.

McDonald met me and said, "How did you get along today?" I said, "We got it in, but I don't know yet what was accomplished." He said, "That is up to you now, as from now on you are foreman of this camp until it is finished in the spring. You can pick who you want to help you and I will look up a camp clerk who we can break in to scale logs."

I informed him that I thought Ernest Anderson, one of the cookees would make a good clerk, so McDonald talked to him that night and he was glad to get the chance. I told McDonald I would help him all I could, and Ernest made it fine. He worked for the company the next four years as clerk or scaler and sometimes both jobs, as we had all done before him.

I have used the words camp clerk often in writing this logging history. The word "time keeper" would be more appropriate. A camp clerk was both a time keeper and a clerk. The word clerk was always used in large logging camps, probably because those camps always had clothing, tobacco, and other often used accessories which were sold to the employees. A camp clerk would be in charge of the handling of such items along with his work as time keeper.

8

A New Challenge

I really didn't want the foreman job as it had never appealed to me, and I realized that logging camp foremen were underpaid for the amount of work and responsibility they had. In fact, I was getting as much salary as the foreman at the time because I was willing to fill in on any job they assigned to me, which was getting more important now with the U.S. being in a declared war, which was going to take many young men. Imagine, a foreman, with a crew of 75 to 100 men, ten to twelve teams of horses scattered out a lot, rough country, lots of snow, sleigh-haul roads to look after, all for $75.00 per month and board, with board amounting to about $4.00 to $5.00 per week. Did they earn more money? I will let you be the judge. It was the same old story in those days. Money wasn't the most important part; it was the challenge of accomplishment that kept many able-bodied men in the woods along with the clean, exciting outdoor work.

In spite of the salary, being made camp foreman in January, 1918, was a challenge to me, especially because I was only twenty-one years old, with four years logging camp experience.

I was the youngest man in the crew outside of Ernest Anderson, who hired out for a clerk from the kitchen crew, and Wilson White the other cookee. I realized that some of the older men resented taking orders from me because of my age. Some showed it; others didn't. For a while, I went out of my way to show them I would go more than half-way to get their respect, until I began to find out that a few men were taking advantage of it, especially a couple of teamsters. I began to follow up on my suspicions. There were only trivial incidents at first, but before long they were more bold. I then told one of the teamsters, "I may not make good on this job, but I'm not going to let a few men make it miserable for me. You just do your job and I will do mine, then we will get along fine." He worked a few more days then quit and never bothered me again.

The other man had worked under other foremen for McDonald,

even before McDonald had come to the Foster-Latimer Lumber Company, and he got the idea that I would overlook his actions on that account. I decided to just quietly let him go. One afternoon I told him to take the team rigging along to camp that evening. He said, "Am I going to have a new job?" "No," I said, "you just don't care about taking orders from me so it is better that you work under someone you enjoy working under."

I had no more trouble and kept a fairly steady crew the rest of the winter. With the deep snow of that winter, we had about 20% of the crew changing often and it was here I learned another good lesson.

I would sit down in the evening after a visit to the barn to see that all teamsters were taking proper care of their horses. They didn't have to feed the horses or clean the barn, as we had a barn boss, but they were required to clean off the horses and check the harness at night so they wouldn't get a mile or two away from camp then find a weak part in the harness. While relaxing after a visit to the barn, I planned my work for the next day. One morning, however, after I had made all plans the night before, a half dozen men quit. Then I had to make the plans over; so decided it was better to make final plans in the morning.

Another evening, after a few tough days of much snowplowing with a small production of logs hauled and a few more men than usual quitting on account of too much snow, I was down in the dumps a little and showed it.

My straw boss (as the assistant foreman was called in those days) Jack Reardon, a typical old-time Irishman said, "Say, what salary do you think Harry Latimer (vice president and general manager of the company) gets?" "Gee," I said, "I have no idea, possibly $5,000 or $6,000 a year," a lot of money in those days. Then he said, "What salary are you getting?" I told him and he then said, "That is why he is getting that big salary, to do the worrying. You just do the best you can with what crew you have, so stop worrying, go to bed, get a good night's sleep and things will look different in the morning."

He was right. The weather cleared up, some good new men came in the next day and in a couple of days we were hauling in good shape and made up for the bad days in a hurry. It was a good lesson, but I still say there has never been a successful woods logging foreman who didn't worry.

McDonald came to camp one afternoon to stay overnight to see how I was getting along. That evening he said, "George, I had a chance to hire a foreman last night." I said, "Did you hire him?" He said, "No, but John Broadwell called me up and said he would like to come back." I said, "I told Broadwell when he left that he should let you know he wanted to quit, that it would be easier to come back sometime." He said, "That is always the best way."

The next big problem I had was a change of cooks. Ernest Smith, the good boat cook we had, wanted to spend a month away from cooking before going back on the boats on the Great Lakes. At that time of year, about five or six weeks before the spring breakup, it was hard to get a name cook. We decided to try to break in a cook. When Ernest Anderson, one of our cookees, took the clerk job, his older brother, Elmer, who had been doing some short-order cooking at the depot restaurant in Mellen took the job as cookee at Camp 34.

When we put on additional men around February 1, 1918, so we could clean up the logging at Camp 34 by breakup time, Elmer Anderson took the second cook job. He listened to our cook, Smith, with interest and Smith gave him all the chances he could. When Smith decided to leave, he told me Elmer should be able to handle it.

The camp crew had started to get smaller due to the sawyers being laid off as the logs were all cut. Elmer took over the cook job until the breakup and got along okay considering his inexperience. He also took up boat cooking later and became an excellent cook.

Even with a change of supervision at Camp 34 at mid-winter, we cleaned up camp logging by breakup time. We had very good luck in hauling the logs in the rough country and didn't kill or cripple any men or horses. The year before, two horses had been killed and two crippled badly. This could easily happen on a log sleigh haul, as just a strap breaking a neck yoke might come loose, or a sleigh jumping the rut could make the difference.

To show what a difference World War I was making in the timber industry, I quoted some headlines:

January 24, 1918: Flour and sugar situation critical.

February 7, 1918: Food situation serious in Ashland Co. Two pounds sugar per person a month to be rationed.

February 21, 1918: Cut wood and save coal next winter.

March 28, 1918: Daylight saving time to go in force Sunday, March 31, 1918. Will remain in force until October 27, 1918.

This brings to mind an incident in early October, 1918. I had been sent to Hurley to hire a few men for Camp 36. I came back with the men on the afternoon Scoot, walked them about four miles to camp, arriving in time for supper. In the morning when the wake-up horn blew at 5:00 a.m. one of the men turned over in his bunk and said, "What are they doing here, stealing these old logs, getting up in the middle of the night to get them?" Of course, with daylight saving time, it is dark at 5:00 a.m. in October in this area.

Daylight saving time was only in effect the one summer. It was a World War I idea in an attempt to accomplish more in the daylight hours. It made no difference in the woods at the time as they worked daylight to dark anyway.

Another amusing incident which shows how resourceful people were in the early part of this century.

Around the middle of March, 1918, it was getting near break-up time so Aristo called me up one morning saying he would pick me up with the gasoline railroad speeder. We would make a trip to Camp 36 where all the equipment, supplies, horses, etc., would be moved to from Camp 34 after the break-up. Camp 36 had been built in the spring of 1917. It had been used by the men to peel bark and make railroad grades only during the summer of 1917.

In the fall and winter, the William Strick family, who lived near Weber Lake had moved in to dray out and load the hemlock bark onto cars. Their son, Ed Strick, and William Blise sawed the hemlock logs and made railroad ties.

I didn't know what kind of a set up the Strick's had, until I arrived there with Aristo, as I hadn't been that way since August, 1917 and Aristo didn't tell me. To my surprise when we arrived at the bark loading landing, I saw a team coming in with a bark jumper load of bark, with a young girl driving the team. She jumped off the bark load, unhitched the evener, turned the team around, hooked onto the cable used to pull the bark jumper onto the car, as quick as any man. As she left for the woods, another team arrived with another girl driving them, who repeated the same performance.

William Strick had skidded and loaded all the bark at Camp 36, with himself and four daughters doing the work, and his wife doing the cooking. They moved a lot of bark. It didn't seem to hurt them as they were always good, healthy girls. All members of a family worked together and all are still living.

Aristo and I went about our work of looking at the condition of the camps. We then arranged with Ed Strick and his partner, William Blise, to do what work was necessary to put the camps in shape for the move to Camp 36 in early April.

The camp kitchen and bunkhouse supplies were moved out of Camp 34 to Camp 36 as soon as possible so as to be ready for railroad logging when frost was out of the ground, as there was more of a demand for some species of lumber and veneer logs due to the war.

Up until this time the Foster-Latimer Company had never sorted out and sold veneer logs as they needed all the better grades of lumber they could get to help sell the lower grades of lumber because the higher grades were in more demand for furniture, etc.

The first veneer logs they sorted out were yellow birch with only perfect logs accepted. They had to have 16" top and up and 12' to 16' long almost perfectly straight with no defects, which they sold for $100.00 per 1,000 board feet. Those same kind of logs today would bring around $600 per 1,000 board feet at least, possibly more as you never see that type of birch veneer log today in Ashland, Iron, or Gogebic counties.

I worked the spring of 1918, getting Camp 36 ready for summer logging, then turned the foreman job over to James McLeod as I was going to be in charge of bark peeling again during the summer. There were three camps peeling bark and some jippos[1] besides who batched or lived in scattered locations. The camps peeling bark consisted of about twenty-five men at Camp 36 located one mile west of Highway 122 near the Potato River. There were about forty men in the car camps located just north of Alder Creek on Highway 122 and about fifty men at Camp 37 located one mile east of Highway 122 near Alder Creek. Around 5,000 cords of hemlock bark were peeled that summer. The price for peeling bark ranged from $2.75 to $3.25 per cord, the highest price paid up until that time. All wages were higher, so naturally meal costs were higher as all supplies were costing more.

With jobs more plentiful, men gradually became more independent with an increasing turnover of men in the crews. Camp cooks and helpers were harder to hold so that the company began hiring more man and wife cooks. They built little shanties or used small boarding cars for the couples to live in.

Camp 35, located southeast of Upson Lake between the lake and Upson on a railroad branch of the company, was run by Bill Richardson of Mellen. The company had a good name for feeding well and for having good horses, and equipment which helped to keep full crews most of the time. There was a good walking trail from Camp 35 to Upson about two miles which came out on Highway 77 after crossing the old Jack Johnson farm where the highway turns directly east just before entering Upson.

Upson was the leading stopoff junction due to the fine passenger service between Mellen and Hurley.

Automobiles were beginning to show up more in the rural areas where roads were improved enough to use them. The highway between Mellen and Hurley was one of the first highways to be improved for automobile traffic due to the many mines in the area. The waste ore from the mines was used in place of gravel. It was easier to obtain ore and there were no rock crushers in those days. When gravel pits were available, it was used for the final surface covering.

My headquarters for that summer was located at the car camps on what is now Highway 122, as it centered well for all the bark peeling activity. To say I was busy that summer would be putting it mildly. There was not only a lot of bark to be scaled, but often a change of camp clerks would make extra work for the bark scaler. On real busy days, the clerk at each camp was supposed to help the bark scaler.

As bark peeling was all contract work with one-, two-, or three-man crews, the scale would have to be divided evenly, then see that board and wannigan charges were deducted before completing the time sheet. Once in a while a new camp clerk or timekeeper, while in a hurry, would get confused and put the wrong number of cords down on the time sheet. The men would then take the time sheets to the main office at Mellen to get their checks. Most of the time the error would be discov-

[1]Jippo loggers are two- or three-man crews who contract to log on a small scale without having financial investment.

ered but every once in a while one would get by.

I remember once, two men at one camp peeled 28 cords of bark, which was 14 cords each, but the clerk put down 28 cords each on the time sheet at $3.00 per cord. The two men kept still about it and were paid off at Mellen for the 28 cords each which amounted to a difference of $84.00. In checking over the scale that evening, the camp clerk noticed the error and called the main office at 8:00 a.m. the next morning. The men had walked from camp to town and were paid just before the office had closed for the day. It was a lot of money in those days but didn't break the company. All the clerks, timekeepers, scalers and camp foremen were advised to be more careful.

The camp clerk at the car camps where I made my headquarters was seventeen-year-old Mark Ferrando of Mellen. He had one more year of high school but wanted to earn some money toward going to college after finishing high school. The car camps needed a clerk for the summer only and Aristo David recommended Mark for the job. Mark did very well and had a splendid personality with a fine sense of humor. He was a lot of help to me that summer, never complaining if we had some bark to scale after supper.

Weber Lake was about as beautiful a lake as one will ever see. It was located at the foot of White Cap and Radar Tower mountains. There was a fine stand of virgin hemlock and mixed hardwood on the sides of those mountains. It is beautiful again now, but doesn't compare to what it was then.

The one thing that saved the beauty of Weber Lake was more an act of God than good planning. When Foster-Latimer logged White Cap Mountain, the price of mixed hardwood lumber was very low. Yellow birch, hard maple and basswood being the only species in demand, except for the hemlock which went for pulpwood to paper mills.

The area was a very rough logging risk as horses were still the most power available, as it was just before the coming of gasoline tractors. This, combined with the low hardwood lumber price, and the higher cost of logging, resulted in leaving a good stand of hardwood around the lake. Only the hemlock and birch were cleaned out with just the very best hard maple, basswood, and oak logs taken.

Weber Lake also missed the heavy forest fire which swept all around it -- another act of God, it seems to me. The weather being favorable, the fire burned through the top of the mountain very slowly and didn't do too much damage to the trees. It was a light ground fire.

The second growth trees kept on growing and produced a good mixed hardwood forest. It all made a beautiful setting for the White Cap Mountain ski area and chalet, and the Iron County Recreational area. Weber Lake is mostly a spring water lake with no regular inlet outside of springs, with some runoff from the hills. It has a good outlet with a creek running into Alder Creek at the northeast corner of the lake, so there is fresh water all the time.

The beauty of this north country, even in winter, came to me vividly one afternoon in January, 1970. I had been writing on this logging history rather steadily but did have to get in some outdoor exercise at least every second day, as I was used to it. I still continued regular outdoor exercise.

I threw the snowshoes in the car at 1:00 p.m., drove out to where the Hoyt siding road leaves Highway 77 going north. I carried the snowshoes as I wasn't sure the snowmobiles had been traveling regularly in there. I didn't need the snowshoes as there was a good snowmobile trail to walk on, so I walked north to where a mapped hiking trail crosses east and west from Weber Lake to Montreal. I walked the trail west about a mile then back to Hoyt, at least six miles, and it made me feel real good. The weather was just right at 31° above zero. The scenery was beautiful with the snow-covered trees; I met only two snowmobiles. I arrived home in time for a good supper.

There were many families on small farms all around Iron Belt and Upson. The men and older boys would take jobs in the woods for the winter while the women and girls took care of the chores at home. Most of those hardy pioneers were very friendly. Another good all-around jippo, or piece worker, of that era was Edward Strick of the Iron Belt region. Ed had just been married to Edith Moerke of Highbridge. Ed had a helper, William Blise, also of the Iron Belt region.

The distance was short from Iron Belt to the Copper Hill logging setup of the Foster-Latimer Lumber Co. It was too far to commute morning and night so Ed decided to build a log cabin. He decided on the location at the turn of the present Highway 122 where County Trunk E branches off to White Cap. It was a good, dry location with fine spring water just across the road.

When working in the woods in the days I am writing about, there was never a dull moment, which is why it was so interesting.

During the spring of 1918 while scaling bark, I often worked late at one camp; then after having a late lunch with the cooks, would walk to the camp of my headquarters. One night I finished up at Camp 36 late, visited at the office a while, then started for the car camps a mile away, walking on the railroad. The track hadn't been in very long so it didn't have much ballast between the ties, making it hard walking, especially in the dark.

I was walking carefully, not paying any attention except to see that I didn't step between the ties, when a terrible scream sounded just over my head. I believe my hair stood up enough to push my hat off (I had some hair then), as it was so sudden. Then I realized what it was -- a screech owl had evidently been hunting and flew so close to me before seeing me that it was as surprised as I was, resulting in the terrible screech. I guess this was really the biggest scare I ever had.

While working as a fill-in man during the late summer of 1918, I had an interesting experience. Just as I finished dinner at Camp 36, a phone call came from Camp 35 asking if I would go to the loading crew at Camp 35 at once. The top loader had quit and they had no one at the time to replace him. I hiked a mile or so to the loading crew, grabbed a peavey cant hook and climbed on the Russell car which had no stakes so it required more care when loading. You would build up the load on 8' wide bunks, 3 or 4 log tiers high by placing the logs to match so as to be solid, with no crowding, especially of the face logs. One chain or cable wrapper would be put around the center of the load. Then you would build up another tier of one or two logs, then put another wrapper on each end of the load tight enough to hold the load. You would then fill in the center with logs to hold the wrappers tight and place one more log to fill out the load in a solid position.

When the load was completed, it usually contained an average of 4,000 board feet of logs with about 40 to 50 logs. When building up the first three tiers of logs, I noticed the hoister was dropping the logs a little too hard, so I motioned him to drop them more easily. He wasn't one of the better hoisters, except at a bar. A log was then brought up for the outside face, which I was able to hold until the hoister brought up a log for the front face, which he was supposed to hold until the wrapper was put in place. This time he brought the log up too fast and missed placing it on the front face. Then, in fear of hitting me with the log, he let the slack loose, dropping the log hard onto the load, which jarred the log I was holding loose and I had to take to the brush or get covered up. Luckily there was a brush pile on that side without any large hard obstacle underneath and I made a good leap without getting anything hurt except my feelings.

I said to myself, I'd better see what is going on here, before I do get hurt, as I have always put a priority on my arms and legs. I talked to the engineer, then I realized he was getting over a Sunday celebration and was in no shape to be hoisting logs. About that time, the foreman, William Richardson, came along. He sent the hoister in to sober up and told me to hoist the balance of the afternoon and load what logs we could, so we finished the day with no more trouble. The hoister was very repentant and back on the job the next morning. It shook me up a little, but made me more careful.

Shortly after this episode, the same hoister wished to have a week's vacation, so Aristo told me to plan my work ahead so I could take over the hoisting for a week. It was during a period of hot weather and one very hot day, just as the train crew was in to switch out the loads and spot the empties, the steam injector began giving us trouble. I didn't want the water to get too low in the boiler and I didn't want to delay the train crew more than was necessary, so I tried all the methods used previously, but none would work. I then grabbed a wrench to take the injector apart and found the wrench in very poor shape. The gear to loosen and tighten the wrench was badly worn and it would not hold. After one slip, I threw the wrench across the top of the water tank, and it went over the edge of the tank, dropping between the tank and wall of the loader with no room to reach it.

The engineer on the train let me use his wrench and we got the injector working. While the train was switching, some of the loading crew helped me work the wrench out from behind the water tank. I controlled my temper better after that, at least when around machinery.

During the summer of 1918, the car camps were located on the county road that is now Highway 122, just north of Alder Creek. Part of the crew was laying steel and part of the crew were station workers, grading the right-of-way. This is a part of County Highway E, east from the road to the site of Camp 38, which was to be built the following spring. It was built near where White Cap Mountain Ski Hill Chalet now stands and the railroad continued along the south shore of Weber Lake to the west side. The old grade is plainly visible and used by Dave Lundberg to get machinery and equipment to the west side of the ski hill.

There were also men hewing ties for the right-of-way with a broad axe. In order to hew ties, a man had to be exceptionally good with an axe. One such man, at the car camps that summer, was Charles Woodward of Coria, well-known around the Mellen, Highbridge and Marengo areas.

While I was scaling bark for Herman Christenson on the south side of Copper Hill, now part of White Cap Mountain, we heard what sounded like a man hollering for help. The sound came very faintly at first, but when we neared the Camp 38 right-of-way, we could hear it more clearly. We figured at once that it must be Charles, so we started out in that direction on the grade. We hadn't gone far when we met him dragging himself down the right-of-way, with one foot broken badly.

He had already dragged himself a good quarter of a mile on the grade, which had a lot of hemlock trees felled cross-wise across the grade, some of which he went over and some under. He was now getting weak from pain and loss of blood. Herman and I made a tourniquet on his leg. Herman stayed with him while I went to camp to get a horse and jumper. I called Dr. Lockhart at Mellen so he could get started with a driving team and ambulance. I went back with the horse.

I brought Charles to the car camps. To say Charles was tough would be putting it mildly, as he stayed conscious all the while, with no complaint on the handling. Herman and I could never figure how he made that first quarter of a mile alone.

The injury happened while he was cutting down a hemlock tree to make ties. The tree got hung up when falling, and kicked back enough to come down on Charles' foot, pinning him to the roots of the tree. By using the axe while pinned, he somehow worked himself loose and dragged himself prone on the ground that first quarter of a mile.

Dr. Lockhart left Mellen immediately and was at the camp in about three hours, a distance of fifteen miles, with a horse-drawn ambulance and gave Charles first aid.

Dr. Lockhart took one look at the bandage I had put on, after taking orders from him over the telephone and I'll never forget what he said, "That is a genuine lumberjack bandage, if I ever saw one, but it has answered the purpose." It was the first serious accident I had ever worked on and it was some experience.

Charles Woodward survived the accident and his foot was saved, but it was badly crippled. The next summer, he was back at camp making ties again. He was really a tough guy.

It was very lucky for Charles that the Workmen's Compensation Law was in force at that time, as he was laid up for a long time. The compensation itself was very little at the time, but the doctor and hospital bill amounted to a good sized sum.

The accident to Charles Woodward in August of 1918, brought home to me the importance of workmen's compensation in the forest industries.

The wages were so small that the compensation was very small, but it helped. The doctor and hospital bills were very important.

Before the start of Workmen's Compensation in 1911, the only thing a woods worker had to depend on was a Hospital Ticket, in case of accident or illness.

In my research on the date or year the Hospital Tickets were first used, I was unable to find an exact date, but the year seemed to be 1905.

The St. Joseph Hospital in Ashland, WI was the first hospital to use it in the four county area of which I am concentrating on in this logging history.

I talked to some of the last hospital personnel who were employed until the closing of the hospital a few years ago. There were no records they could find back to 1905. They did know that the tickets were in use up until the late 1920's. It was real good insurance.

I found out that in 1905, when the hospital board was arriving at a decision to sell tickets, a man with a badly broken leg, by the name of Ed Hickey, was brought to the hospital with only a few dollars, coming from a logging camp he was working at when he was injured.

Ed impressed on them that when he got back to work, he would pay; and he did, in a big way. He could neither read or write, but like so many in that era, he could count and add up money.

Ed asked them about getting a job selling tickets on a commission basis. There is no record of what the commission was, but it had to be small, as the price per ticket was small. The board accepted his offer with no regrets.

Ed was a full-blooded Irishman. He was a small man, about 5'6", weighing about 140 pounds. I knew him from about 1913 until his disappearance in the mid 1920's. He disappeared under mysterious circumstances. He walked from camp to camp, by day or night; he had no fear of man or beast. After the first year on the job, he knew more lumberjacks than any man living.

I have been told that from 1905 until 1911, the year Workman's Compensation came into effect, he sold thousands of tickets each year.

As near as I could find out, the tickets were priced at $5.00 each per year, from the date the tickets were sold. It was a fantastic price for the benefits the men were able to receive. The lumberjacks realized what a bargain it was and did not go to the hospital with each small injury or minor illness.

Ed sold many tickets after Workmen's Compensation, as the ticket covered the men when not working, from injury off the job, or illness. It seems to me that the tickets did raise in price to $10.00 a year after World War I.

Ed enjoyed getting out over the area, visiting the camp crews and giving them the news on current events. He was very witty and could be sarcastic when the occasion called for it. A camp foreman told me about a cook who, when in town with a few too many drinks under his belt, gave Ed a hard time. Ed held his temper without exploding. Sometime later, Ed stopped at a camp where the cook was employed. He walked into the kitchen for lunch and let on he did not know the cook, who happened to have a soiled apron on.

Ed said, "Who is the cook here?" The cook said, "I am, who do you think I am?" Ed said, "By the looks of you, I thought you were the blacksmith."

Another time, a foreman that Ed liked asked how a foreman that Ed disliked was getting along on a new job. Ed said, "You should know; he doesn't know enough to pee a hole in the snow."

Sometime during the mid 1920's, Ed Hickey was seen for the last time at Eagle River, WI.

He had come to Eagle River from a camp tour with several hundred dollars on his person. He planned to go towards Watersmeet, MI from where he would take the passenger train to Ashland.

He was never seen after that. The law officers who checked up on the case figured that it became known he had money on him, was followed out of town, was held up on some trail, robbed, and thrown into a mucky swamp.

It was a sad ending for a man that did so much for the lumberjacks. I am sure no real lumberjack had a part in his disappearance.

ED HICKEY STILL MISSING - MAY, 1922

Ed Hickey, well-known throughout this country as the Hospital Ticket man is still missing. Hickey has been reported missing for about two weeks. As yet, no traces of him have been found. When the report first came out, there was not a great deal of anxiety for his welfare because everyone was confident that he would show up sooner or later. But now, after a careful seach and an exhausted inquiry has been made, and no signs of Hickey are apparent, there is a great deal of anxiety in evidence.

Hickey is known by practically every resident of Mellen and vicini-
ty. He has made this section of the country for a good many years.
Everytime a few established residents of the community get set for a
yarn-swapping party, the name of Ed Hickey is sure to be mentioned.
from Mellen Weekly - May, 1922

By late summer of 1918, my home problems had diminished. I asked for a re-classification of my draft status, which was 3A at the time. It was then changed to 1A and I received my first call in September, 1918, but a flu epidemic had hit the Mellen area and a few days before I was to report for induction, I came down with a fever. The doctor said it was the flu and that I would be unable to report at that time. After a ten-day sick period, I was told I could work again until the next draft call.

I reported back to Dan McDonald on a Monday morning at the Mellen office, and Dan said, "By cripers, I may need a brakeman this a.m. as one had threatened to quit," I said, "Oh no, that is completely out of my line and I'm not at all interested; any job in the woods is okay." "Well," he said, "seeing you may get another call soon, you'd better go up to Camp 36 and get the gasoline wood-sawing drag-saw rig in shape; pick up a crew, and start sawing winter wood for the camps."

This was a big job in those days, cutting the wood for three large camps. The sleeping camps, kitchen and office were made of one layer of lumber with heavy tar paper on the walls and roofing on the roof put on with lumber strips where the paper lapped over. It is safe to say that each camp burned between 1,000 and 1,200 cords of 18 inch length wood for the kitchen and 30 inch wood for the other buildings in one year. With winter coming on, when more wood was used, it was always wiser to get the winter wood cut ahead, if possible. In the spring, when the camps were shut down for the break-up, with no unemployment compensation at that time, the companies could always get men wanting work to saw wood ahead for the summer months with the cross-cut saws.

Dan said to try to get at least 1,500 cords of wood cut for the three camps. I picked a gang of sawyers to cut the logs into 12 to 20 foot lengths, a teamster and team to skid the logs to where the wood machine was spotted and three men besides myself to operate the drag-saw. When all was running smoothly, we cut about thirty cords of wood a day with seven men and a team, for an average cost per cord of about $.75.

Some of the splitting of wood into smaller pieces for the stove would be done whenever we were moving the wood machine to new locations or when a breakdown of some kind occurred. When the foreman wanted to keep a few extra men on the payroll for emergencies, he would put them on the wood pile until needed at other regular jobs. It was figured at that time to cost about $.25 per cord to split and pile the wood. The chore boy would split the kitchen wood. The total woodcutting cost came to about $1.25 per cord at the camps, which was not bad for that kind of wood.

We were just finishing the wood-sawing when I got my next draft call for November 18, 1918. I was at home in Mellen, preparing to leave when, on November 11, the armistice was signed, which ended my chance of getting into the service. I was just as well satisfied, for it was obvious that the war was nearly over. While I was anxious to get in previously, when most of my friends were in the service, it didn't appeal to me when the war was over. I received a notice at once not to report; so back to the woods I went again where I was always at home.

The car camps were moved from near Alder Creek on what is now State Highway 122 to a location where they had been the previous winter on Potato River, near the outlet of Upson Lake, which empties into the Potato River. The cars were to have a logging crew there for the winter again.

There was a barn, blacksmith shop and office already there from the previous winter, so it didn't take long to get the cars ready for a logging crew. Henry Cronk was camp foreman; Steve Ferkovich the cook. I did the clerking for the cars and Camp 36 and filled in as spare man when needed at other occupations. Men weren't plentiful yet, so I put in a busy winter with my headquarters at Camp 36.

We didn't have much excitement that winter as men were just adjusting back to peace time work. Not many young men were coming back to the woods. My good friend, Aristo David, who had been assistant superintendent to Dan McDonald, had a disagreement with Dan and decided to make a change.

William Richardson then took over Aristo's job. It made no difference as far as the work was concerned as I could always get along with any of them, but Aristo and I were more than friends. We had a track speeder bike together, which I took over, we had a group who hunted or fished together, etc., but those things happen, so we made the best of it.

Aristo and I had always worked for the one company, except the short time I had worked at Mellen Lumber Company camps before going to the Foster-Latimer Lumber Company operations.

It seemed back in those days, when promotions were slow in logging operations, that the company officials would have the idea that because you had only worked for the one company, you weren't as well equipped to handle the new jobs. Sometimes they would pass over men who had always worked for them to take on a man with more experience, which is what happened in Aristo's case.

Aristo went on to a better position, first with the Mellen Lumber Company, then with the Twomey Williams Company of Duluth, Minnesota, then on to the Northern Logging Company at Marenisco and Ontonagon, Michigan. He ended up as woods superintendent in the 1940's. We always remained friends however, until his death.

I survived the winter of 1918-1919 without too much trouble, and went on to a busy summer in 1919 in the Iron Belt-Upson-White Cap

Mountain area.

While making my headquarters at Camp 36 with the car camps one mile away on the main line railroad, I had the option of staying at the car camps at night or going back to Camp 36, as I was working at both camps as steam loader engineer.

Steve Ferkovich was the cook, and although very young, a good cook. He had already worked for the Foster-Latimer Lumber Company and the Mellen Lumber Company camps out of Mellen and Glidden and at the Rib Lake Lumber Company at Rib Lake, Wisconsin.

George Taylor, a camp foreman, who had worked in logging of pine in northern Michigan, said this was the largest white pine log he had ever seen. George Corrigan was engineer on the skidder when the log was pulled out of the bog near Camp 31 on the Potato River. 1918

9

Summer of 1919

In the spring of 1919, the car camps were moved back to Alder Creek, just north of the bridge on what is now State Highway 122. They remained at the same location until the spring of 1922, as it centered well for a lot of railroad building in the summer months and was used for large landing crews in the winter months.

It was a good location for a headquarters camp, with Upson less than two miles distant and camps located to the east and west of the highway. It was easily accessible for men traveling looking for work. The county highway (now State Highway 122) was being improved also with good prospects at that time of beginning automobile traffic.

The Mellen Cedar Company followed the logging of the Foster-Latimer Company, taking out the cedar poles, posts, shingle-timber bolts and pulpwood. They bought this stumpage from Foster-Latimer and paid so much a car load for hauling on the company railroad. This company moved a set of boarding cars in and set them on a siding about twenty rods from where the other cars were located. A few men who were working steady moved their wives out to camp, sometimes with children. It didn't cost much to build those cottages as the company furnished the lumber and nails and some of the men in the crew helped on the buildings just for pastime.

One family who moved in and made a fairly nice little three-room building and stayed the three years the camps were located there was the Ed Pray family from Mellen. For many years, Ed was a steam shovel and log loader steam engineer for the company.

Mrs. Ed Pray, being an ambitious woman, did the laundry at a modest charge for the men at camp. Most of the men took advantage of it, so she did well.

Tom Hicks and his wife took over the cook and cookee positions at the Foster-Latimer cars. She was the former Maud Brown of Upson, Wisconsin. They were a fine couple around the kitchen, very accommodating, and she was an excellent cook. Tom was handy so they made the work easy.

I will say we had a very fine little settlement with all families getting along well; guess they were all too busy to get into trouble. Since Upson was such a short distance away and all the people there at that time were very friendly and sociable, we had a pleasant three-year camp life. We were just starting to get good radio reception at the time but still had to depend on batteries for power as there was no electricity in camps. We did have gas lanterns and lamps, though.

The demand for forest products started to pick up again after a short period of adjustment following the end of World War I, which made everyone busy during the summer of 1919.

I was very busy all spring, running out railroad lines, section lines and cruising the prospective logging sites for the summer. Camp 36 was again the summer logging camp and was to keep the sawmill going one shift after the decked logs, piled up on landings from the winter sleigh hauls, were loaded out.

The hardwood logs, cut in the fall and winter season from October to April, which is the time the sap goes down in the deciduous (or hardwood) species, will hold up good for sawing into lumber until around July first. From that time on, log grade will deteriorate very fast. The company always planned to run the mill two shifts, at least from January to July. During that period the lumber cut from the hardwood species grades out much better than when cut from logs during the spring and summer season when the sap is up in the trees.

The foremen in the camps would put more of their attention on bark peeling during May and June. The one camp was to keep the mill going from summer logging getting the skidways built ahead, etc., in order to be ready when called on to supply the mill with logs. This would take about 75 men and 10 to 12 teams of horses for the balance of the summer and the fall.

Camp No. 37 was located about one mile east of Highway 122 leading off on a town road just south of the bridge over Alder Creek. A kitchen, two men's camps and an office were built during the spring breakup so as to be ready to peel bark by May 15. The remaining camp buildings were finished during the summer and a crew put in to cut, skid and deck logs after the bark peeling season ended in August, 1919. August Schwartz of Mellen was the camp foreman.

There was some fine hemlock at Camp 37, so we had no trouble getting bark peelers. We also got a very good cook and his wife named Christie from Minnesota. When the crew was increased in the fall, a cookee was added.

Matt Mylykangas and Fred Harma who were loggers at Iron Belt did some jobbing for the company that summer farther east on Alder Creek and in the Iron Belt Mountains. My job again for the summer was helping to look after bark peelers and scale the bark. I would make a trip to Hurley for men once in a while, especially later in the season, as men were starting to look around to see where wages were better as there was a greater demand for woods workers. Good timber helped us get the required number of bark peelers.

An incident to show how carefree some of the men of that era were comes to my mind here. John Maki, a tall, well-built, hardworking man of Finnish descent, peeled bark all through the season or around sixty days during the spring and summer of 1919 at the car camps. At the end of the season, he settled up one morning with a time check of around $110.00 net due him. It doesn't sound like much money today but it would be equal to $1,000.00 of today's value.

He walked to Upson, took the Scoot to Mellen, where he received his check, then boarded the afternoon Scoot for Hurley. The next day he returned on the afternoon Scoot to Upson, walked back to camp for supper. He was broke, having been robbed at Hurley, the first night in town. He was so disgusted with himself that he wanted to get out of town at once and back to work. He didn't blame anyone, only himself.

The incident of John Maki's loss happened after the evening of Prohibition, July 1919. The following article from "The Miner" of July, 1919 may be of interest as the time of prohibition begins.

HOT TIME IN HURLEY ON EVE OF PROHIBITION
(Miner Files of July, 1919)

The streets of Hurley presented a busy scene Monday evening on the occasion of the closing of the saloons in accordance with the war time prohibition law. Crowds thronged the streets early in the evening and remained until the curtain was dropped. Many came out of mere curiosity, while others came for the purpose of "loading up" for the impending dry spell. The "loading up" process, of course, was underway for several days, but it became exceptionally heavy as the eleventh hour approached. Some carried the stuff in shoe boxes, a great many carried it in suitcases, but the most popular way of getting it out was by automobile. Cars of all sizes and makes came from all sections of the surrounding country. One person stated that he counted two hundred automobiles parked on the main street of the city during the evening. Saloons were open until midnight, one hour longer than usual. The hour of grace no doubt being granted on account of the momentous occasion.

But in spite of the government closing order, quite a number of saloons are still open for the sale of light beer and wine. Others are open for the sale of soft drinks. A total of thirty saloon-keepers decided to take a chance along with those in other cities of the country who will sell beer of 2¾ percent alcoholic content, pending the decision by courts as to what constitutes intoxicating beer. That number planked down the $500 which entitles them to a city license. Others have not yet decided to take the chance and are closed. So, while hard liquors are tabooed, you may still get your war time beer and light wines."

I also noticed that many times at Hurley and Mellen the lumber-jacks would help each other, especially those who always spent their stakes foolishly. I have seen men go to town with their checks, get them cashed, then meet a few men who they knew previously and not only buy drinks, but hand out a few dollars to his pals so they could buy once in a while. What is more generous than that?

Near the close of the bark peeling season, the summer of 1919, Mark Ferrando and I had an interesting experience. We went out to scale the two-men crew of John Perkela and Oscar Markula. They had peeled bark all season, but were doing a rough job of peeling bark although they knew better. They peeled a lot of bark but weren't careful to get some sheets for covering the top of bark piles. They let bark dry too long so some curled and looked more like stove pipes than bark sheets. The results were terrible-looking bark piles.

The foreman, Henry Cronk, had warned them a few times but hadn't followed up to see that they changed their method of peeling. I had a lot of bark to scale, so Mark had come out to tally the bark pile measurements. When we finished scaling their bark, it tallied out that we had quite a lot less bark than they had figured. It didn't take long for them to tell us, then curse us in the Finnish language. They both grabbed their axes threatening to see that Mark and I would scale no more bark. We stood our ground, as I was sure it was a good act by them. Possibly we both turned pale, but it showed more on Mark, as he had a darker complexion. We finally walked off to the next crew, although a little shaky.

The two men settled up and also worked for me a lot in later years. In fact, Oscar worked at the Corrigan and Organist Camp at Rouse in 1948 or 1949. Just a way of life in those pioneer days, when making a living wasn't easy, but oh, what fun!

One day in the fall of 1919, I was out with Dan McDonald to look over some log roads which had to be ready for the winter haul from Camp 37. The road workers had felled some trees, some were good logs and some culls, but were sound enough for wood. Over near where County Trunk E now runs to Weber Lake, we noticed a man and boy sawing wood out of the cull logs, so we asked them their names. The man said, "Franzoi, and this is my boy, Bruno. We didn't think you would care if we cut up some of these cull logs for wood." McDonald said that it was okay but to see that they didn't cut good logs. He then turned to me and told me to check up once in a while to see that no good logs were cut. Then to show how he wished to help, McDonald pointed out some cull trees along the road which they could cut.

The boy was Bruno Franzoi, then about twelve years old, who now with his wife, have the Belle and Bruno Restaurant and Tavern on Highway 77 as you enter Iron Belt going east. Bruno and his dad cut a lot of wood that fall with a cross cut saw. I think Bruno stood up better on the end of a cross saw at that time than he would now, even though he does some hard work to help keep in condition. Of course, like most men, he turns the hardest work over to his wife. They run a good eating place and tavern. It comes in handy, being the only eating place between Hurley and Mellen. It is a good place to stop for a visit and reminisce on the past. Sometimes many of our current events are settled there, especially political events.

Bruno did a lot of woods work in his early days, but was smarter than some of us and got away from it at a younger age.

After bark peeling, I moved into Camp 37 for my headquarters, where I looked after log sawyers and sleigh road building until the sleigh haul started in January of 1920. I was then sent to the car camps to run the landing crew, with Phil Boissoneau of Mellen scaling the logs at the landing and doing the clerking at Camp 37 in the evenings. All logs from Camp 37 were loaded out at the car camp landing.

Immediately after Christmas 1919 was a busy period for me as getting a sleigh haul landing ready for the first winter is a big job. There were no bulldozers, and the landing had to be leveled, some of which had been done by hand before the freeze-up. Then skidways had to be built, spaced a car load apart, with the sleigh road coming in on the other end of the skidway with the skidway high enough to be about even with the sleigh bunks. This made it easier unloading the sleighs.

I was fortunate in having a good landing and loading crew. My old friend, Harry Frost, the perfect cant hook man mentioned earlier, showed up again and immediately after Christmas went to work with another man and a team getting the skidways built.

When the sleigh haul started in the early part of January, 1920, I put Frank Harris, Frank Wavernick and Earl (Dutch) Blank of Mellen, all back from World War I, on the landing with Harry Frost to unload the sleighs. Ed Pray was the steam loader hoister with Victor Nurmi, an excellent top loader. The loading crew was made up of three additional men, all good lumberjacks. With a good crew like that I was able to put in a pleasant winter, with a minimum of problems.

It was a welcome relief when one morning just after breakfast a phone call came from the foreman, Henry Cronk, at Camp 37, asking if I could send him a sleigh haul teamster. This was a pretty hard assignment from a landing crew. I thought for a minute, then told Cronk, "I have no one to send, but how will I do?" He said, "You, what will I do with you?" I said, "Listen, if you have any kind of a team to drive, I will haul as many logs as any man you have." He answered the way I expected, "The team knows more about hauling logs than you do, but you come anyway as we have to keep the loading crew busy in the woods." I had to put in a parting shot at Cronk, so said, "You see that the team is cleaned and harnessed when I get there as I refuse to drive team any other way. I am a professional." Then I hung up the phone.

I left for Camp 37 immediately and found out there was a good team ready to go. I hooked onto a sleigh, drove out to the loading crew where a sleigh load of logs was all ready for me. I hooked on and went through to the railroad landing all okay. I then went back for another load, which was only partly loaded as the loading crew had put what was left from a deck of logs on the sleigh, then had to move to a new deck. I moved the sleigh to the next deck of good sized hemlock logs, which made a good chance for a nice big load of logs.

The loading crew took up the challenge to try for a record load of logs from that camp. They kept loading logs on, putting the wrappers on carefully until they had 51 good average logs loaded. It was a beautiful load and just as we finished the load, Cronk came along and said, "George, you will never make it to the landing." Well, I had some doubts also but didn't let on. I got onto the sleigh and with the help of a good start got the sleigh load to the ice road.

The landing was two miles away and the sleigh teamsters usually stopped once to give the team a breather. That was where I was expecting trouble in getting the load started again, but I was able to stop gradually in order to be on a little down hill when breaking over the little raise. After we got started again, it was easy sailing as the ice road was in excellent condition.

The weather was just about right for good slipping. When it is really cold, the sleigh runners will not slide easily. When I landed the load, the landing crew wanted a picture, so one of them ran over to the kitchen where Tom Hicks had a camera, and Tom came out and took a picture. When the load was unloaded, it scaled out at a little over 6,000 feet, equal to just about a flat car load in those days.[1]

I'm not saying that load of logs was a record load, but there have never been many larger loads of logs hauled by one team of horses. I'm not saying either that I was the only teamster hauling that day who could have hauled that load; there were three other better teamsters hauling that day.

I got the breaks by being at the right place at the right time and to have some nice large long logs. I made it a point to help the sleigh top loader to pick and place the logs in order to get a big load. It gave me a chance to have some fun with Henry Cronk, the foreman, who said I would not make it to the landing.

In January, 1920, a news item mentioned that Manager J. D. Twomey of the Mellen Lumber Company was getting almost as much publicity in the newspapers throughout the state as were Jack Dempsey, George Carpenter or Babe Ruth. The cause of J.D.'s sudden jump

---

[1]I had the picture along with many others I would never have parted with until the fall of 1942. I had a trunk load of pictures, maps of all the Foster-Latimer operations, including all railroad branches and camp setups, etc., which we left at the farm that winter. In some way late that fall, the house caught fire and burned completely, trunk and contents included; otherwise, there certainly would be more pictures with this write-up.

into the limelight was through an idea of establishing a home for aged woodsmen, to be built near Glidden.

Twomey had obtained a tract of land from the Mellen Lumber Company at the junction of the Augustine River and the east branch of the Chippewa River, which he felt was an excellent site for the proposed home. The project never did get started, however. John Twomey had a good idea, but he was looking farther ahead than most of the lumbermen of that era.

One home for woodsmen did get started later out of Hayward with some success until the Social Security Law of 1937 became effective. Then in later years, the Unemployment Workman's Compensation Act took up more of the slack, but the woodsworker was one of the last to be covered by the Act.

During the winter of 1920, I made a very interesting two-day trip at the request of McDonald and Richardson who asked me to go out of Saxon to observe an experimental steam-powered sleigh log hauler. The landing crew at the car camps were all set with a good crew with the sleigh haul moving into February. Richardson said he was not too busy for a few days and was going to send me over to Saxon to spend a couple of days on that logging job and he would take care of the landing for me.

A logging company had been organized at Mellen consisting of the Cordy Brothers - Frank and Walter - George Schuler of the Mellen Cedar Company, and Nels Ledin of Mason who had been connected with the Charcoal Iron Company of Ashland. They bought the stumpage on a good-sized area of land between Saxon and Lake Superior. It consisted of some pine, hemlock and mixed hardwood species of logs with a fair amount of good white cedar which was in demand for telephone and power company lines, as well as for shingles.

The company had good timber, but a rough logging chance, not rocky like the Foster-Latimer Lumber Company logging chance, but large ravines with a clay soil, making it hard to lay out sleigh haul roads without many heavy uphill grades.

The first couple of miles out of Saxon were not bad, but they had no stumpage those first couple of miles so that didn't help them much, except that it was easier to make roads. Once up to the ravines it was different, as the ravines all lead toward Lake Superior which would have made a much longer haul and the forest products would still have to come back toward Saxon in order to get to a railroad siding.

It would have been almost impossible to get the logs and poles out of those ravines with horses, so those men decided on leasing a steam-powered sleigh log hauler and a fleet of sleighs.

On a winter's day I took my little packsack after breakfast and started for Saxon, nine miles away, where I was to catch a ride to the woods with one of the bosses from the railroad landing. It was a cool day with the sun shining when I started out, making it a nice day to walk. The road was good and I made Saxon before 10:00 a.m. On arriving at the landing I found George Schuler there with the driving team and sled.

The steam hauler had just arrived with ten sleigh loads of logs with about 3,000 feet of logs on each sleigh. The steam hauler, when having no trouble, made two trips a day. The logs had to be hauled out of steep ravines in some places.

Part of the sleighs had to be set out at an appointed location, one load at a time, then coupled with the four or five other loads so they could be hauled out at one time. Time was lost in this way and there were some days when only one trip was made to the landing.

The steam hauler was shaped like a railroad locomotive, but in place of wheels it had rollers and a track like the gasoline tractors which started to come into use at about this time. The fire box was made so either soft coal or wood could be used for fuel. Wood was used on this job as a lot of it was piled at different locations along the road.

The company also had one gasoline tractor on the job on a trial basis. I am sure it was a ten-ton Holt tractor, one of the first gasoline tractors used in the woods. The day I was there it seems they were having some track troubles, so I wasn't able to see much accomplished under gasoline power. I had plenty of experience with Holt tractors two winters later.

At the time I was, of course, more interested in the steam hauler, which happened to do some good work the couple of days I was there. Nels Ledin, in charge of getting the logs out of the woods, informed me that there had been plenty of trouble with the steam hauler at times. He didn't recommend it at all for the kind of country the Foster-Latimer Lumber Company was logging in, and George Schuler informed Dan McDonald in the same way.

After watching it perform two days, I was of the same opinion. With Dan McDonald and Richardson not too optimistic about a steam hauler in the first place, the Foster-Latimer Lumber Company never did use one.

The gasoline-powered Holt-Caterpillar was gaining recognition in that period, which Dan McDonald believed was going to be of some use in the woods.

Disappointingly, Cordy Brothers and Nels Ledin were unable to get all their forest products hauled on the Saxon job before the breakup.

Notes of interest from "The Mellen Weekly" files:

April 29, 1920 -- Timber Workers Union has served notice on lumber and shingle manufacturers and veneer mills of Minnesota, Michigan and Wisconsin that an eight-hour workday will be demanded on May 3, 1920. The mills have said the demand will not be granted.

May 6, 1920 -- Men didn't report for work on May 3rd.

May 13, 1920 -- All mills are still shut down tight.

May 27, 1920 -- All mills not running in Mellen area.

June 6, 1920 -- Some mills start on small scale.

June 24- 1920 -- More mills are getting started, all on a ten-hour day.

August 12, 1920 -- Foster-Latimer sawmill to start running after being almost entirely rebuilt during the past three months.

When the sleigh haul was completed on the car camp landing around March 15, 1920, I was sent over to the Tyler Forks Landing to scale out logs the company was buying from William Layman, Mose Meredith and Earl Poundstone. This partnership logging company had stumpage and a logging camp about one mile southeast from Tyler Forks Siding. They had hauled the logs out and decked them on the siding during the winter. Foster-Latimer Lumber Company let them use a steam loader and crew to do the loading out.

It was one of those springs when a lot of log loading was going on and a serious railroad car shortage developed. The loading crew was capable of loading around eight car loads a day or about 50,000 feet. Some days we would load eight cars. Other days we would get from two to eight empties which made it very bad for Layman, Meredith, and Poundstone, three very fine men. I remember Mose Meredith taking it very hard.

It would have been worse if they were compelled to load with their own crew, but the Foster-Latimer Lumber Company loading crew had put in a hard winter and didn't care if they lost a little time. They would stay in Mellen and wouldn't go out to load unless at least six empty cars were spotted. When they didn't go out to load, I wouldn't go out, so I had a little vacation out of the deal.

Finally around the middle of April, we finished the job and I went back to the car camps to get ready for the summer bark peeling. There was always a lot of very interesting work.

The car camps continued as the headquarter camp for the spring, summer and fall of 1920 and the winter of 1921. There was a lot of railroad building to do in the area which could be handled by having a Lima engine tied up in the woods at this location. The car camps, therefore, were operated strictly as a railroad building camp for the summer months.

Camps 37 and 38 were bark peeling camps again. The summer logging was done from Camp 38. Matt Mylyakangas had a logging job from the company and peeled bark during that summer between Iron Belt and Weber Lake.

In the spring of 1920, the company added another logging contractor, John Dunn of Mellen. They placed him about a mile southwest of Moore at the end of a railroad spur. The Soo Line ran in from the main line at Moore. Moore was a railroad station at that time. A man named John Moore who had a combination small store, rooms and meals lived there with his family until the middle twenties.

John Dunn's crew peeled bark that summer. They skidded and decked the logs on sleigh roads in the fall, then kept on sawing and skidding hardwood logs to the roads all winter.

Henry Cronk was foreman at Camp 38, with Ernest Anderson, scaler and clerk. Smokey Ferrando took care of the cars with William Richardson, the woods walking boss. Mr. and Mrs. Tom Hicks continued to be the cooks at the cars, and Mr. and Mrs. Christie at Camp 37. Martha Peterson, a very young girl who lived at Upson, helped as a cookee at Camp 37 during the summer school vacation. She became a very good cook a few years later and cooked a year or two for her brother, Joe Peterson, in the middle 1920's when he was a contract logger.

After the bark peeling season, I was put to work running out section lines and quarter lines -- that is, blazing lines to cut the section into four quarters of one hundred sixty acres each. You always could see these blazes when you were crossing a certain section. We blazed the lines with an axe. Paint is now used to mark the lines. The spring, before leaves are on the trees, or fall after the leaves are off, is the best time to run lines or picket out a railroad, as you can see so much better to get an idea of the terrain and contour of the land.

We had no photos of the timberlands from the air as we have today so running out railroads was a very particular job, especially in rough country. If you don't believe it, try walking cross country, skiing, or snowmobiling any place north of the Tyler Forks River to Gurney, Hurley, Iron Belt, Saxon or Upson and the area in Ashland County of Mellen to Mineral Lake, Sanborn, Marengo, Highbridge and Odanah, using the old railroad or sleigh roads where possible. For people who haven't lived in the northern part of Wisconsin or Michigan, it will be a treat they will never forget, as the scenery is outstanding along any of the rivers or lakes.

It is especially beautiful along the Bad, Potato, and Tyler Forks Rivers at any season of the year. The one thing that has helped to keep the Tyler Forks and Potato Rivers so beautiful is the hilly, rough, winding country they flow through. Another thing, the species of timber which grew along those rough areas adjoining the rivers wasn't much sought after in the early days. When the companies logged near those rivers with oxen or horses, it paid them to log only the most valuable species such as white pine and yellow birch, so much good cover was left. Again an "Act of God" helped along those rivers as in only a few spots did the fires burn really close to the rivers. Now with the new second growth getting more mature, the area presents many worthwhile sights to see.

There is another Wisconsin area I would classify as the second most beautiful, and it could possibly be first except for the heavy population. That area is along the western side of Wisconsin from Trempeleau to Prairie du Chien. I always enjoyed traveling this part of the state almost as much as my own area.

When running section and railroad lines, I was furnished a helper most of the time, but not always the same person, as the foreman at the camp furnished the best man he could spare at any given time.

Blazing section lines wasn't hard as the helper could use a light hatchet and simply watch the compass man ahead of him who placed one hand on the trees in the line on which the helper was to knock enough bark off to show where the line was located. These blazes were so other men connected with the company could follow the line. Those lines were also handy if a man happened to get lost, as they would generally lead out to a road.

Picketing out a railroad was much more important and harder work, as you wanted to keep a straight line wherever possible. In doing so, you had to cut smaller trees. When your line came directly into a large tree, it was a case of cutting it down or measuring an offset line on each side of the tree. Off-setting required very careful measuring or when the railroad steel was finally laid, you might have a small kink in the track. This was a very serious error, especially on a main line track.

The pickets were set each fifty feet, measured by pacing on straight lines and by a tape line on curves, in order to get the curve more accurate. Being careful with the pickets, you could run a good, even line.

Running lines required a lot of walking. On virgin timber land away from the rivers, there were very few roads. We worked in from whatever direction we could catch the line picketed the previous day at the shortest point by using a Box Gurley Compass.

It was work I enjoyed very much, and it surely helped to know the area in which you were working. Foster-Latimer Lumber Company owned most of the stumpage rights from the Tyler Forks River on the west, to a line north and south from Hoyt to Kimball in the east, north to Gurney, Saxon and Kimball, and south to State Highway 77, covering the towns of Anderson, Gurney, Knight and Saxon.

Since I started working for them in January, 1914, I worked steadily in the woods until April 1, 1926 for all but ten months. I also worked on the laying out of railroads and section lines during that twelve year period, so I know that area very well. In fact, I will say that I could be dropped from a helicopter anywhere in that area in the morning without a compass and I would get out before nightfall. It is really home for me, as I have logged pulpwood and some saw logs the second time in that forest area.

Just as the fall log decking season was going in full swing around November 1, 1920, Bill Richardson and I had a real bear experience. We took the No. 2 spot railroad engine over to old Camp 31 on the Potato River near Foster Falls where the old office and barn at Camp 31 was still standing.

The company was able to pasture horses not working in the spring and summer. An old-time barn boss named Joe Bauer was left there to take care of the horses. There were no fences, but the company always left plenty of oats so Joe was able to feed them a little oats morning and night. The horses had luscious grass in those old slashings, especially a year after the forest fires had gone through. A little oats morning and night would keep the horses coming back regularly. Only a few crippled horses were there at this time.

Bill and I got off the engine about one mile east of Potato River where we were going to set pickets for the new main line going through to what is now State Highway 122. The railroad line we were running is now the Sullivan Fire Lane with a direction sign on Highway 122 just south of Sullivan Creek.

We started setting pickets just before the line crossed Sullivan Creek about two miles west from Highway 122. About 2:00 p.m. after setting pickets for about one-half mile, we had to walk to the highway about one and one-half miles away, then five miles to the car camps for the night.

We decided to run the compass in the direction our railroad line was going to see if we were coming out at the spot where McDonald and Richardson had picked for the site for Camp 41 to be built.

The Airdale dog had followed us this day and was keeping close to us. I was running the compass and Bill was carrying the two little blazing axes when we heard the dog barking in an excited manner. It was the first time we had missed the dog, but we paid no attention for awhile. The dog kept on barking and seemed to be getting closer. Bill, looking through an opening in the trees where the conifers weren't so thick, saw the dog coming with a bear chasing it. The dog circled a little, then came toward us.

It all happened so fast, I can truthfully say we didn't have time to get scared. The dog stopped at our feet and I thought for a second the bear was going to run over us, but she stopped too. Seeing us, she stood up on her hind feet, ready to strike at the dog who had chased her two cubs. We were all on about a three-foot space. We could easily have shaken hands with the bear or the bear could have slapped Bill or I easily, but she took one look at us, dropped down on her four feet and took off.

It was a good lesson to us, as I have studied black bear habits ever since and have had from one to six bears at one time at our cabin on Weber Lake each summer since 1954.

The lessons I learned by that encounter in 1920 with bear, and I have met hundreds of them in the woods since that time, never run from a bear unless there is a real small tree handy, which will hold a man and too small for a bear to climb. If you run any distance and they want to catch you, they will anyway. I clocked one running ahead of a Ford pickup on the Island Lake County Road at thirty miles per hour, and when it left the road it looked like a big black ball rolling into the woods. Phil Boissoneau, our camp clerk, had a different version, which he put in the "Mellen Weekly." I stand by my description of the event.

WOODSMEN GAVE BEAR AWFUL CHASE
One day during the past week Bill Richardson, walker for Foster-

Latimer Lumber Company and George Corrigan, scaler and utility worker for the same company, accompanied by their Airedale dog, left the camp cars to round up a bear that had been seen in the vicinity. Everything went all right with the hunt, and for several hours the three brave hunters showed wonderful bravery.

General Pershing or Frank Kapellan had nothing on them when they were in search of the enemy. Suddenly the bear was located by the dog. The dog took one look at Mr. Bear and without hesitation reversed his course and began beating it in the opposite direction with considerable speed. George unlimbered his long legs and began stepping over windfalls in a manner that would do credit to a fair-sized buck deer.

About this time Bill got a glance at Mrs. Bruin who was just starting to throw herself into high and coming in his direction. Bill tore up a couple of saplings getting started and he set sail in the direction of Corrigan and the Airedale. As he caught up to them, he brushed them aside and in passing them, said, "If you can't run, get out of the way and let someone run that can." The bear gave up the chase after a half mile or so and went back to continue her search for a hollow stump to hibernate in, thoroughly satisfied that she had no chance in a race with those fellows and would need the balance of the winter to rest up.

All the meetings I have had with bear since that time bears out my theory of not to run. The next best thing some say is to faint or play dead. Some people may faint without trying. I have also found out that in the spring of the year when the mother bear has her cubs with her (they are born in February but still very small in the spring) is the most dangerous period. People acquainted with wild animals know that all animals, however small, will fight for their young. Another thing which makes bear more dangerous in the early spring is that they are hungry after the long winter hibernation and food is scarce until the new crop of vegetation has a start. Bear aren't a real carnivorous animal and prefer some vegetation growth, berries, fish, pastry, fruit, etc., in preference to meat. They will tear apart old decayed stumps or logs to get at a nest of ants.

In the spring of the year when food is scarce or after the berry and fruit season was over, we would have to watch our pigs at the farms, camps and the screen meathouses at camp, as bear loved smoked ham and bacon. Other times of the year I have seen bear eat swill with the pigs and never bother the pigs.

The one important thing I attempt to impress on my own children and grandchildren and tourists who come to our summer cottage on Weber Lake is that bear are wild animals so treat them as such; don't try to make complete pets of them. I always have a bear feeding place in the summer. When there are small children at our summer cottage, I feed them farther away and only once a day in the evening. They do not stay around all the time. I miss a day or two without putting out food so they don't get to depend on it.

Bear are one of the better tourist attractions we have. A few times in 1968, we had up to thirty young people at one time at the lake and on nice evenings they would line up near the feeding grounds to watch the bears eat. That summer one mother bear came regularly with two cubs which were the centers of attraction. Another summer we had a female with three cubs. Bear study has been a hobby of mine for years. I get carried away once in awhile. I do wish to give a couple of illustrations on being careful when you see cubs alone, as generally the mother bear is not far away.

My wife and I were driving to Upson for the mail one day when we saw three cubs playing on the road at the foot of Copper Hill on Highway 122. We went on into Upson, then on going back the three cubs were again on the road. I stopped the car some distance from the cubs so we could watch the performance. When the car stopped, however, the mother bear soon came out to scatter those cubs.

Another time Leo Lipske and I saw a cub cross the Rouse Fire Lane. We stopped the pickup to investigate, but it didn't take mother bear long to let us know we weren't wanted so we didn't argue with her. Some people think I just feed the bear so it will be easy for me to get one in bear hunting season. Not true. I could no more shoot one of the bear which I feed than to fly. In fact, I try to discourage the bears from being around in the hunting season, so they will be harder to get.

Items of interest from "Mellen Weekly" files:

October 14, 1920. Man tries to wreck log train of the Stearns Lumber Company, Odanah, on a sixteen-foot high trestle over a gulch on the Bad River Reservation. He was picked up. It resembles the try a man made to wreck a Foster-Latimer log train a few years ago.

October 14, 1920. Forest fires cause heavy losses for Cordy Brothers and Nels Ledin interests near Saxon. Unable to get a lot of their forest products out before the breakup last spring, it was left on skids to be hauled the coming winter and this was about all destroyed. The loss included 500,000 feet of saw logs, 15,000 railroad tie cuts and 10,000 pieces of cedar poles and posts. It was a real loss.

November 18, 1920. Wages in woods are being cut. New price schedule into effect November 15, 1920. Notice as follows:

The following wages will apply to all men hired after this date (a cut of $15.00 per month):

Swampers - $60.00 per month, plus board. Tailing Down on Skidways - $60.00 per month, plus board. Teamsters - $65.00 per month, plus board. Sawyers - $65.00 per month, plus board. Signed: Foster-Latimer Lumber Co.

I remember putting up some of the signs. The reduction affected men hired after November 15, 1920. Men that were in the employ of the company previous to this date and order are not affected by the change of wage scale.

Wanigan prices also cut 20%.

Personal Comment: You can be sure this wage reduction was decided on at the Wisconsin Loggers Association meeting at Ashland on September 20, 1920. It also shows that the woods worker was always the first to get a cut in wages and the last to get a raise. It seems to be the same today in the 1970's. It also goes to show that a war-time economy is never reliable as it is almost always an inflationary trend, caused by worker shortages and a high demand for goods for a few years after a war.

I have always had the impression that the woods worker was treated unfairly on the wage scale, as I don't believe that any segment of our labor force works harder for the money they receive than the woods worker and works under more unfavorable conditions. In the summer, it is insects, flies, heat, rain, and in the winter severe cold, winds, snow, ice, etc.

One day in the fall of 1920 Dan McDonald said, "We're now using the County Road (State Highway No. 122 now) more for a starting point when running out our lines as a lot of the section and quarter corners have deteriorated so much it is hard to distinguish them." This was before the days of steel corner posts. This was a total distance of eight miles and it was quite a job, as it required walking back and forth to the headquarter camps near Alder Creek. I did hit a spell of nice weather which helped make the job pleasant as I worked alone on it.

In December, it came time to get ready for sleigh hauls again, so Dan McDonald told me to get the car camp landing ready again, but I wouldn't be there the winter of 1921. He said, "I'm sending you over to John Dunn's camp out of Moore to see that they clean up that job this coming winter, as we don't want to go back there another year." John Dunn had some trouble keeping a foreman during the summer and fall but finally got a capable man named Jim Scott who had worked some for McDonald in his younger days around Newberry, Michigan.

Jim Scott took care of the woods and I took care of the landing and scaled the logs and billed out the cars daily at Moore. We put in a nice winter. The camp was close enough to the landing, so we could coffee up once in a while. It was also handy to catch the Scoot home on Saturday evenings and back on Sunday nights. I was able to get in for a wrestling match or basketball game during the week, as we could take the Scoot to Mellen in the late afternoon, then catch the daily freight out in the morning early enough for breakfast.

We had a good loading crew, with a team of horses for power in the cross haul. A James McBride from Sanborn had hired himself and a good team to John Dunn for the winter. Ed Spray, a very capable young man, landed at camp one day and told Jim Scott he was a top loader. Jim was doubtful and mentioned it to me that night. He said he is only a boy twenty years old. I said, "Well, Jim, you know there are a lot of young men who are working in the woods now; he may be better than he looks."

Back when they decked or loaded with horse teams, a good crew would handle a lot of logs at a low cost. It served a purpose when really needed.

Ed Spray had been working in the woods from a very young age and was a really good cant-hook man. He was also very good in all woods work, as I found out in later years. With Ed Spray top loading and Jim McBride and team in the cross haul and two good hookers along with another good hook man unloading sleighs, the crew loaded from six to seven flat car loads of logs amounting to 40,000 to 45,000 feet daily. This was very good loading with a team and side jammer loader. We also had a bark loading crew, as there was a lot of bark to load out.

John Dunn had a good cook that winter by the name of Frank Gilcrist which helped to keep a steady crew.

We had one very sad accident at the John Dunn camp in late February or early March, 1921, which really upset the landing crew for a few days. Ed Spray, the top loader, loading cars on the landing had gone home on a weekend and didn't get back for work on Monday morning. A young man from Birch Lake in Bayfield County, Clarence Olson, was unloading sleighs on the landing and offered to top load until Ed Spray got back or the foreman put a new man on the job. Clarence was a good able young fellow but had no experience at top loading. I wasn't in favor of him taking over top loading on a side jammer with horse power as this was about as dangerous a job as a man could pick out.

The foreman told him not to take chances but to stay on the safe side all of the time, even if they didn't load so many logs. They loaded one car of logs and all went well, until the next car. When loading cars with a side jammer, the top loader placed the stakes on the car next to the jammer, then put up as many logs as they could safely pile up on the car before placing the car stakes on the front face of the car. This saved the team from lifting so many logs over the stakes and they wouldn't have to back the team up so much.

They would try to get the larger logs on the car before putting up the front stakes. Clarence had piled up what came handy and then had a large yellow birch log to put on the car before placing the car stakes. There were other logs on the skidway behind the large log which could be loaded easily after the stakes were up, so the loading crew looked carefully that the skids from the skidway to the car were in a skid position.

The hookers placed the loading hooks on each end of the large log and hollered to the teamster to go ahead. The team started off easy with the log going nicely until it was up on the last log on the middle of the car, where it wouldn't balance over the last log. Clarence then got behind the log, put his peavey in place to give a little push, when suddenly one hook pulled out on the end of the log, letting the weight on Clarence. It looked for a couple of seconds that he would make it, but there was too much weight against him so he had to let go and jump off the car with no time to pick out his fall and the log rolled back down the loading skids, pinning him between the logs, crushing the left side of his upper body.

We placed him on a sled and took him up to the Moore Station to wait the arrival of a doctor from Mellen. He never gained consciousness; although, there were some signs of life from around ten o'clock until three o'clock p.m., but the doctor said he had been crushed too badly around the heart and lungs to survive.

It was a sad loading crew for a few days as they all liked Clarence very much. If he had just fallen off the car, his life might have been saved, as the log would have rolled down the skids over him but he jumped a little too far. There is no "second guessing" in a situation like that as you have no time to think out your next move. I know from experience, as I had a real close call on a load of logs many years later.

The following paragraphs record a few notes of interest from the "Mellen Weekly" in the winter of 1921:

January, 1921: Joe Kannia who is logging with his brother, Walter, in the Ballou area, received a serious injury when operating a snowplow which hit a limb breaking a piece of the limb, which was thrown up and hit Joe."

The Kannia Brothers operated a logging camp a couple of winters in the Hoyt-Kimball area of Iron County.

Sam Giovanoni, a well-known Hurley resident, a good semi-pro baseball player, was a sheriff for two or three terms, later took over the former Christenson Hardware Store on Silver Street and started what is now the very successful Giovanoni Tru Value Hardware business. At the age of 16, Sam worked at odd jobs for the Kannia's the winter of 1921.

When I was a logging contractor in the Island, Moose and Pine Lake area of Iron County, Sam Giovanoni and Jerry Lawler, another Hurley businessman, would always spend a few days at our logging camps in hunting season. We always enjoyed them.

We were reminiscing one evening in a gun-hunting season when Sam told me about his logging experience. I had remembered seeing a young active boy getting on and off the Scoot passenger train with the Kannia crew but did not know his name in 1921. Sam is now semi-retired with the business managed by his son, Jack.

February 3, 1921: John D. Twomey resigns his position as General Manager of the Mellen Lumber Company Logging Operations at Foster Junction and Glidden after twelve years on the job. To be replaced by Ed Mercier of the Stearns Lumber Company, Odanah, as Woods Superintendent with Fred Keller, Office Manager of the Mellen Office, taking over the additional duties of business manager.

April 28, 1921: Otto Grieser, employed by the Foster-Latimer Lumber Company as a railroad and shop maintenance worker and living in a company house in White Row, was held up by a masked man opposite the company office at 9:30 p.m. and relieved of $8.00. In telling me about it, Otto said, "With a gun pointed at me, I put up no argument!"

So we had large and small robberies, murders, suicides, etc., probably as many in proportion to the population in those days as we have today.

10

New Challenges

The spring and summer of 1921 was a real challenge as it really tested my stamina. I moved back from the John Dunn Camp at Moore to the headquarters at the car camps out of Upson on what is now State Highway 122.

William Richardson, the woods superintendent, and I got busy at once laying out a main line railroad from about one mile north of old Camp 31 near Foster Falls, east to what is now State Highway 122. This branch crossed Highway 122 again, one-half mile north of the main line railroad and went on east about three miles across Mud Creek and ended in the Kimball farm area. There were three or four branch lines running off this main line. This was all a heavy virgin hardwood and hemlock timber stand, with most of the logging done by cutting and skidding to railroads. A small block was left for winter sleigh haul on the east end of the two branches.

Another problem the company had that spring was to build two sets of logging camps, with the lumber to be unloaded at the car camp landing on Highway 122. The lumber was loaded onto wagons to be toted to a point about a quarter of a mile, just east of Iron Belt where the tote road angled northeast until it came out on the old wagon road from Hoyt to Kimball about one-half mile north of Hoyt. It then continued north another mile and a half to where the marked hiking trail from Weber Lake to Montreal crossed the Hoyt to Kimball road, just north of Alder Creek, then west about one-half mile to where Camp 39 was to be constructed. It was a distance of about eleven miles and the team made one round trip a day with all the lumber and equipment to be used at that camp. The man who drove the team was my brother, Bill Corrigan.

The other camp was to be located about four miles out of Upson on the Upson to Morse road and about two miles southwest of Rouse. The logs and bark were to be loaded out during the winter of 1921 and 1922. It was to be Camp 40. It was only a small one-year camp, with six 40's of good timber to be logged. Henry Cronk was the foreman in that camp.

A man named John Hanson from the Houghton, Michigan area was hired as foreman for Camp 39. A couple of tents were pitched for the camp building crew, one for the kitchen and one for sleeping. Hanson had a crew of eight men and started to clean camp grounds the same day the first load of lumber was hauled in.

The tote team kept him in lumber until a kitchen, men's camp and office were complete enough to start a crew peeling bark by May 15. Bill kept on hauling lumber, equipment and supplies until another men's camp, blacksmith shop and barn were constructed. It was a one-year camp also, but housed a crew of about 80 to 100 men, as there was a large block of timber to be logged out of extremely rough country.

During that spring and early summer, my sister, Mrs. Ida Bell and her two children, Joe and Bonnie Bell, arrived from Valdez, Alaska for a visit with our mother, sister Ann, brothers Bill and me at Mellen and sister Frances at Warren, Minnesota. Ida Bell had gone to Alaska from Bibon, Wisconsin in 1905 at the age of sixteen, a few years after our father's death, to work for an aunt and uncle in a hardware store at Valdez. She later met Joe Bell from Lancaster, Wisconsin who had gone to Alaska with a brother a few years earlier when the gold rush was on.

The two men stayed in Alaska, although they did not hit it rich. Joe Bell became a mail and gold carrier with a dog team in the mining area around Valdez, and was the driver of the first horse-drawn coach from Valdez to Fairbanks, Alaska, a distance of about 400 miles. From viewing the road he drove over when I was in Alaska in the late summer of 1968, I would consider it a great feat to just walk over the road, let alone drive a team over it.

Each day when Bill Corrigan left the car camps with a load of lumber or other supplies on his wagon, for the round trip of twenty-two miles to Camp 39 and back, young Joe would be there. He liked to take a turn at driving the team.

About once a week, Ida Bell and daughter, Bonnie, often accompanied by my mother or sister Ann, would also spend a day at the camps. Ida had the same opinion of our scenery in northern Wisconsin and Michigan as did Joe, Jr. She said the only difference was that there were glaciers and more large rivers and lakes in Alaska. Our timber, at the time, was better here.

Soon after the bark season opened, I became extremely busy on bark peeling. I had much hiking between camps that summer as the camps were so far apart. I walked more those next two months than in any other two-month period of my life, although walking always was a part of my job in the woods.

I made a schedule to be at the large bark peeling camp (No. 39) two days each week, with one day at Camp 40, one day at Camp 38, one day at the jobbers, and one day wherever needed. Some days I would walk thirty miles, in addition to scaling a hundred cords of bark. My headquarters were centered at the car camps on Highway 122. Many times I would sleep at one camp and walk to the other camp before 5:30 a.m.

In scaling, it was necessary to wear calk shoes because the hemlock trees would be extremely slippery after the bark was peeled until it dried out towards the fall of the year. I wore good, light walking shoes when not scaling bark and carried the calk shoes. I tied them together, then used the scale stick to carry them over my back to the next camp. I weighed 180 pounds when I started that summer's work, which was the most I ever weighed, and around August first, I was down to 160 pounds.

I ran into some poison ivy one day, which in my run-down condition really knocked me out; but I survived the ordeal, although I never weighed 180 pounds again. I settled at 170 pounds, which has varied only a few pounds a year since 1922, so weight has never been a problem to me, even though I am a good eater and can eat or drink whatever I like, whenever I want to. It was always great to be that way in the logging camps with all the rich food available.

During the fall of 1921, I had the good fortune to pilot Alvin Rabbideau a couple of days while he made some changes in the camp bookkeeping methods at the camp offices. (Alvin was now working in the Foster-Latimer main office in Mellen.) I had known Alvin for a long time, but was never around him much, as I was working in the woods and he was working in town. I really knew him as a good semi-pro baseball player.

In the two days he spent at camp, I learned that Alvin was an all-around good scout who seemed to enjoy every minute he spent at the camp. Since it was late fall, with the season open on deer and snow-shoe rabbits, the rabbits just turning from brown to white, we carried a rifle as we hiked from one camp to another, in case a deer was chased out some place. Along the trail one day we saw a big snowshoe rabbit sitting up in a swamp, so I took a shot; the rabbit did not move. Alvin took a shot; the rabbit still did not move. "Gee," I said, "it must be in a snare or killed by someone who set it up there." When we went to investigate, we found out it was alive, as it raced away. It was just as well it was not a deer.

That summer we were so busy that there wasn't much excitement, but one day going from Camp 39 to the car camps, I saw the largest black bear I have ever seen. I was walking a ridge looking across a flat, when I saw what looked like a high black charred stump. No fire had been through there so I took a better look. As I moved closer, the bear evidently heard me as he sat there on his haunches looking more like a horse than a bear. When I moved again, he took off. I never did see one as large again although I have seen many bear. There was much wildlife in that area at the time: bear, deer, timber wolves, coyotes, fox, beaver, snowshoe rabbits and other small game, including lots of partridge.

After getting back on the job after the poison ivy attack, the company gave me a helper to run out railroad logging branches in the area northwest of Foster Falls, which was to be logged the following summer after bark peeling.

The boarding cars were to be located on Sullivan Creek in the spring of 1922 as headquarters for building railroads and peeling bark. One evening, when I got to camp from work, Bill said, "You'd better hike over to Camp 39 after supper as Hanson, the foreman, sent word that he might need a cook at once." If the cook left I would be able to look up one for them.

I hiked over to Camp 39 and sure enough, the cook told Hanson he wanted to leave at once, but would stay another day or two. A lumberjack came into Camp 39 from Saxon that evening and told Hanson there was a good cook in Saxon named Joe Dawson who was on a little vacation but was broke. We all knew he was a good cook, so Hanson told me to go over to Saxon in the morning and see if I could hire him.

In the morning I took off for Saxon. I took the Hoyt-Kimball wagon road trail north from near Camp 39 to old Highway 10, then west to the Kimball Railroad Depot where I caught the morning passenger train to Saxon. I found Dawson at the Pat Auger Bar and Hotel, but getting him out of Saxon was another problem, as there were some jacks with money in town and Dawson was still thirsty. By staying around Dawson, I was able to keep him spacing his drinks enough that he was able to take the evening passenger train to Hurley where I kept him overnight.

We took the Scoot to Hoyt in the morning where I walked him into camp in time for dinner. He was fairly sober by evening, but sick, and not ready to go to work the following morning. Hanson let him stay in camp figuring he would be okay the next morning. Joe had different ideas. He took off again for Hurley during the day. Even though I had spent a day and a half getting him over from Saxon, Hanson still did not have a cook! We didn't try to track him down and I believe either Art Kenney or Tom Padjen finally took the job, so the problem was solved.

A few weeks later, John Hanson, the foreman at Camp 39, decided to go back to the Diamond Match Company in upper Michigan. The country there was not quite as rough as around Camp 39. Bill Richardson sent me over to take Hanson's place until they could get a foreman. He and McDonald decided to leave me there so there were some new experiences as I was once more a foreman.

For about eight years, I had been working in logging camps for the Foster-Latimer Lumber Company and the Mellen Lumber Company. It was all in very rough country, but not comparable with the area north of Iron Belt which takes in the Iron Belt, Upson, and White Cap Mountain Range. This terrain should be called mountains to give the area some deserved prestige.

Camp 39 had begun the fall logging season. After the completion of bark peeling, sawyers were cutting the peeled hemlock trees into logs and making sleigh roads. It was strictly a sleigh haul camp, with emphasis on getting all the logs possible, cut, skidded and decked on the sleigh roads before the snow. It was important to get the peeled hemlock logs and mixed hardwood from the roughest spots, although it was all rough enough.

There were six teams of horses and about forty men at camp 39 when I took over, which was increased by six teams and thirty men as fast as we could get ready for them. A fair share of our crew coming from Iron Belt, Pence, and the Upson area. Some were good, able young men who had some logging experience and were willing to work.

We had one problem not encountered before when the camps were further into the wilderness. It seems the people on the small farms and others in the region figured that Foster-Latimer Lumber Company, being a large company, could afford to furnish tools and logging equipment for all, free of charge. First we started missing an axe or a cant hook, then our cross-cut saws, then it was team rigging or tongs, and skidding chains. It got so bad that the men had to hide the tools or carry them back to camp each night. The teamsters would hide the team rigging, chain, and tongs a short distance away from the skidways.

I remember one morning the saw boss took four gangs of sawyers out to saw hardwood logs. The tools consisted of eight new D.B. axes and four 5½-foot cross-cut saws. It was within walking distance of camp for the dinner meal. When the crew went out after dinner, the tools were gone. Someone had carried some of them away and had hid some of them. The saw boss watched that afternoon and early evening but no one came back. In the morning, while looking in the woods, he found two of the cross-cut saws, but the others saws and eight axes were never found; the thieves had carried all they could. It was not a huge loss, as axes and saws were not really high priced at that time, but it was very inconvenient.

By all of us keeping a close vigil and letting the crew know it would have to stop, the thievery gradually tapered off. I have thought while logging the modern way you could leave an axe or a cross-cut saw right in the road and no one would bother to take it as it does not have a motor on it. Very few would know how to use those tools anyway, but leave a power saw handy and you will see how quickly it will disappear.

We kept at the skidding and decking steady. We were fortunate in having a fairly dry fall, which surely helped in those hills and ravines.

There were places where logs had to be skidded and dumped once and skidded and dumped again before getting the logs to a road where they could be decked for the winter haul. To add to the logging problems, there were many flowing springs. The spring water coming out of the hills made it difficult for good ice roads. Some real spring water does not freeze solid. It tends to crystalize. In many places, we would have to pole the roads cross wise, placing the poles about two feet apart, so as to hold the sleighs up with heavy loads.

The good weather continued through October and into November. We kept the skidding and decking crews in the roughest places, which we finished around November 15, 1921.

Deer hunting season was coming on the weekend and I planned to join Aristo David, Mike Donahue, Oscar Auley, and Roy Gonia, a guest, at our hunting camp on Potato River near the outlet of Upson Lake. The lodge was also on the Foster and Latimer railroad track, but that did not help us at that time. The four men mentioned above were coming from Mellen on the Scoot to a spot about two miles west of Upson, where a wagon road ran off north to Upson Lake.

The men had almost three miles to walk from there. I caught the Scoot at Hoyt on its return from Bessemer and got off at the same location, then walked to the lodge, arriving a couple of hours later. The men had a good meal ready. We did not have much work in preparing the sleeping quarters. It was a good gang to be with in a hunting camp, even though they were not the best of hunters. They all had a real good time, which was almost always the case in the old time hunting camps.

A little incident happened the first night at the lodge, which was a sample of what was to be the next few days. We still had the old two-story double bunks. Oscar Auley and Mike Donahue took a bottom bunk with Mike sleeping next to the log wall. We all heard a mouse gnawing toward morning but paid no attention to it until just before breakfast. Oscar Auley, a pretty fair hunting lodge cook and myself, were preparing breakfast when Mike rolled out of bed and someone said, "How did you sleep Mike?" "Sleep?", Mike said, "Sleep?, how in hell can a man sleep with a mouse on one side of him and a lion on the other side?" Oscar could really snore by note.

Ray Gonia, a railroad telegraph operator, who lived in Mellen, was a good semi-pro baseball player but never took up hunting as a hobby. He told me after the hunting season that he never spent three days at any place that he enjoyed more. He laughed himself sick sometimes. It was the arguments and sarcasm of Mike and Oscar that kept us all in good humor. Even the last day in camp, a day of hardship, could not dampen the comradeship shared those few days.

A heavy snow started to fall on Saturday night and continued all day Sunday. Right after a full Sunday noon meal, we packed what had to be carried out, left the two deer, the results of our hunt at a Foster-Latimer Camp close by, to be loaded on the log train on Monday. We started for Rouse, four miles away, with a foot of snow or more to walk in and still falling, to catch the afternoon Scoot. We left the lodge early enough for ordinary walking, but with our heavy packs we could not make time. Aristo and I were in good shape for walking but the other three were not. It was all uphill going out. We got to Highway 77, about a miles from Rouse, where the highway and railroad were side by side, when we heard the Scoot whistle at Upson and knew we would not make it to Rouse. We spotted ourselves near the railroad track, waving our lantern. The train crew knew it was our gang and stopped for us, as they had let us off there when we went to camp, but we had not told them to stop for us on Sunday night. The Scoot's crew were good about that service any time of the year.

It is too bad that feeling isn't exhibited more in this day and age. Very few people had much money in those days, but there was much more friendly feeling for each other; the kind of human feeling which is disappearing so fast.

After we were picked up by the Scoot, I rode into Mellen with the gang. I took the Scoot back to Hoyt on the evening run where I had nearly a three mile walk back to Camp 39. The snow was deeper, about eighteen inches by that time, and to say I was tired when I got back to camp would be putting it mildly. After a good night's sleep, I was okay again.

I did not turn the crew out on Monday morning as it had turned into a fine wet snow, making it a miserable day out. Our office crew made money for the company that day by selling clothing and footwear. We sold out of rubbers, socks, underwear, wool shirts, etc., which we had in the wanigan. When the first real snow storm hit in those days, the lumberjacks that made the camp their home would buy the work clothes they really needed. Some would not trust themselves to buy the clothes when they got to town. A wanigan was a must in logging camps in those days.

The next morning, after the first big snow storm, the sun came out and it warmed up some. The snow, being wet, settled fast as the ground was not yet frozen. It made a lot of mud. In other words, winter had not settled in for keeps. In fact, most of the snow from that storm melted, which happens quite often in this snow belt of northern Wisconsin when the large snow storm comes in the late fall. That is the reason why loggers depending on sleigh haul for the hauling of logs, would plan to have the roads ready to haul by the first of January of each year. Four out of five years they would be unable to haul before this, as we generally do not get steady, cold, dependable weather until around December 21, which is the shortest daylight time also. There is an old saying which goes, "When the days begin to lengthen, the cold begins to strengthen."

Before the machinery and heavy equipment period, the winter season was very important in logging. It is the reason so many old-time loggers and foremen were bald or had gray hair so young. George Taylor, the camp foreman I worked under for so many years would say, "A gray horse is just as good as a black one." I do not know about a bald one.

The loggers would start getting the roads ready in the middle of December when the weather looked favorable, then if winter set in early, they would gain a few days of good hauling in late December. During the Christmas holidays, when most of the crew would go to town for a few days before settling in for the winter's work, a few men would be left in camp to take care of the horses and tramp roads for the sleigh haul.

The company camps planned on six to eight weeks of good hauling in January and February. If March continued to be cold they might get another week or two. Then again, they could lose a week or ten days during January and February thaws. A winter sleigh haul had many complications.

The winter of 1921-1922 was no exception, as the Camp 39 sleigh haul had rough country in the woods, with the main sleigh road in open country from the headwaters of Alder Creek to the car camp landing on what is now State Highway 122, about a quarter of a mile north of the Alder Creek bridge. For a distance of five or six miles, it was a good level road after the log loads hit the well-iced main road.

The Prohibition Act also brought new problems to the logging industry.

The Prohibition Act became effective by Federal Law June 30, 1919, after being tried out some as a war-time measure in 1918. Stricter enforcement began in 1920, but many still looked on it as a joke until November 23, 1921, when the government ordered it enforced by all state and federal officers or penalties would be assessed against them.

The men who were in charge of logging operations, who thought they had trouble with liquor at times in logging camps from licensed saloons, had not seen anything yet because the saloons were generally not that close to logging camps, they were only in scattered settled spots. After Prohibition many people living in the country anywhere near logging camps made moonshine liquor. Some of the cooks in logging camps made it while cooking the meals.

It was not long before some men, looking for an easy way to earn some money, were looking for abandoned small farms or hunting shacks near good water, but away from main traveled roads. They would then pack in the equipment necessary to make moonshine. Some of them that made a business out of it were real careful, made some money, and held onto it, then started a legal business. Most of them made some easy money but spent it just as fast. Others were caught by revenue officers, paid a fine or were jailed.

After Prohibition, a foreman in a logging camp would never know how many men he would have ready to work on a Monday morning.

When the camps were near farming country or accessible roads, it added to the problems. With a crew of men, whether in the woods or in a factory, there are some who like to believe they are shrewd and are looking to make a little easy money. Once in a while a man working at camp would steal some camp equipment and exchange it for moonshine.

I remember a cook named Leonard Woods who was cooking for John Broadwell. John came back to the office one morning after breakfast and said, "Did you see any new men at the table this morning?"

"No," I said, "Why?" He said, "Our cook is staggering drunk." I hadn't noticed it. After the crew had gone out to work, John went into the kitchen to investigate. Sure enough, the cook had made up a little batch of moonshine on the kitchen range. Broadwell, knowing very well that Woods, who liked his liquor, would keep at it, notified McDonald to send him a dependable cook.

During the fall of 1921 when Dan McDonald, Wm. Richardson and myself were making plans for the winter haul, the subject of how many teams it would take to haul out the logs from Camp 39 was discussed. Then a steam sleigh log hauler was mentioned such as I had visited in Saxon a couple of years previously. McDonald spoke up and said, "I am going to a demonstration of gasoline Holt-Caterpillar tractors put on by the Drott Tractor Company at Butternut this coming week. It may be the answer. We will make a decision on what to use for power after I see the demonstration.

Dan McDonald returned from the demonstration confident that the Holt-Caterpillar tractor would do the job satisfactorily, with his mind made up to get two, five-ton Holt-Caterpillars to do the main line sleigh log hauling.

Just a note here to show how sharp Dan McDonald was regarding logging equipment. When at Butternut, for the Holt Tractor demonstration, which was a log skidding show, the salesman, in talking to the group of loggers, made the statement, "One thing about these tractors, when you are skidding you do not need much swamping as they will run over old logs, brush piles, stones, stumps and other debris which you cannot do when skidding with horses."

Not one of those other woods superintendents or loggers contradicted him, nor did McDonald until after the meeting when he went up to the salesman to talk a little more about the tractor, as he planned to buy two tractors.

McDonald said to the salesman, "You made one statement about what the tractors will do that you will live to regret." "What was that?" the salesman replied. Dan said, "When you told them they did not need a road or trail. Your machine may do that for a short time, but it will not hold up without some care and attentive, careful driving. No machine will run over obstacles of that sort in complete abandon." The salesman thought about it for a minute, then said, "You are right, Mr. McDonald. I was carried off by what the machine would do. Thank you for calling it to my attention." He thanked McDonald again about six months later and said he found out the hard way.

McDonald then told me to have my blacksmith figure out a sleigh-haul hook-up between sleighs in order to make up a train of sleigh loads to haul on each trip.

Along with this, another big problem came up. We were planning to use horses to set the sleigh loads out from the woods roads to the level "set-out" landing on the marsh. This required poles on the sleighs to help hold back the sleighs on the hills.

In working out these problems, we were very fortunate in having one of the better all-around blacksmith and "wood butchers" in the business by the name of Louie Hines who worked the year around for the Foster-Latimer Lumber Company until it finished its operation in 1932.

The following morning, Richardson came up to camp. He, Louie and I went over the problem nearly all forenoon, with the result of a combination, two part pole for the sleighs. The pole was made separately from the sleigh with clamps to fit over the roll of the sleigh, with reinforced chains to the sleigh runners, so the pull would not be all on the sleigh roll. When the team set the load out, the teamster unhooked the pole and went back for another sleigh load. It was tried and it looked good. Louie and a wood butcher helper, Frank Posnell, got busy equipping the log sleighs accordingly.

McDonald ordered the two five-ton Holts for immediate delivery, so we received them in early December. They were then used in packing the main road through the Alder Creek lowlands, which is not a marsh, as it has a good solid ground floor with the water coming mostly from springs in the mountains. Melvin Hovde of Upson and Gunnard Osterberg of Cedar were the first operators of the machines.

We had the machines, sleighs, and roads all ready when the freeze-up set in around the middle of December. The machines packed the roads, the water-tank plow and rutter were ready to pour the water on so we had a fairly good road ready by January 1 when the machines started to haul. The first day they took one sleigh load at a time, directly from the woods; the second day two sleigh loads at a time directly from the set-out landing; and the third day, three sleigh loads at a time, but not maximum loads. Then they continued to haul three loads at a time, increasing the size of the sleigh loads until achieving what we all figured was a maximum load.

Then we had a rude awakening. The road was getting real good, but it was found out then that three sleigh loads was all the five ton Holts could handle. We further found out that in hauling three sleighs at a time, the tractors might not hold up. This would really handicap the hauling when there were so many logs to haul.

McDonald spent a day up in the woods observing, then decided he would have to exchange the two 5-ton Holts for two 10-ton Holts, which he did. We then started to move logs. Oscar Peterson of Upson, later a ranger for the State Conservation Department, was conductor for Melvin Hovde that winter and Clyde Williams, a capable tractor operator, was conductor for Osterberg, which made a capable relief operator on the job.

The sleigh haul troubles were not all on the main line as we had some rough, crooked roads to haul the logs out of the woods. There was one hill which was fairly steep and almost a mile long to come down which required two ruts, one for each side of the sleighs. Even then, hot sand was needed the first few trips in the morning.

I was very fortunate in having a very good sand hill man to take care of the hills. He got up at 4:00 a.m., ate a little, took his lunch pail and went to work. Then in the afternoon, when his helper could handle the hills, he prepared the fires for the night by piling up huge green blocks of wood onto each fire so it would hold until morning, heating the necessary sand. When it was snowing at night, he sometimes went out to check the fires after supper. The man's name was John Koski of Iron River, Wisconsin. As he was a superior worker, I did not fail to reward him accordingly. Since going wages were from $40 to $50 per month with board and room furnished, I paid John at the rate of $120 per month when he was on sand hill winter hauling roads and he still made money for the company. McDonald and Richardson knew I was doing it and I got around the wage schedule, set by the company, by keeping him down as a contract worker, which he was, since he usually worked 16 hours a day.

McDonald said when talking about the arrangement with me one time, "I know how good a man he is. I also know that logging chances being equal, your logging cost is less than the other foremen, as the company keeps monthly logging costs of each operation. I also know that a good sand hill man on a hilly sleigh haul is the most important man you have." I appreciated what he said.

Whether running camp for the company or my own camps later on, I never did attempt to get by with the lowest wages possible, but I always looked for production. This fact always made for a smooth running, low cost operation.

The company set up schedule of wages, generally with a $5 per month spread to work on. Some of the foremen thought by paying the lower wages their logging would be cheaper, but I had followed Richardson's philosophy - pay the extra $5 per month to the good man.

One man, Louis Gottwald, who worked all winter at Camp 39, still lives in Iron Belt.

To explain more fully about the variables in winter weather in northern Wisconsin and upper Michigan, I will tell about two changes in February, 1922.

Around the middle of February, we were far enough away from the camp to dinner-out the crew. We did not have a dinner shack as we were changing dinner locations too often, but we did have some logs to sit on with a brush fence with a big fireplace in the center. This day was real cold but we did not know just how cold it was as no thermometers were allowed in logging camps in those days. The cook always tried to send out a hot lunch in a horse-drawn jumper with the food containers well covered with blankets to keep the food as warm as possible.

The man got out to the dinner place on time okay, but it was so cold the food in the jumper was cold when we opened up the containers. The cook had sent out some baked beans which popped out on the plates like bullets when we stuck a fork under them. We had a short, snappy dinner that day and naturally much griping as there is never money made working on a logging job when it is that cold. All chains, tools, harness and rigging breaks easily. When one of the tractors came back from the landing after the train had come from Mellen, we found out it had been 54 degrees below zero at Mellen, so it must have been close to that in the lowland around Iron Belt.

When the crew heard that, they all wanted to go to camp even if it was not so cold by that time. It was near 3:00 p.m. with a cold wind, so I let the crew go to camp. It just goes to show it was a very good idea not to have thermometers in logging camps.

Of course, today footwear and clothing of all kinds is more effective without loading one down for weight, so the temperature has to get very cold before outdoor work gets unbearable.

About a week later, on February 23, 1922, we had a three-day blizzard. It had warmed up after the extreme cold day and we had a February thaw, ending up with a blizzard.

To show you how authentic I am on this item, the following news item was in the Mellen-Weekly, February 23, 1922:

The Worst Blizzard in Years Hits the Area. Trains Buried For 3 Days.

I also have many witnesses about this storm. Old-time Mellen residents, myself included, remember that you could stand on the street snow banks and touch the telephone lines.

Norman Warren, now an executive of the Northern State Bank, Ashland, Wisconsin told me he was living at Butternut at the time and put on snowshoes to go to see the passenger train stalled near the Butternut station.

After the breakup in March, 1922, I scaled out some peeled hemlock logs going to the Nash Paper Company at Port Edwards and Nekoosa which helped me to get a change of scenery about six months later.

After the peeled logs were loaded out, the car camps were moved over to the new main line east of Foster Falls on Sullivan Creek near where the creek runs into the Potato River, so I was living in the same office car only at a new location.

The car camps were to have about forty men building railroads and thirty men peeling bark with Sam Johnson as the railroad crew foreman and me taking care of the bark peelers, the contract loggers and scaling the bark at Camp 41.

Since many people have the impression that woods or logging operations require no management skill or brains, just muscles and a strong back, I want to pass on a lesson on this issue given to me by Dan McDonald during the summer of 1922.

A logging operation always required a woods railroad section crew of three to four men in the summer and two in the winter. Dan always picked the section men by taking the advice of Sam Johnson. This summer, Dan had put on a new section foreman, Charles Howe, a very good worker with all the know-how needed about a section crew. Charles had two men working with him at the time, but it seemed that whenever Dan would pass Charles' section crew, Charles would be working and the other two men were taking it easy. So Dan said to Charles, "What wages am I paying you?" Charles replied, "$60.00 a month plus room and board." How much are the two men paid?" He answered, "$45.00 per month plus board and room." "Then," said Dan, "from now on you see that those two men do more work or I will put you back to their wages. From then on he did boss the men more.

That summer was not bad for me as the camps were not scattered out, and it was not necessary to peel as much bark. The company was getting farther ahead of the hardwood logging crew, so I put in a pleasant summer until about August 1, 1922.

We did have to change cooks at the cars. Tom Hicks' family decided to make a change as the car camps now were more in the wilderness. So, Mr. and Mrs. Christie took over at the cars and Tom Padjen took Camp 41 for the summer.

The Christies got along well at the cars until a tragedy occurred early in the summer. The water for the camp was coming from a spring over which a box had been sunk which had a cover to keep it clean. Someone left the cover off one day and the Christies' little sixteen or eighteen month old girl rambled away from the kitchen car when no one was around. Her curiosity headed her to the spring where she fell in and drowned.

Naturally it was a hard blow for the Christies. He came back for awhile after the funeral, but Mrs. Christie was not able to come back to live, so he gave up the job. Leo Miller of Upson, who also was an excellent cook, took the cooking job.

After the bark peeling was completed, I was told to get a crew ready for logging so I put log sawyers on. I also had to build a barn, a blacksmith shop and an extra shanty to hold more men. We would have continued to do well except for two changes during that spring and summer. First, Wm. Richardson, the woods superintendent, and Dan McDonald had a falling out and Richardson resigned. He was replaced by Oscar Barnhardt, the foreman who had been at Camp 38, who was a big "blow" with little ability. Richardson could stay in camp and get out more logs than Barnhardt.

Then to make matters worse, Dan McDonald had been up to camp the latter part of July with his gasoline speeder and was supposed to be back in town at 4:30 p.m. for a meeting at the main office. He left soon enough, but being behind schedule, he may have been traveling a little too fast; his speeder jumped the track between old Camp 31 and Casey Switch, throwing McDonald into the woods. With no crew coming from that direction to camp, no one knew about the accident, but when Dan

McDonald did not show up for the meeting, Mr. Latimer called the camps. We informed him from the car camps that Dan had left the cars around 3:00 p.m., which gave him plenty of time to be at Mellen for the meeting.

Harry Latimer immediately got in touch with Joe Landry, the railroad superintendent, who jumped on his gas car and took off to see what had happened. When Joe was nearing Camp 29 Creek (now Vought Creek) about a mile west of where Dan's gas car jumped the track, just east of Casey Switch, he met Dan walking slowly on the track. Dan did not know Joe Landry and did not know where he was. He had been knocked out completely and lost his memory for some time, but his intuition and woods knowledge of the area had evidently saved him. He had a fractured wrist, bruised leg, and a head concussion which laid him up for about two months, with his memory gradually coming back. It was his second bad accident in twelve years, but he was as tough as they come, so he survived once more.

Talking with Jasper Landry, Joe's son, now Editor of the Mellen-Weekly Record, about this accident some time ago, I learned that Jasper's dad had said, "Even if Dan was woozy from the accident and did not know Joe, he said 'You railroad men will have to do a better job on the tracks.'" Those first gasoline railroad speedsters, however, were light and would jump the rail rather easily.

The injury to McDonald gave Oscar Barnhardt a chance to throw his voice and he made the statement he would make a complete clean sweep of the woods personnel, "starting with that long slim Corrigan," a statement made in the presence of the train crew. It was okay by me, but to this day I do not know what he had against me. I hardly knew the man, only seeing him once in awhile when scaling bark at Camp 38 where he was foreman.

I just went ahead doing my job, getting ready to keep the mill in saw logs when needed. Then one day, Harry Latimer came up to camp and Barnhardt was there for dinner. After dinner, we talked about the size of the extra sleeping camp I was building. One of them said, "How many men will you need for the logging crew?" I said, "Around sixty-five to seventy and a railroad crew of about twenty. The cars with the addtional men's camp will hold ninety-six men, giving Sam and I about six extra beds, which we figured was enough. After a couple of months when the railroad crew will be laid off, there would be plenty of room." Barnhardt spoke up, speaking to me, "You can't keep the sawmill going with seventy men." All I said was, "Oh yes I can. I have done it before with a harder logging chance than this is." He said, "You or no one else can do it." Harry Latimer said, "George is right, Oscar, he has done it before!" That ended the argument, but it was the beginning of the end for me working under Oscar Barnhardt. I could see that after the way Aristo had been given a bum choice two or three years before. I thought to myself that it might be all for the best, as that was practically the only company I had worked for and I would have liked to see if I could work for another company. I felt I would let the chips fall where they would.

The teams and men were moved in and I started skidding and loading the logs for the mill. After the first month of logging, we had kept the mill going, had built up an inventory of extra logs in case of a lost time because of rain, and the best part of it for me was that I did not have over sixty-five men at any one time!

At about that time, Dan McDonald began to get around again and one day he said to me, "What is the trouble between you and Oscar?" I said, "As far as I am concerned, nothing. Of course we have a difference of opinion at times, but he has the final say." Then I said, "Why?" "Well," Dan said, "Oscar claims you will not cooperate with him." "Oh. That's it," I said. "I guess I have been here too long, so it is okay with me; you can put a new man in my place by October 1st." "Oh," Dan said, "You don't need to quit; we will put you on another job." "No," I said, "that won't work when I still have to take orders from Oscar! It is better if I try another company for awhile. It will do me good."

11

Hired Out To A New Company

With my time not scheduled, something new for me, I rested up at home in Mellen a few days, then spent a week at the hunting lodge with Oscar Auley and Mike Donahue. When I arrived home again, there was a letter from Lon Leavitts, Wood Superintendent for the Collins Lumber Company of Rhinelander who had a logging operation of three or four camps running the year around out of Pine Lake, Wisconsin. I had known Lon Leavitts for some time. I had met him the first time when he was a logging superintendent for the Gurney Lumber Company at Gurney, as their stumpage joined the Foster-Latimer Lumber Company stumpage in places and we sometimes met in the woods while cruising timber.

When Gurney closed down, he accepted a job as camp foreman for the Mellen Lumber Co. out of Foster Junction. In the letter he asked me to call him; I did and we made a date to meet at Hurley on Tuesday of the following week to talk about a job with his company.

I took our favorite mode of travel in those days, the Scoot, to Hurley. I visited with Leavitts, had lunch, and hired out to him. He hired me to be foreman at one of his camps December 1. He wanted me to go hiring men for him at once. He would pay me foreman wages plus my board and other expenses at Hurley until December 1st. I agreed to start November 1, 1922, at $125.00 per month with board and room at Hurley or camp, whichever my work required. That was the going wage for camp foremen in those days until a man had been with a company for some time, so it was okay.

There was a train through Pine Lake each way morning and night, so generally I would take the men I hired down to the headquarters at Pine Lake in the afternoon where Leavitts would have a team and sleigh ready to take them to camp. Arthur Anderson, now a retired yard superintendent of the Rhinelander Paper Company, Rhinelander, Wisconsin, who now lives in Ashland, was in charge of the headquarters and was supply buyer for the camps. He was a very capable man.

Once in a while I would take some special workers needed at once down on the morning train. Then I would spend some of the day with Arthur, and Lon would take me for a drive into the woods operation so I would know what it was like. The land was not as rough as at the Foster-Latimer operations, but there was a lot more lowlands and swamps. It was all a sleigh-haul chance with the hemlock logs and the pulpwood going to the Rhinelander Paper Company and the hardwood logs to Collins Lumber Company sawmill at Rhinelander.

The man-catcher job was not bad, as my nine years' wood working experience started to pay off. I knew a lot of lumberjacks, was able to pick out the better ones, and hired my share of men, so Leavitts was completely satisfied.

I stopped in a barber shop at Hurley for a shave one day and got acquainted with Harry LaFave who owned the shop and Harry Clayton, who was LaFave's right hand barber. LaFave, a very friendly fellow, asked me what I was doing and I told him. We then visited while he gave me a shave. I said, "Where can I find a good, clean rooming house for a few weeks?" He said, "Go east to the corner of this block, turn south two blocks to the last house on the left side of the avenue, across from the court house. Ask for Tim Nolan and you may get a good room and also meals if you wish." I went right there and was able to get a good room in a nice and quiet neighborhood.

While boarding and rooming at Nolan's, I had the good fortune to meet J. E. Murphy, Superintendent of Schools at Hurley. A fine outstanding gentleman. He was a very progressive educator. He was a well-built man of average height, very pleasant and a neat dresser. He carried himself well at all times; with most all people he came in contact with becoming admirers of his.

J. E. Murphy was also a famed orator, which resulted in his becoming well known all over upper Wisconsin and Michigan. He retired many years ago and passed away only recently. The Hurley High School has been named the J. E. Murphy High School.

There were a lot of men coming and going out of Hurley at that time and, with the heavy concentration of logging in the area along with the heavy iron ore mining, it was a busy city but a little rough at times. The rough city never bothered me in any way and I have lived in Hurley two different periods of nine years and eight years besides being in and out in the earlier logging periods. I had no serious trouble, but have seen many lumberjack incidents -- some of them comical and others not so funny.

On my first weekend home in Mellen where I was staying with my mother as I was not married at that time, there was a letter from a Hugh Boles of the J. B. Nash Paper Company, later the Nekoosa Edwards Paper Company, asking if I would be interested in a position with the company in the yard at Port Edwards. It would be checkscaling on logs and pulpwood during the winter season. I then would have the chance to be yard foreman under a yard superintendent. I felt I had to give this offer some real consideration.

Around 1920, a young man by the name of Elmer Boles of Port Edwards who had completed a business course, was hired to keep books at the Mellen State Bank. Through church and sport activities, Aristo and I became acquainted with Elmer and liked him very much. With Aristo and I being friends of Mike Donahue, Elmer got so he would drop into Mike's tailor shop for some words of wisdom, for which Mike was noted.

Aristo by this time had an automobile and even though there were few roads to drive on, we were able to make the Iron Range cities, Ashland, Glidden, Butternut and Park Falls, to see baseball games at least in the summer dry weather. Aristo would furnish the car, the riders the expenses, which was not a bad deal.

Then Elmer Boles decided to take an office position with the Nash Paper Company at his hometown of Port Edwards. Hugh Boles, father of Elmer, was a long-time employee of the Nash Company and for a couple of years had been sent out to the logging operations where the company was buying its pulpwood to see what quality of wood was being produced and how it was being scaled and graded. At that time, pulpwood was cut in 55" or 100" sticks with the 55" wood loaded in box cars and the 100" wood on flat cars, with the company putting a solid end on the flat cars to be used. These same cars would stay in service for the same company as long as they kept the cars moving. A sign with the company's name and home city would be nailed on each car so the car would be returned. The pulpwood would be scaled at the mill and paid for by that scale. Of course the producer had the privilege or right to scale it himself in order to have a check on it, which a man should always do before complaining about an unjust scale. The logs were scaled when loaded in the woods by log scalers agreed upon by the two companies, then scaled again at the mill unless it was found over a long period that a conscientious job was being done with the same scalers on the job steady. Once in a while a log scaler would get careless and think he was so good he could just count the logs and put scale figures down to cover the total scale he guessed was there.[1] This works out once in a while if logs are running a uniform size, but it is often inaccurate. This is the reason Hugh Boles was sent out to check on scaling procedures.

Hugh Boles was a real gentleman and it made me feel good that he had recommended me to his company so highly. If I accepted the job, it would also give me a chance to see if I would be satisfied working out of the woods and, of course, I could always go back to the woods if it didn't

[1]I never used it on a buying or selling basis. The only place I would use it would be on a skidding and decking job in woods or on a landing where an estimate was needed and logs would be scaled before a settlement was made.

work out. I found out after three or four more trials it was next to impossible to keep me from being connected with logging operations in some way; it was in my blood from an early age.

On my return to Hurley after the weekend at home, I hired some men for the Collins Lumber Company and sent them down on Monday afternoon to Pine Lake. Then I hired some for Tuesday morning and went down with them and spent the day with Lon Leavitts riding around in the woods. I informed him of my decision, to go with the Nash Company, which he could see was worth a try by me at my age of twenty-six years at the time. I agreed to stay on another week or ten days and Lon said that if it did not work out satisfactorily at the mill, I should see him before I hired out again. I thanked him and many years later he hired men for me after his full-time retirement. The following week on my return to Mellen I began packing in readiness for my trip to Port Edwards 200 miles away. The highways were not dependable yet and automobiles were scarce. When I left, I did not plan on being home before Easter as it was too hard to make train connections and also because we worked Saturdays at that time. I left right after Thanksgiving Day on the evening train and was met by Elmer Boles at Wisconsin Rapids, where we took the street car to Port Edwards, arriving around midnight. The Nash Company was running a company hotel at Port Edwards at the time and a room had been registered for me, so no problem on my arrival. On Friday morning, I reported to the superintendent at his office, from where he took me on a tour of the plant. It was the first pulp and paper mill I had been in, so this was a treat. Then Hugh took me out to the Port Edwards log yard and to the Nekoosa log yards three miles from Port Edwards to the other mill.

After lunch Hugh told me to spend the balance of Friday and Saturday with the log and pulpwood scalers in the yard and mill, to get better acquainted with the company methods and procedures before starting on my own on Monday morning. I also visited with Hugh Boles and family over the weekend, who made me feel at home.

This company had two locations to scale logs -- one at the mill and the other in the yard. The mill deck, where the logs were cut into blocks before going to the splitter, chipper and digester, was an ideal place to scale and grade logs. There was a good long log deck under cover and all logs and pulpwood that could be handled in the mill by direct shipment were unloaded at that deck.

In the winter season, the yard deck was also a busy place for scaling. So much wood was shipped on railroads from logging companies who had to depend on sleigh hauls to get logs out of the woods, that the mills had to have a lot of yard room and the J. B. Nash Company had yard room.

In the yard the crew was using an electric carrier, which took large bunches of logs and put them in long high piles directly from the cars. Crewmen were also using a steam-powered loader with a long boom which they could move around easier than the electrical log decker. When decking with either one of the log deckers, a scaler had to scale the logs on the car, which is an extremely hard way for one man to scale logs accurately. The logs were loaded by the company on flat cars, some equipped with patent stakes and bunks, with top chain or cable to be used at its mill. Some, however, were loaded on regular flat cars with three-car stakes on each side of each tier and two tiers of logs on each car with car wire used to keep the loads from spreading. No gondola cars were used for shipping logs at that time. Another thing which made for bad scaling conditions was that a lot of the cars were 36', 38', and 40' long, with the logs cut 12', 14' and 16' long, with 3" added to each log so the logs could be trimmed to the even number of feet allowed. For pulpwood, of course, it made no difference if the logs were a little short as far as usage was concerned, but all buyers liked to get the scale they were paying for. You can see how tough it was to scale two tiers of logs on a 36' or 38' car, as most of the logs were cut in 16' lengths. The two tiers of logs would be tight together at the center of the car. The company had its own train crew to do the switching between the two mills. They would switch the short cars out so they could be put at the unloading deck at the mill. When scaling the cars to be decked in the yard, the company did furnish a light loader for the scaler to climb around on, so he could get the length and top end of logs to be scaled. I will say one thing, no one crowded the scaler when scaling in the yard. All knew it was a tough job, if a scaler was conscientious about doing his work. Of course, the 40' or longer cars were much better to work on and usually there were more of the longer cars. Scaling at the mill deck was ideal as the logs would be unloaded all laid out flat where the scaler could see the full logs and scale them the way logs should be scaled. Some of you may wonder why the logs were scaled at the mill again after they were scaled when loaded up in the woods. There were generally five or six different scalers for the companies who were shipping logs to the J. B. Nash Paper Company who were employees of the companies shipping the logs. They were more interested in seeing that their companies received a fair scale, so once in a while a scaler would lean too far to the side of his employer. Or on a real cold day in the winter when it was warmer in the steam loader than out at the skidway, a scaler might say that the logs being loaded that day were running about ten logs to the thousand feet, so he might count what went on the car and mark down scale to cover the average. This might work out well once in a while but most of the time when a scaler did that he got too liberal on the scale, and that might be the car that showed up with a larger overrun on scale, when scaled at the mill. Most all companies allowed up to about 3% over or under on a carload of logs, but if the load ran 3% consistently one way or the other or up to 7% or 8% once too often, a company would immediately make a thorough check on all the carloads coming from that scaler. In that case they would put the loads from that scaler all at the mill dock, then have someone whom they considered one of their more consistent scalers do the scaling. A scaler might scale a carload of logs in the woods, then go down to the mill, scale the same load, and be off from 1% to 3%, as he might put the scale rule on the logs at a little different angle, but that would not happen too often on peeled hemlock logs. I have a real illustration of this latter.

The middle of the first week I was scaling on the log deck at the mill. The superintendent left a message for me to stop at the office after quitting time. Of course, I did not know what was up. I stopped and he said, "Do you know where we might get another log scaler? We will need one at the Nekoosa Mill just as soon as possible." It came to me at once that Ernest Anderson of Upson, who had been scaling at the Foster-Latimer camps from the time I started him in January, 1918, until September, 1922, when he could no longer stand Oscar Barnhardt, had resigned his job. I said, "I know of one man you might get at this time." I told him who it was. He said, "Can he do the job?" I said, "Yes, or I wouldn't recommend him." He said, "Will you write to him? You can explain what the work is like now." I said, "Okay, what wages should I tell him?" He replied, "$100.00 per month, plus board and room at the boarding house." I wrote to Ernest that night telling him about the job. He wrote back that the offer came at just the right time as the road crew he was working with would be laid off at the end of the week, and he would come down on Tuesday morning. He met the superintendent after lunch, who kept him in tow during the afternoon, arranging for a room and all other details. Almost immediately after supper I was in my room reading a newspaper when there was a knock on the door. It was the superintendent. After he sat down and we had a little conversation, he said that the new scaler, Ernest Anderson, was very young. I said he was twenty years old but that he had four years' experience. Ernest did look younger than he was, as he had a very light complexion and smooth face. I asked what that had to do with the job and whether he had tried Ernest on scaling. He answered that he hadn't yet, so I said, "You should try him before complaining." He then said he could use Ernest but that he would have to pay him only $75.00 per month to start with. At this I asked if he had told the young man that and he answered, "No, but I will in the morning." Although I agreed that was between the two of them, right there I lost all respect for the superintendent. My mind did not change later, as that was not the only small thing he did that winter. A short time after the superintendent left my room Ernest came for a visit. After we had talked about news around Upson, I asked him how it looked so far. He replied it seemed okay. Then I told him about the conversation with the superintendent which had me on the spot. Ernest said, "What would you do?" I said, "I would tell him, 'try me first the rest of this week; then if you are not satisfied I will go back home.' " I told Ernest I knew he could do the job so call his bluff. Ernest Anderson was sent to Nekoosa the next day to work under a man by the name of Arthur

Goddard who was yard superintendent, a fine gentleman. He received the original $100.00 per month salary, and Ernest repaid the Nash Company and the Nekoosa-Edwards Paper Company by working for them until his retirement forty-five years later in 1967. He had worked up to yard superintendent many years ago and still makes Nekoosa his home where he lives on a little piece of land.

The next incident by the yard superintendent, who was already lowered in my estimation, lowered him some more; in fact, it lowered my feelings for him so much that I decided I would put in the winter at Port Edwards but that would be all. The work was fine, the company was first rate, but I just could not work under a man who would use such small tactics.

On the scale sheets coming from one of the Mellen Lumber Company camps, there began to be a steady increase in the difference on scale of the two companies, always in favor of the Mellen Lumber Company with one carload running up to 800 feet. Bill Donaldson, a former Mellen Lumber Company scaler, and I had scaled some of the cars and the difference was the same whether scaled by Bill or I, so the yard superintendent said he was going to scale some of the same loads. In order to scale the same loads, he would have to scale at the time we scaled those cars, which was okay for Bill and I. But he never did scale the same loads we did, or we would have known it. The yard superintendent then sent Bill and me a comparison on ten carloads of logs scaled by the man he wanted checked. The comparison showed the scale of the man in the woods, then of Bill or I, and another scale by the superintendent. He had taken the easy way, sitting in his office just marking the same number of logs on his scale sheet but showing his scale to be between the man in the woods and Bill or I. In other words, he was supposed to be the more accurate scaler. It works out okay when you are the boss.

Later on in life I found many people that way, as will come out later. It may be that I spend too much time on those events but it is important to me, as too many old timers try to give the impression that there were no dishonest people in those days. From that time on, I did my work and gave a good honest day's work, so I would not have to back into the office on pay days.

Elmer Boles and I spent an evening in Wisconsin Rapids once in a while. I also had dinner with the Hugh Boles family occasionally and spent a Sunday with Ernest Anderson every few weeks.

The winter passed rapidly for me, and I was glad I had the opportunity to work at a pulp and paper mill as the experience gained that winter paid off for me when I started contract logging. During the winter I was at Port Edwards, the Nash Paper Company started to talk about reforestation on their lands around Port Edwards-Nekoosa. They began to have meetings on the subject and invited their employees who were interested to attend the meetings. I took in a few before leaving and kept up my interest in conservation from then on.

I had been corresponding with Aristo David during the winter and when I informed him that I was going to stay until spring at Port Edwards, I got a letter back in which Aristo stated he told Gust DeLene, the woods superintendent, that I would be returning north. Gust told Aristo to write me that there would be a job open for me at the Mellen Lumber Company camps out of Foster Junction under him when I returned home. I readily accepted this offer, as I knew Gust and Aristo very well, and also knew all their foremen, clerks, cooks, and trainmen. I was sure I would enjoy working with that gang and I did, as you will see later. Near the end of March, 1923, when the log and pulpwood cars were all unloaded so one scaler was all that was needed, I began to pack up my belongings. I left in good grace with no hard feelings toward the company and they seemed to feel the same about me.

12

Logging In Native Home Area

The first weekend I was home from Port Edwards I met Aristo David who informed me that Gust Delene would like me to report at once, as Joe Langlois, his foreman at Camp 22, wished to take a few weeks off to visit relatives and friends in Minnesota. Gus Delene, walking boss for the Mellen Lumber Company, was a short, well-built, stocky man, very strong. He was of dark complexion and carried himself well. Woodsworkers would recognize at a glance that he was a man of authority. Supervisory employees seemed to enjoy working under him and he held onto them well. I enjoyed working under him the short time I was under his charge. On Monday morning I reported to Gus at Foster Junction and we took the train to camp arriving in time for a good dinner put on by Art Kenney of Mellen, cook at Camp 22. Joe Langlois took me around a few hours after dinner but there was not much to show, as the camp only had a log loading crew and a bark loading crew at the time. It was spring breakup time so there were a few extra men cutting camp wood, washing blankets, and other "housekeeping" jobs, plus a blacksmith and two men taking care of horses -- about twenty-five men in all. Joe Langlois left on the log train, and I was back in the woods where I felt I belonged. There were good crews loading logs and bark so I had time to spend in the woods with Aristo running out railroad lines and bark strips for the coming bark peeling season. My job was to be the bark scaler for three camps and help supervise the peelers during the season as the company planned to peel around 5,000 cords of hemlock bark as well as summer-log from one camp during the peeling season.

The Mellen Lumber Company was logging in an area where I had lived as a boy until I was eleven years old, which made me feel really at home but there were only a few of the families left at that time who had lived around Mineral Lake when my family moved to Mellen after the death of our stepfather, James Doyle, in 1907. Some of the old landmarks were still there, though, such as Spring Brook Trout stream,

Lake 3 and the trout fishing spot at the outlet which runs into the Brunsweiler and Mineral Lake. On the Brunsweiler River, both the inlet and outlet had trout, black bass, and pan fish in the early days. When I lived at Mineral Lake in 1907, there were many trout in Spring Brook. One early morning in May, 1907, Frank and Robert Moder, my brother Bill and I caught sixty-six trout in an hour, only fishing from the bridge at the old Olson farm on the Mineral Lake - Marengo road to the meadows. Please do not mention that to the game warden at Mellen now! George Moder, an older boy, and I caught thirty nice large trout at the foot of the old dam on the Brunsweiler one day in a short time. We also caught a lot of nice large trout at the outlet of Lake 3 many more times.

George Moder, Fred Jensen, and Harry Baker were the model hunters and fishermen in the Mineral Lake area when I lived there as a boy.

In 1923, with the roads a little better, a few fishermen in automobiles could make it into the area, and some of the men in the camps would fish for pastime. It was not as easy to get a good mess of trout, but a lot easier then than now, I assure you. The men from camp would always turn their catch in to the camp cook so there was no waste.

To get back to logging, we did not have as much time for fishing as the people do today, even though many do argue with me on that point. We had to work six long days each week. The Mellen Lumber Company was going to have logging operations at Camps 22, 23, and 24, plus the railroad cars out of Foster Junction and about the same number of camps out of Glidden. Camp 22, located in what was called the Klondike area when I lived at Mineral Lake, was on the bank of the Brunsweiler River with a spring of fine drinking water. It was a real nice camp location. This camp had been in operation for one year and had one more year to go. It was to be the summer logging camp and also the base for some bark peelers. I was to supervise the peelers when bark peeling started at Camp 22 and was also to scale the bark at Camps 23 and 24. Joe Langlois was to be back to take care of the logging crew. Camp 22 was to be my headquarters, but with beds at Camps 23 and 24 I would generally sleep one night a week at each camp. This way I had a change of cooks a couple of days a week, which was always welcome, especially in the summer.

Camp 23 was in a rough canyon near Morgan Creek which was also a good camp location. John Reed, the camp foreman, was a character in his own right; a little different in his style than most foremen I had been around, but he got results which was all that was necessary in those days. There was no tenure or security for woods workers . . . it was every man for himself.

The fellows at Camp 22 told a good yarn about John Reed, which may have been true as he never liked being kidded about it. It seems he had a crew summer-logging near the Marengo - Mineral Lake town road the previous summer. One day when John had been around the crew near the road a few hours, he noticed one man walking around from one skidding crew to the other, but he did not seem to be working at any job. Finally John walked up to him and said, "Are you looking for something?" "No," he replied, "I am working here." "Well," John said, "where is your axe?" The fellow said, "I don't have an axe." Then John said, "How long have you been here?" He replied, "Two weeks." At which John said, "It's about time you get an axe; come into the office at noon and I'll fix you up." They told that John took it as a good joke and said, "Jiminy cripes! The man was not to blame; if I could get along working in a logging camp without tools, I would be doing just that, as it would be much better than being a foreman!"

Camp 24 was located northeast of Long Lake over toward Sanborn. Sandy McDonald was foreman there. He was a real old timer and had been with the Foster-Latimer Lumber Company and the Mellen Lumber Company for years, living with his family at Mellen, Wisconsin. He was a brawny man, but age was beginning to show on him, with his legs giving him a lot of trouble. He was like almost all woods workers of that era, never able to save money. It always took all a man's salary to live on, but it was not large by any standard so he had to keep on working.

Cases such as Sandy's often made me think what are these woods workers going to do when they get disabled entirely? We often saw old men looking for work and working when every move they made was misery for them but they would keep at it as the next stop would be the jungles or the poor farm. We also saw foremen who were lucky they had a foreman's job, as they would not have been able to do actual work any more and would get by for a while as foreman on their know-how, as they could pick good straw bosses, as assistant foremen were called. Some of these foremen would be the roughest on the old, crippled-up workers and those foremen paid for it later on. I could understand the impatience in young men, when they got out-of-sorts if some older or partially disabled man might not move fast enough to suit them, as most young able bodied men figure they are always going to be that way. This seems to be natural. I was the same way, although I was not built for power. Now when I hear young men ridicule older men, I laugh a little inside and once in awhile I tell them, in a nice way, "You may change your way of thinking when you get up there."

Of course, workman's compensation, widow's pensions, Social Security, unemployment compensation, and Medicare have eased the lot of the working man or woman tremendously today. I have lived through all the changes and feel those laws should be classified among the greatest human laws on the books.

As I have said previously, the Mellen Lumber Company or Foster-Latimer Lumber Company always seemed to have good log loading crews and Camp 22 was no exception. Once again Shorty Pollock was the hoister, with Sam Bonovich the top loader using a Clyde Steam Loader with a swing boom, a great invention especially when loading stake flat cars. With a steam loader such as this, a crew could load one flat car with four bunches of 3,000' to 3,500' of peeled hemlock; an extra bunch or two could be handled when loading hardwood logs.

A very handy Clyde Steam Log Loader for railroad loading of standard flat cars. It is built heavy and strong and pulls itself from car to car with a heavy cable and sheave blocks. We had one on our contract logging jobs for six or seven years.

The crew at Camp 22 was loading about seven carloads a day that spring, about 50,000' from logs decked on a landing during the winter. The empties were spotted around 10 a.m. The crew of five men would start loading at once and have the cars loaded by quitting time in the evening, which gave them a few hours of spare time in the a.m. Shorty and Sam would spend this time fishing unless the loaders needed some repairs.

One morning when Sam came in from fishing, I said, "How many fish did you catch, Sam?" He answered me, "Oh, not such a hell of a much." Is it any wonder I use poor grammar some times?

Trout season opened that spring on May 1st. Naturally, Shorty was looking forward to a good catch, as the snow was off the ground and the water in the Brunsweiler River was about right. Then on the last day of April it started to rain in the morning turning to snow after lunch. Snow kept falling all afternoon, all night, and on into the morning of May 1st, when we could measure about 14" on the ground. Since the snow was very wet, the crew was not turned out. Shorty borrowed a pair of snowshoes from Aristo and decided to go fishing on snowshoes. He would have had a lot of fun and a good story had he managed to catch some trout, but he did not "catch such a hell of a much" that time either.

A few weeks later when the trout fishing was very good, Shorty set out three fish poles in three good holes in the river which he could see from the sleeping camp. After Shorty had gone to bed, Byran Callahan, the fireman on the 3-spot, and I went into the roothouse where the cook had a box of good-sized smoked herring with heads on; we picked out two nice ones and put them on two of Shorty's set lines. In the morning when Shorty looked out he could tell something was on the two lines so he hurried out and was extra careful in pulling up the first line. The disgusted look on his face was something to see!! Then he broke into a good laugh. Life at Camp 22 was that way all summer.

By the middle of May we started peeling bark with men coming in from all over the area. The company even started a bus service with Bill Corrigan driving the panel bus which had curtains for sides and tailend. The roads from Marengo or Mellen were just barely passable at the time and after a heavy rain a driver could expect trouble. Bill made a trip to Marengo in the morning and if a full bus load of men got off the South Shore train from Duluth, Bill would take them on to Mellen and make up a load there in order to save one trip. This system worked out fine and the bus was kept on all summer. Times were good in the 1923 to 1929 era and men moved around a lot, so man-catching was a steady job.

The company filled up the camps with bark peelers in a hurry and in a few weeks I was moving from camp to camp scaling bark. Once in awhile though my turn would come to spend a Sunday at camp to take care of wannigan sales. One Sunday when it was my turn to be at Camp 23, I made it a point to get there on Saturday afternoon to get some instructions about which men did not have enough credit to buy much and to settle myself in.

Felix Baker, the cook, had been feeding the bears around camp, even had a nice feeding place picked out for them up on a ledge overlooking the camp. Felix took pancakes, meat, bread, and pastry scraps up to the ledge, knocked on a rock with a pan and maybe three or four bears might come at one time, even going under his arm to get at the food, so tame were they. Well, this Saturday night I was waiting on some customers when I heard a lot of hollering and laughing by the crew out in the yards. I took a look and there was a mother bear standing on her haunches with a couple of cubs looking on; the men were throwing small stones or sticks up toward the bear; she would pick one up and throw it back. They kept this up for fifteen minutes when the bear got tired of the game, took her cubs, and left.

Another day a bear watched two men and I scale bark for two hours, never coming real close but following close enough to see us at all times, appearing as though it was supervising the job!

One night I took Ernest Hennell, a jewelry salesman from Mellen, out to watch the bears come to the feeding place. We were sitting on a peeled hemlock tree near the butt end and a big bear crossed the tree on the top end. I think Ernest would have taken off, but I advised him to hold still and we watched the bear eat a big meal.

Another day during that summer, I was going across country from one camp to another when I came out on the Mineral Lake - Marengo road. I walked it a short distance when I noticed an elderly man sitting outside a little log cabin on what was the old McLain homestead on top of Klondike Valley. He looked familiar, so I walked over to the cabin to fine Joe Moder, a real Mineral Lake character. His family and our family had been neighbors at Mineral Lake in the late 19th and early 20th century. His family had married and were scattered out, but Joe had to spend the summers at least in the Mineral Lake area.

One morning around the middle of July Aristo David, the assistant woods superintendent, wanted to know if I'd heard the latest news of the change in our woods setup. John Carlson, our railroad building foreman, was going to retire. That was news to me, as he had been with them since the company started. Aristo said, "How would you like to take his place?" I thought he was joking and told him so. "No," he said, "Gus Delene told me to see what you thought about it." I said, "Well, you know I have had experience in surveying and grading railroads, but have not had actual experience in laying steel." He said, "We know that but we also feel you can grasp that part in a short time." Then I knew I was backing into a trap although I believe this would be a challenge, I do not believe I would care about it. Then I said to Aristo, "What other plans do you and Gus have for me after the bark peeling season?" He said, "Gus figures Sandy McDonald is not able to handle a large crew any more and had figured you for that job up until John Carlson's plans were made known." I did not say anything at the time but later when thinking it over I thought, "Gee! I would hate to take his job" and the more I thought about it, the decision to be made later was not easier. That weekend while in Mellen, I was walking down Main Street when I met Dan McDonald, the woods superintendent of the Foster-Latimer Lumber Company. We stopped for a little conversation and all at once he said, "What are you going to do when bark peeling season is over?" I said, "I'll be okay as they plan on something for me." He said, "We would like to have you come back for us if you are going to be through out there." Then I asked, "What has happened to Oscar Barnhart?" Dan replied, "He didn't measure up and we have William Richardson back in his place, who also would like to see you back. We would place you in charge of Camp 41 for the fall and winter, then have you laying out railroads and setting up locations for us and building a couple of sets of camps." I said, "What will the salary be?" He said, "We will give you a $15 per month raise over what you were getting when you left last fall." I told him I would let him know the next week after I had a talk with Gus and that I also would want to talk it over with Bill Richardson. The first part of the next week I was talking with Gus, so I asked him what the plans were for me. He said that they would keep me busy and then he told me he was planning on me taking over as foreman at Camp 24, and, if Sandy wished and I was willing, I could have Sandy for assistant or straw boss. I said no more at the time, as I wished to talk to Aristo first. I made it a point to meet Aristo the next day. I told him I hated to leave, as I had never enjoyed a summer more, but I also hated to take Sandy's job and by taking the other job offer it might save him for the coming year. Another thing I was taking into consideration was that the Mellen Lumber Company was in its last camps at Mineral Lake, after which all personnel would have to move. I told Aristo I was aware that Gus and he would be the first to take over new jobs and that I also knew I could work for either one of them, but I still did not like the idea of replacing Sandy. After thinking it over, I told Gus it would be better if I took the other job for all concerned, as much as I liked working for him. Gus could see my point as it was a hard decision for him to make in letting Sandy go after he had been with the company so many years. I think possibly he was glad I made the decision I did, which was to take the other job and I told him so.

I finished up the bark scaling the following week with an incident which touched me very much. There was a big Finnish bark peeler who had shipped in from Duluth at the start of the bark season; John Salo was his name, and he peeled at Camp 23. The foreman, John Reed, and I had mentioned many times the fine job he was doing, both in peeling and piling his bark; always piling at the right time without being told. John had not asked for a scale that summer and he was the last man I was to scale. On Friday afternoon I went out to his strip to start scaling with him marking one side of the pile. After scaling a half dozen piles, I said, "Your piles are all running over the regular size pile in height and length." "Oh!" he said, "Some may be a little larger, some a little smaller, so I scaled them the way they were all the way through, as the piles were solid as a brick wall with no air holes and being well covered. When I added up the scales, I said, "How many cords do you think you have?" He said, "Sixty-five cords." I asked, "How many piles?" He replied, "One hundred four piles." That was exactly what I had, but I had seventy-three cords of bark. John smiled and said, "You are a fair scaler, not like some who have scaled my bark other summers." I assured him, "I didn't give you a thing; I just scaled it the way it was." I was wishing at the time that I was going to be around when that bark was skidded so it could have been loaded separately, because I know the bark weighed out more than the scale. There were very few men who ever put up bark in better shape and it would have been most unfair to scale those piles as just regular piles. Sad to say, there were some scalers who would do it, just thinking it would help them to get a stand in with the company, which is part of the reason so many men did not fill their piles well.

I said goodbye all around the four camps on Saturday as they had all treated me fine all summer, including the good humorous cooks and office personnel. I have never disliked leaving a woods job more than that one and almost decided not to leave at the last minute, but I had made a solid commitment so went through with it.

However, that is one part of my way of life -- I never look back, only to compare, as what is past is gone forever. There is no way of changing it, so what is the use of dwelling on it. I say, use that energy in the future, which is where it might help.

I went home to Mellen on Saturday afternoon and then spent Sunday at home and with the old hunting gang. We even rode out with Aristo to the new hunting camp near Lake 3 and Spring Brook on the Mineral Lake - Marengo road which could, at times, be reached by automobile in 1923.

On the first Monday in August, 1923, I arrived at the yard headquarters of the Foster-Latimer Lumber Company where I met Dan McDonald and took my first automobile ride to one of the Foster-Latimer Lumber Company camps. Dan McDonald had a four-cylinder Oldsmobile and the road to Upson on Highway 77 then (now State Highway 122) had been made passable for automobiles in dry weather, but still very troublesome in wet weather. Winter driving was not attempted between Saxon and Upson until the winter of 1926-27 and then only on a limited scale, late fall and early winter. After Dan left his orders with the train crew, he told me to get in his automobile and we would try to beat the train to Camp 41 where he was taking me. The train had about seventeen miles to go to the camp and we had twenty miles to travel on a very poor road, but it was dry weather at the time so at least I didn't have to do any pushing.

Camp 41 was on what is now State Highway 122, where the Sullivan cottage is located on Sullivan Creek and where the Sullivan fire lane leaves Highway 122 going west to Foster Falls on the old Foster-Latimer Lumber Company right-of-way. The kitchen, two large bunk houses, barn, and blacksmith shop were on the west side of Highway 122 with the kitchen near the creek. The office and filing shack were on the east side of 122 with a two-room cottage on the little knoll where Wm. Richardson and his wife Lottie lived. Richardson was again assistant woods superintendent.

Of course, I was right at home with the Foster-Latimer Lumber Company except that their camps were now on a new main line leading into the Saxon-Kimball area. I had helped run the main railroad line up as far as Highway 122 the year before and had scaled bark at Camp 41 at that time.

Most of the key men, especially the train crews and steam loader engineers, had survived the Oscar Barnhart era, as had Henry Cronk and Ray Scribner, two of the foremen.

Camp 41 was a well-located camp, centered in a nice block of hemlock and mixed hardwood timber, with very good water. The spring had flow enough so a pipe was run into the kitchen so water could be diverted into a tank at the will of the kitchen crew. Then the water was run on through to the outside again, where a cold water refrigerator was fixed up so cooks would be able to keep butter, lard, pudding, etc. in hot weather. There was no ice in camps, just the water cooler, root house and screened-in meat house. The water from the spring then ran on into a water trough for the horses so it was an ideal water location, even a nice little trout stream now called Sullivan Creek running by the side of the office and kitchen.

The road going by the camp also was being improved all the time.

Wm. Weber, the Iron County Highway Commissioner, lived at Weber Lake in the big white house that is still standing, where Highway 122 swings west to get around Copper Hill now White Cap Mountain ski area on the way to Upson.

With the Foster-Latimer Lumber Company owning so much stumpage in Iron County and putting a lot of men to work, Wm. Weber had good leverage to get Highway 122 improved. Of course, the fact that he lived out there didn't hurt either. He drove a Model T Ford at the time.

The clerk, who had been the bark scaler at Camp 41 during the summer, was John Nordberg, a long-time resident of Saxon and a fine man. We hit it off together in good style and were good friends up to his death a decade or so ago. The log scaler was Frank Falkman who had worked for McDonald in Michigan many years previously and had come up from Newberry, Michigan, in the spring of 1923. He was a good log scaler and helped with the clerking when necessary that summer, a very good man in every way.

The cook was Sherman Frank, one of the best bakers I had encountered up until that time, who always had a fine assortment of bread, pastry and pies. He was not bad on meat and vegetables either. When the crew was around one hundred men, as at Camp 41, the company furnished a second cook and two cookees, with the second cook generally a good meat cook. The name of the second cook was Dan McPherson, Sr., of Mellen. Dan now lives between Mellen, Wisconsin and the Lake Superior District Power Company power plant on the Montreal River out of Saxon with his son, Dan, Jr., and family. (Dan, Sr. passed away this past spring in 1976.) This cook, Sherman Frank, revolutionized camp meals by talking Dan McDonald into using butter on the tables in place of oleomargarine. He told McDonald that pastry and potatoes were cheaper than meat and if the crew ate a lot of bread, potatoes, and vegetables they would not eat as much meat. He convinced Dan to give it a trial and he proved right. With the change to butter, an immediate reduction in the amount of meat consumed and a big increase in the amount of flour became evident. The average cost per meal to feed the men dropped sharply. Figuring the meals for one hundred men, quite a savings occurred, just about enough to cover the wage of the cooks and one helper. From that time on, not only McDonald but I as well, when hiring a cook, would try to get one who was an excellent baker, although in those days many were good all-around cooks.

Sherman Frank, cook, center of picture, with two helpers. This was at Camp 41 on State Highway 122, now at Sullivan Creek, in 1923. Screen meathouse in background.

Foster-Latimer Lumber Co. Camp 26 around 1910 in the Cozy Valley and Moore area. The young fellow in the center of the picture was Dan McPherson, Sr., of Mellen at the age of 14 years. I believe the man holding the horn was the cook Archie.

The car camps at that time were on a spur off the fire lane road which leads to the Weber Marsh and which formerly led to the State of Wisconsin fire tower site. They were only a quarter of a mile from Camp 41, but they proved handy as there was only a railroad building crew of fifty to sixty men in them during the summer.

The cook at the cars was Louis Lesperence, as game a man as I have ever seen to overcome a handicap such as he was afflicted with. While cooking at the Stearns Lumber Company camps out of Odanah, the affliction hit him. After lunch one day he laid on his bunk to take a nap as almost all cooks did, as they had to get up so early in the mornings. This day he laid flat on his back and crossed legs just below the knees and when he woke up an hour later, he was paralyzed that way and was never able to walk naturally again. By daily practice he was able to shuffle around that way and by using a cane and crutches occasionally, he went back cooking again for a limited size crew. He was a very good all-around cook and always did his share by working longer hours, but once in awhile a cookee would take advantage of him by not cleaning the tables right or letting the root house and screen house get messed up, as they knew it was hard for him to get around to check up. When he did check up and found they had been taking advantage of him, he soon set them in their places. If they took it all well and good; if not, they might as well move at once. Louis was very good natured, considering his handicap, and Dan McDonald took a liking to him, keeping him on the job whenever the boarding cars were in use as landing crews in the winter and railroad crews in the summer with a crew running from forty to sixty men.

Camp 41 was just starting to do the summer logging as the company had a large supply of logs on skids in the spring of 1923, which needed to be loaded out and sawed up at the mill by August 1, 1923. We also had some hemlock logs and a little white pine to saw out from decks. I got busy at once putting on more men and teams to get some logs ahead on skidways to keep the mill running in case of fall rain. Since there were many lowlands on both sides of Sullivan Creek, we kept at these during the dry weather in August. This area also had a scattering of real nice white pine logs. I remember one perfect white pine log sixteen feet long which scaled 1,610 feet.

We had a lot of bark to get out and along with keeping the mill in hardwood logs we had to produce three flat carloads of peeled hemlock logs a day. Altogether, the job required eighty-five to one hundred men. John Nordberg took over the saw boss job along with the clerk duties, and Frank Falkman did the log scaling as well as the clerking for the car camps.

Since Highway 122 ran by the camps and they were close to Hurley, Saxon and Upson with many other company camps scattered through the region, we were able to keep a full crew most of the time. I also began to get many young farm men from around Saxon in the fall after the crops were harvested.

The Brown Lumber Company of Rhinelander was running the Defer Mill at Saxon, buying local logs and shipping in some from the Mercer area. That mill kept the local Saxon, Cedar and Gurney sawmill employees working steadily, and there were two hotels open for transients.

There were many small farms between Saxon, Cedar, and Gurney with families living on them. The men often worked at the mill or in the woods, the women and children farmed on a small scale with the men folks helping in the evening with the barn chores, as they always had a few cows and a horse or two on those small farms. I dare say the Saxon, Cedar, and Gurney area at that time had at least double its present population.

Logging moved along at Camp 41 without any startling events. The weather stayed fairly dry through August, September, and October which made for good railroad logging, especially in the heavy, rocky soil we had to contend with. One afternoon in October, I dropped by the camp just as Wm. Richardson was coming out of one of the bunk houses. He was laughing so I said, "What are you laughing at?" He told me to go on in and see. I did and there was Frank Banko, the loud talker, but a very good man whom I mentioned some back in 1916 and 1917 and had not seen since. He had been working as a top loader and then brakeman on the Willow River Lumber Company train crew at Grandview, Wisconsin. The Willow River Lumber Company was finishing up in the Grandview area so Frank decided to try the Foster-Latimer Lumber Company again. I visited with him for a short time and told him I would put him to work. He said, "That's what I came here for!" The next morning I put him out with the skidway building crew. He was very good at this job and we began to get one or two more skidways per day and also a better job done on them. After building skidways a few days, a teamster quit who was driving a good team but hard to drive. No other teamster who was working there wanted to drive that team so I said to Frank, "You see what you can do with them. They are a good heavy team and should make a good sleigh haul team for the winter." "Okay," he said. He took the team and in two weeks it was the best team on the job. They were just a little too fast for most teamsters but that is what Frank liked. He drove them skidding all fall and all winter on the sleigh haul without going to town. He hauled in a lot of logs with that one team on a short sleigh haul and kept the team in good shape.

With Camp 41 a main traveled road, with moonshine stills being located on or near every available hunting shack or abandoned building where there was water and away from the main roads, a foreman just had to be around some on weekends to avoid trouble in the camp. I know at times I wished that the camp was 'way out in the wilderness some place. Finally I made a decision and decided no matter what, I would live up to it if it cost me my job. I told Richardson and McDonald what I was going to try and asked them to back me up for a trial of four or five weeks. I had posters made that we posted in all the camp buildings which stated that starting with the coming weekend any employees at this camp who were not in shape to go to work on Monday mornings might as well call for their time, with no favoritism to be shown.

The plan worked surprisingly well, much better than I had expected. Of course, there were always some in a crew of lumberjacks who would say, "Who the hell does he think he is, telling me what I can do on my own time?" I told one who brought it up on a Monday morning that I was not telling him what to do on his own time but only telling all the men to be ready for work on company time which we were all getting paid for. Logging is a dangerous occupation and men needed to be alert at all times. A foreman never had trouble with good lumberjacks on that subject as I have known many of the heavy drinking hard-working jacks who would drink heavy when in town but did not want to look at liquor when in camp. Some of them would say it only caused trouble in camp which was true. I would always tell the men I do not care how much you drink in town or away from the job, and I feel the same way today. Most of the old-time jacks respected my position on the subject and I was always fortunate in having a steady crew of good men. I tried to treat the men the way I would like to be treated and it worked out very well.

During October, 1923, the car camps were moved from Highway 122 east to the Weber Marsh near the headwaters of Sullivan Creek on the north side of Radar Tower Mountain. The cars were set up for a landing crew with a foreman by the name of Dan McDonald, called Black Dan by the jacks, as he was very dark for a Scotchman. He was a former Stearns and Schroeder Lumber Company camp foreman, a very capable man but getting up in years. With no retirement setup or no social security at that time, woods workers worked as long as they could get a job. Dan and I got along very well, with some of the logs from Camp 41 landed at what was called Camp 42 landing. The cars would be moved out in the spring and back the next fall again.

In November, 1923, we had much change of weather as so often happens in northern Wisconsin and Michigan, especially along Lake Michigan and Lake Superior. The month started out with rain and snow, then followed with some real nice weather for a week, followed with cold down to the middle 20's. A few inches of snow at times made it a miserable month. We were very fortunate that we had some extra skidways filled with logs, or the sawmill might have run short of logs.

The month of December opened about as an average December, remained dry, then got real warm for a week or ten days when it seemed more like early fall. Then about the middle of the month a change to rain occurred and we had rain almost continuously until around December 20, 1923.

Wm. Richardson, the woods superintendent, met me out on our

railroad skidding job where some of the teams were wallowing in mud skidding logs. He asked me what I thought of it. I replied that if it was near spring and we were going to be breaking camp, it would be the right thing to keep on working, but with a long winter ahead in a snow belt, work in such conditions was going to play out the horses. I told him that during the nice weather we had gotten a lot of extra logs on skidways, along with thirty or forty extra carloads on sidings and that we had enough logs to run the mill a week or ten days. I felt that surely the weather would change by that time. I also reminded him that it was Christmas week when the men who had been in camp for some time wished to get away. For those reasons, my opinion was to stop all the skidding crews and let those who planned to go out for Christmas go the next day, while those who wished to stay could be used getting ready for the sleigh haul and the sawyers who wished to stay could keep on cutting logs. Bill thought that sounded good and said we would make a decision at the camp that evening. Bill stopped at the office after supper. It was still raining. He said, "You may as well stop skidding until the weather changes or, better still, until after Christmas." I took my evening trip to the barn to tell the barn boss to cut down on feed to the horses as when horses are doing heavy work steady they need plenty of oats and hay, but when they stop work you must cut the amount of feed -- not to save money but to keep from having sick horses. Horses are not like cows, but will eat more than is good for them, especially oats. You also have to cut down on hay; I had an experience about this which will come out later on. In those days when you had over five or six teams in a camp, it paid to have a barn boss who knew horses and also able to take criticism, as many good teamsters had no judgment when it came to feeding horses. In fact, some would be caught trying to give the team they were driving more oats, thinking they were being good to the horses.

The next morning we had an exodus of lumberjacks, not to Israel but to Saxon, Hurley, and Mellen, with no complaints about a layoff. The weather stayed wet up until December 23rd when it started to cool off and on December 24th around noon the snow started and kept up all afternoon. On Christmas Eve we had about eight inches of snow by midnight . . . I remember it well. The reasons I can remember that Christmas Eve so well are first, the steam loader engineer wanted to go out for Christmas and I told him as long as I was going to be at camp I would take care of the steam boiler for him, keep a fire in it, so there would be no freeze-up. Secondly, a few of us at camp planned to attend Midnight Mass in Saxon and with no automobiles yet available and no road to use them on in bad weather, I said I would hitch up a team on a lumber wagon. By 10 p.m. Christmas Eve we could use a sleigh instead of the wagon so I hitched up the team, threw some blankets and hay into it, picked up Mrs. Wm. Richardson and a couple of men from the camp, and then stopped at other farms where we picked up some more passengers and on to Saxon. The snow had stopped by that time so we made it to Saxon for the midnight mass and back to camp by about 3:00 a.m. Christmas morning for a few hours' sleep.

At that time there was at least sixteen families from Weber's home to Saxon on what is now Highway 122, not including the homes on old Highway 10. At the present time, there is no family on that stretch of highway. Now with lake property hard to get and this whole northern area a tourist attraction, people from the larger cities are buying some land to build cottages where there are solid roads and good water, as with a car they are able to drive to assorted centers of interest. Another thing they like, which is obtainable, is electricity and a telephone. I am getting inquiries right along for from an acre to forty acres of land, if not priced out of reason. I look for this area to be settled again as it is blessed with some of the best spring water in the north, flowing out of the ground everywhere. To let you know how odd this is, the city water at Hurley and Montreal is not fit to drink but Pence, Iron Belt, Upson and Saxon have good water which is easy to get. I wondered why in 1960 when they were talking about a pipe line from Lake Superior to Hurley and Ironwood when, according to my estimate, there is spring water enough in those hills from Iron Belt and Upson to Saxon to supply the range.

Following the light snowstorm of December 24, the weather turned colder, so between Christmas and New Year's while the crew was getting back to normal, we had a few teamsters exercise the horses by tramping the sleigh roads which had no chance to freeze with the snow coming after a week of rainy, warm weather. It was done by placing skidding chains on the ends of a log, then hitching a team on it so as to drag the log angle-wise on the road, using a light log the first day as naturally the first day the horses would break through in the soft spots which would help those spots freeze up the next night. Once in a while we would have to tramp a soft spot with men first, let it freeze, then go over with a team. The company was not using tractors for skidding at that time. The weather was just right that week for tramping roads, getting a little colder each night and not snowing, so that by New Year of 1924 the sleigh roads were in good condition. We were not making ice roads at Camp 41. Our sleigh roads were all short haul with many odd patches of stumpage to sleigh out. We had been logging in high land area where railroad branches were made whenever possible. We were cleaning up the patches of timber too rough or scattered for a railroad.

We were logging west of Highway 122 and south of the Sullivan fire lane in a block of a mile square, or one section, reaching up to Weber Lake corner. The landing for that block of timber was in about one-half mile west on the south side of the Sullivan fire lane. The hemlock and some hardwood logs were loaded out. Some hardwood logs were decked for summer loading. It ran about 500,000 of hemlock, so we decked about 500,000 on the landing of good hemlock and mixed hardwood logs; at the same time sorting out the basswood logs which deteriorated rapidly in the summer so they could be loaded first in the springtime.

We were very fortunate that winter in not having much snow, but it was plenty cold which is generally the case when you do not have much snow. Just like it was the winter of 1970. We had decked no logs on this block of timber. The peeled logs had been cut but were not skidded as we needed to use all the horses we had until January 1, 1924, to skid the logs to keep the mill going. Now with the freeze-up, we had to send five of our teams to Camp 42 on the Weber Marsh as some hardwood logs had been decked in the woods for the sleigh haul there. The hemlock had been decked. All the logs at Camp 42 were to be loaded out when hauled as the landing reached in on the marsh and it would be too soft to load in the spring. Therefore, they had to get busy on cutting and skidding hardwood logs as the hardwood logs from Camp 42 were to go to the mill at once, with Camp 41 loading what additional hardwood logs needed to keep the mill going one shift. Camp 38, where they had been decking logs all fall, was to keep the mill going the other shift with the mill only scheduled to run two shifts through March, 1924.

The Camp 41 crew was back on the job by New Year's. Our sleigh roads were ready so we started hot logging at once, which means cutting, skidding and loading onto sleighs, hauling to a loading onto cars. Once in awhile logs cut in the morning would be into the sawmill at Mellen in the late afternoon, which you can call really hot when all logging up to the landing was done with horses and men.

Frank Banko, the sleigh haul teamster, was all ready; his team had been sharp shod for the sleigh haul, was rested up some, and from the first of the year until around March 15 that team of dapple grays with Frank sleigh-hauled all the logs from that block of timber.

We had two skidding gangs in the woods with three teams skidding in one gang and two teams in the other gang with a side tip-up boom, jammer, or loader powered by a team of horses for each gang. We kept the two side loaders as close as possible to each other so that one cross haul team and four men would be able to load the logs from the two gangs. It would have been an advantage to have had two more teams but we made out the best we could with what teams we had. The crew averaged 25,000' per day which was very good for that size crew, especially in the winter season.

We were favored with an ideal winter for hot logging, which was a real break as we did not have to dig the peeled hemlock logs out of three or four feet of snow and did not have to spend a lot of time plowing out sleigh roads with teams. For that reason peeled hemlock logs were almost always skidded and decked before snowfall set in each winter in that snow belt area.

Camp 41 also had one woods loading crew east of Highway 122 on peeled hemlock logs which had been decked in the woods during the fall. The logs from that loading crew were hauled by a Holt tractor to Camp

42 landing to be loaded.

John Organist, who was a contract logger, decked the logs he produced on the branch north of Sullivan Creek just off of Highway 122. That railroad branch was extended in 1924 into Kimball Township.

About the first week of March, 1924, the weather turned very warm. It was the first real thaw of the winter but with the ideal winter we had been blessed with, we were in good shape to stop at any time as the log haul was all the logging planned for the winter. It would be on the landing by March 15. It did turn a little cold about the time we finished hauling but not cold enough to plan more sleigh hauls, so we cut and skidded for a short dray haul just to keep the horses busy a little longer.

It was one of the best all-around winters I ever put in at a logging camp.

There were handicapped woods workers in logging operations in those days.

The teamster in the loading crew driving, the cross haul team loading sleighs, was Frank Shultz, who had come over from Poland in the early 1900's, settling at Mellen. Frank Shultz started working at the Foster and Latimer Lumber Company camps shortly after arriving at Mellen. He sawed logs at first, then took a job swamping as he liked horses and wished to be a teamster and it did not take him long to make it. He started practicing with a cant hook and became very efficient with a hook; he took up hooking on steam loaders next and was good at that too as he had a lot of ambition and drive. But one day he had the misfortune to get his left hand smashed badly. It had to be amputated at the wrist. This did not stop Frank. When the wrist had healed, he was fixed up with an artificial wrist with just a plain steel hook for a hand and when the stub had thoroughly healed he went back to camp. It was not too long before he was able to do all the same jobs, but he liked driving team the best so would only take the other jobs if a foreman needed a man badly for a few days to help out. Well, Frank was the teamster in the cross haul at Camp 41 during the winter, with Tony Jesse the top loader. Those men did a really fine job in keeping those two skidding crews loaded out. They always had the side tip-up loaders ready to move and set up again in a hurry without being told. In fact the whole crew I had that winter made it a pleasure to run a camp crew.

A word about some of the leading lumberjack characters of those early days as during the spring breakup most all of them would pass through the area at least once and this spring was no exception.

There was Overland Louie (Louie Johnson) a very good teamster who had the lumberjack record for short stays at a camp. In fact, it is stated on good authority that he once received six different checks from six different camps in one week. That was really getting around. The foreman or men working with Louie would know when he was going to walk away from a job as if any little thing went wrong, he would throw his hands up over his head and that would be all.

Dan Baker, another all-around good man, would make many trips to the camps of this area during a season. He was called the "camp inspector" and "monthly newspaper" as he had a good vocabulary and memory.

Then there was Tommy-on-the-trail (Tom Keegan) who received his nickname by knowing all the trails and shortcuts from camp to camp. He liked the job of swamper and was a good one. If he happened to get swamping for a good teamster, he would sometimes stay for a long period, but a change of teamsters would generally see Tommy move also. He had a habit of talking to himself in a low tone a good share of the time.

Walking John Daley was another man with a short stay record and was a man you would see often and would always be walking across country when not employed. He was a very good axe or cant hook man and, when he did work, did a good job without being watched and always kept his working tools in shape.

Walter Williams was an all-around good blacksmith, mechanic, tractor operator, and gas log loader engineer but also had the roaming fever and would spend about half of his time traveling from one camp to another or in town.

Some will ask a normal question, "How come these fellows were able to get a job?" The men just listed were all good, able men and many times one of them would just happen along when a good man was needed so the camp foreman would be glad to see him and generally one of those men would stay until a replacement showed up.

I know there were many times when I liked to see them show up and during the years I was a contract logger, Dan Baker worked for me and often came along just at the right time.

Another real character was 8-day Henry, correct name, Joe Henry, so nicknamed as he generally worked at one place about eight days. He was a loud, tobacco-chewing jack, a good teamster or swamper, very witty, so was a good camp orator. He was a very good liar too, as he would never get peeved if the men did not believe him, which is the proof of a good liar.

With the coming of nice weather in April, 1924, after a good winter logging season, the supervisory help figured all would be serene at the camps with no change in personnel, but it was not to be. I guess it had all worked out too well.

Wm. Richardson, the woods superintendent who lived at the camp with his wife, Lottie, had, the year before, bought a couple of 40's of farm land in the town of Marengo with buildings on it with the intention of working it up for a few years, then going there to live and farm on a small scale. A man who worked for Bill in the woods in the wintertime had a farm joining Bill's. In fact this friend encouraged Bill to buy the land and said he would work it up for Bill by plowing and seeding some each year on a share basis and he was making progress for Bill.

By this time Dan McDonald had decided he did not need an assistant woods superintendent but offered Bill a job as camp foreman at the same wages. The operation really had not been big enough for two such active men and some of this problem could have been avoided earlier. The fact was, over the past several years, the scattered timber areas had been logged and what was left now was in more of a solid block in the Gurney-Saxon area, with a very good logging chance after about two more years, as the operation would be out of the rough rocky hill adjoining the Copper Hill, White Cap, Radar Tower Mountain Range and not as much supervision needed. Richardson took a few days to make a decision, then he decided to turn down the foreman job and move onto the farm. Henry Cronk, John Nordberg, and I tried to talk him out of it as we not only did not want to see the Richardsons move out, but were convinced Bill would not be a farmer as he was at the age it would be hard to make that much of a change. We could not get Bill to change his mind and he told Dan his decision soon after but he did not move out until the latter part of April as the roads were very bad. They were able to move out by the way of Saxon through Odanah to Ashland on what was State Highway 10, then down what is now State Highway 13 to his farm.

McDonald put John Nordberg and I running section and railroad lines. Henry Cronk was put in charge of building a set of camps to be ready for bark peelers with the other Black Dan McDonald, who had been at Camp 42 on Weber Marsh all winter, helping me at Camp 41 get ready for summer logging.

There was always a clean-up job around camps in the spring of the year, burning the brush in a radius of at least 20 rods in each direction so as to have a chance in case of forest fires. The camps had to be sprayed with a solution to kill bed bugs and lice, blankets washed, and other housekeeping chores completed. We all had plenty of work. I did not take time off as I wanted some time off at the time of my wedding set for June 12, 1924. We were planning to live in an extra boarding car the company had built so it could be moved around.

The time passed very fast and before we knew it, the bark peeling season was here again. John Nordberg had to help Henry Cronk with bark peelers and I took Frank Shultz to help me on the lines.

One afternoon when I came back to camp I saw a familiar face on the bench in front of the camp. I took another look and it was John Salo, the big Finnish bark peeler who had put up his bark so well the summer before at the Mellen Lumber Company Camp 23 and had been so pleased with his scale. I talked with John Salo for a short time and found out he had shipped out from Duluth to the Mellen Lumber Company camps first but when he found out I had moved over to Foster-Latimer camps he decided to try them, too. It made me have a satisfied feeling that I had treated him right when scaling his bark, although I never felt I had given him any more than what he had coming. I told John Nordberg and Henry Cronk about Salo and sent him to the new Camp 43, which Cronk was building for bark peeling. They found out what I told them was true, as they said his bark was put up better than any man they had ever seen. John Nordberg had the same experience when scaling him that I had the year before; a very pleasant experience for a bark scaler as it was usually a thankless job.

We had one other change in Camp 41 personnel when the camp broke up at the end of March. Our good cook, Sherman Frank, decided to give up the cook job for the summer as his wife was not well and he was going to cook at a hotel in Chippewa Falls in order to be home. We hated to see Sherman leave but understood why. We were very fortunate though as Dan McDonald sent us Max Makoske of Upson, who had been cooking at Camp 38 the past year. Max was a very good all-around camp cook and very dependable so we again had good eats.

During the early part of May, I had another interesting experience which happened very often in those early days when large logging companies had stumpage near private lands. In the summer of 1923, Dan McDonald and Bill Richardson had run the railroad branch line which crossed Highway 122 about a quarter of a mile north of Camp 41 going east toward the town of Kimball where the branch ended on Sec. 10T.46N-R1E near Boomer Creek. The branch angled across Sec. 28 and 29T.46N-R1E with Zuchowski owning the SE of SE Sec. 20T. 46N-R1E. There was a high ridge to cross with the east side dropping fast near the section corner. Dan and Bill were able to get a fairly easy grade down over the ridge by crossing the Zuchowski 40 on Sec. 20 right at the Sec. corner so they talked to the Zuchowski family. Mr. Frank Zuchowski, Sr., had died suddenly and the very large family were deciding on what to do with the farm. The Zuchowski family said, at the time, you are no more than touching our 40 so it is doing no harm. Just go ahead as some of our boys are getting employment at your camps. If you want to give us something, okay. So Dan and Bill run the line on through, had it graded, and now in the spring of 1924, planned to lay the steel to set up two camps that summer. The company was able to get the lumber for Camp 44 in the town of Kimball into the camp site on a town road so the crews could peel bark the summer of 1924. All would surely have gone well but Zuchowskis sold out to Anton Gulan, Sr., in the fall of 1923. Zuchowskis told Gulan about the bargain they made with the Foster-Latimer Company and hoped he would honor their word. To be sure how the deal was standing before laying the steel, Dan went to see Anton Gulan, Sr. Well, Mr. Gulan had decided to get something out of it in the meantime so asked Dan for $500, which riled Dan as the line did not cover a quarter of an acre. Dan said, "I will give you $100" which was what he planned to pay Zuchowskis but no papers had been signed. "No," Gulan said, "$500 is the least I will accept." Dan told him, "I will take it up with the company in town tomorrow morning." McDonald came back to Camp 41 at noon and said to me, "Take a man and your compass this afternoon to see if we can get the railroad to miss the corner of Gulan's land." I took John Nordberg and we went over there after dinner, worked all afternoon, found out we could miss the corner but did not get the pickets on the new line all set up. Although we could miss the corner, it would be a heavier grade to pull the loads over and would have to have a reverse curve at the bottom of the hill. We decided to wait until McDonald came out from town and then he could decide what we should do. As usual, Mr. Latimer told Dan McDonald to use his own judgment. Mr. Latimer did not like the idea of paying such a high price either, as naturally he said it would set a precedence for other owners of private lands they might have to deal with in the future. When I told Dan what we had found out he said, "Go ahead, run the new line, put some men grading it out, put a few teams and scrapers on and cut the hill as much as you can." We did this, but the hill could not be cut much as it was rock ledge. We were able to put in some fill to make a more gradual grade for the railroad. When completed, it worked out okay, although the train crew always had to pull four or five carloads of logs, bark or other forest products at one time over the hill to a set out spur at the top of the hill. They would have had to do this with the original grade, but might have been able to pull a car or two more at a time.

The train crew kidded me a lot about the route change, but Dan McDonald never second-guessed me on it, as I had informed him, with John Nordberg as a witness, that it would be a much heavier grade and he also knew it. The company got the logs out from east of the ridge with only one small wreck and that was while laying the steel. The two-spot Lima was spotting a carload of rails and ties at the peak of the hill when the brake did not catch and the car went off the end of the railroad track. The steel gang unloaded the car and the engine was able to pull the empty car back on the rails.

13

Interesting Items
Of Logging Camp Life

One day I took Ed Organist with me to help on some lines as Frank Shultz was taking care of horses, getting them ready to be turned out to pasture. When Ed and I were coming in from work in the afternoon, we saw a mother bear and her cub cross the railroad heading for Sullivan Creek west of the camp. We went on into camp where we had some of the men working around the camp join us to try to catch the cub. One man took a gun, not to shoot the mother bear, but for protection to scare her if she attacked after we had picked up the cub. We got close enough to see them along the creek bottom but the mother bear fooled us. She picked up the cub with her front feet, holding him with her front fore legs, and running on her hind legs only. She ran so fast through the swamps we could not catch up. We had never intended to shoot the mother, and it was a good thing we did not get the cub as we could not keep the cub anyway. Some of those things tried at camp were just ways to have some recreation. I know if those fellows had caught the cub they would have taken care of it or let it go.

Dan McDonald kept me busy running lines until a few days before my wedding was to take place on June 12, 1924. My mother was back in Mellen so I spent a couple of days with her while Mike Donahue, the tailor, was finishing my wedding suit.

It was to be a double wedding as Mary Organist was to marry T.G. Smith on the same day. Tell Smith was a railroad operator on the C. & N.W. at the time. I was to marry Lacarda Organist. In those days a single wedding ceremony was a big event in Saxon so a double wedding of two girls who had grown up in the community added a little to the event, with a dinner and afternoon reception at the Organist farm home.

Dan McDonald had informed me that since the Richardson's moved out of the cottage at Camp 41, we might as well move into the cottage in place of the boarding car, as it would be handier for me to the camps. Lacarda and I had set up the furniture so it was all ready to be occupied on our return from a week wedding trip to Chicago.

While visiting with Henry Cronk, John Nordberg, and Frank Folkman the day before the wedding, Henry said, "Do you know how many miles you walked this past year to see your girl?" "How many?" I said. He answered, "Five hundred fifty-two miles!" and I said, "How do you know?" He said, "John counted your trips until I got here this spring and I have counted them since I got here." Astonished, I said, "Boy! you fellows sure kept an eye on me!"

The big day arrived -- a beautiful sunny June day. After the church service, a quick trip was made to Ironwood for the pictures, then back to the dinner and reception. With such a nice day and big crowd, much time was spent in the apple orchard, which was a dandy at that time. After the guests had departed, Lacarda and I left on our wedding trip by C. & N.W. passenger train for Kenosha and Chicago. We spent a few days in Kenosha as guests of Andrew Organist and his wife. We then spent several days in Chicago as guests of Mr. and Mrs. John Markee. In Chicago, we took in a couple of ball games and some shows which we enjoyed. By that time we were ready to get back to our cozy cottage at the camp.

In our agreement with the Foster-Latimer Lumber Company, we were allowed our living expenses over and above my monthly salary. That is, we could both eat our meals in the camp kitchen, or get whatever we needed from the supplies furnished the camp kitchen so Lacarda could cook for herself, which gave her something to do. We were also furnished fuel and light expenses, so it was a good deal for us. We were able to save a big part of my salary as we did not buy a car while living at camp. There simply were not enough good roads to warrant buying a car at that time.

The balance of the month of June ran smoothly until the 4th of July break which always threw a logging crew out of balance for a couple of weeks.

Ray Scribner was out hiring men after the July 4th break and had just come up from Mellen to see what jobs the foreman needed men for. He was talking to Black Dan, the skidding crew foreman, when I stopped by. Dan was telling him he was in need of teamsters as there were two idle teams in the barn. Ray said, "Well, it's noon now so it's too late to go to Hurley but I will go there tomorrow." Then Ray turned to Dan. "I tell you what I will do; I will drive one of those teams this afternoon if George will drive the other team." I said, "Your bluff is called." I started for the barn because I knew the two teams in the barn and figured I might as well get the first pick. We harnessed the teams and away we went. I was lucky in getting one of the better swampers, little Tommy-on-the-trail, nicknamed because he traveled from camp to camp so much. With Ray and I trying to outdo the other, Black Dan got a good afternoon's work out of us. That night a couple of teamsters walked into camp so Dan was all set again. That's the way it was in the woods those days; a feast or a famine of workers, so it usually kept a foreman on his toes. In addition to the usual woods routine, many amusing incidents occurred during that summer which helped keep up the morale of all of us.

One afternoon as I came down from our cottage near suppertime, I heard a lot of laughing and hollering near the watering trough. I looked and there was Max Makoske, the cook, supervising a half dozen men giving a man a bath. I had an idea who it was at once, as I saw him coming into camp in the afternoon. He was a little fellow, I cannot think of his name now, who everyone working in or near logging camps knew because he never worked, just traveled from camp to camp where he would always get meals but would never wash up. In the summer he would sleep wherever it was handy, so he was filthy dirty. I always believed the poor fellow was mentally unbalanced, although in those days most people other than loggers figured that anyone who worked in the woods was mentally out of balance . . . possible they were. The men gave this fellow a good bath, head and all. Then I donated a light suit of underwear, shirt and pants from the wanigan, as there was no use giving him a bath and then letting him put on the dirty clothes. The cook then let him eat supper. The chore boy gave him a bunk and then some of the men said to him, "Why don't you ever work? It would be better than just walking all the time and never knowing where you are going to get the next meal." He said, "Never mind. If all lumberjacks were like me there would be lots of timber on the reservation yet." The men all had a good laugh over that remark and one of them said, "It's pretty hard to give him an argument on that statement." I would agree, but he was more to be pitied than laughed at.

The work progressed during the summer. The required amount of railroad was graded and the steel laid. The planned acreage of hemlock bark was peeled and enough logs cut and skidded to keep the mill going as well as shipping peeled hemlock logs for pulpwood. Both Camps 43 and 44 were completed with bark peeled also.

During the summer of 1924, Marie Deich came home for a visit in July, and she came to the camp to visit with Lacarda for a day. After the noon lunch, they decided to take a walk to Weber's farm. Just south from Camp 41, Highway 122 had been relocated about one half-mile. The two girls took the new road on the way over to Weber's, visiting a few hours with Mrs. Weber and her daughter, Ester. While there they heard a dynamite blast, which sounded over toward our camp, but they did not pay any attention to it as much dynamite was used in grading railroad or sleigh road grades. When they started back to camp, they decided to take the old road which they had traveled so often a few years previously. They were enjoying the walk and were up almost to the place where the old road turned off when Lacarda, my wife, noticed a man lying with just his feet showing in the road. Naturally her first thought was of a man sleeping off a jag but as the girls edged up a little closer, they could see the blood, which shook them up some. They cut through the little wood section onto the new road and almost ran all the way to the camp about a half-mile away. There was no one at the office yet, since it was almost quitting time, so Lacarda went to the kitchen and told Max, the cook, who laughed at the two of them, so they went to our cottage to wait until I came home. While waiting for me to come home, they saw Frank Botts, the sawyer boss, walking by so they hailed him and asked if he would go up the road to see what had happened to the man. Frank went up to where the man was and came back on the run as white as a sheet. The man had put a fuse and cap in some dynamite and stuck it in his mouth and lit it, so you know what happened. The man had been a section boss for some logging company in Minnesota. He went into Duluth on the 4th of July, spent his money and then shipped out to Mellen. He had just arrived at Camp 41 in the forenoon of the day this happened. The chore boy at camp, Wm. Early, could never figure out how he got that dynamite fuse and caps so fast and neither could the rest of us. The only conclusion we could arrive at was that he had brought them with him. The chore boy said the fellow lay down on a bunk after noon lunch for an hour or two, got up, walked around for awhile and disappeared while the chore boy was carrying wood into the kitchen. The incident gave the crew something to talk about for a few days. One old lumberjack who loved his liquor was heard to say, "I may commit suicide some day but I sure will find an easier way." Of course, those who commit suicide generally do have some way figured out, as I will explain on another case of a man who tried two different ways, then made it on the third attempt.

I was kept busy surveying out new railroad lines all summer in a new location so the season moved along, remaining very interesting and busy for me. A new main line was needed, starting on the east side of the Tyler Forks River where the route to State Highway 169 fire lane turns toward Gurney through what was the Ren Vought farm. From Sec. 5-T 45N-R1W across the SE corner of Sec. 32, T46N-R1E it angled through Sec. 27 across SW corner of Sec. 22, turning east across the Potato River at about one quarter mile in on Sec. 23, then on east across the south tier of 40's, then angled NE across Sec. 24 on into Sec. 19, T46N-R1E to within one half-mile of State Highway 122. It ended in the center of Sec. 19 at the SW corner of the Leonard Chart land. Logging railroad branches ran off to the north, northeast, south and southeast as the larger amount of timber was logged by railroad logging on that block of timber. It was possible to build railroads without excessive cost and railroad logging was always the cheapest when railroad building costs were reasonable. The entire block of timber covered by the railroad in this area was very good hemlock and mixed hardwood, although there were also some good white cedar poles and posts and some spruce and balsam pulpwood which was all marketable.

When a company the size of Foster and Latimer Lumber Company closed down logging camps in the spring breakup, there was naturally a surplus of horses, especially when the company planned to peel a lot of bark and to run the sawmill only one shift. In that case there would be from fifteen to twenty-five horses to go out on pasture. With a camp or two being moved each spring, plenty of pasture land was always available as the grass and oats would grow fast each spring in the slashings where horses were fed out. Even after a forest fire, if the ground had not burned too deep, the grass would grow. Camp 31 on the Potato River just above Foster Falls was the pasture grounds. It was an ideal spot. The sides and floor of the barn and hayshed had been dismantled leaving the roof for protection from sun and storms so the horses could get under cover whenever they wished. Joe Bauers, a good horse man and a steady barn boss for many years, was always picked to be the caretaker as he did not mind being alone. Where horses were accustomed to oats, it was necessary to feed them some in order to keep them in good condition. Such feeding was not only good for them, but it helped keep them coming back at night. Joe would give each horse about a quart of oats morning and night, then when the horses were scheduled to go back to camp, Joe would increase the amount so the horses would be conditioned to work. The horses which were the most run-down from overwork, inefficient teamsters, or injuries, were the first to be turned out and would be kept out until ready for work. A schedule was always figured to exchange the horses first turned out with those kept at the camp so as to have near equal time out on pasture. What a surprise to see what a month or six weeks on pasture would do for the horses! They very seldom would stray very far, since the location with the Potato River on one side and the Tyler Forks River on the other side, along with some large swamps and rough ground, kept Joe from having much trouble.

With the company building the new main line railroad, old Camp 31 became a small headquarters camp. Dan McDonald often came up that far on his gas car when he wished to go with me to inspect the new line or to look over prospective camp sites. He would call up Camp 41 the night before when he was free to go with me. I would then take enough lunch for both of us and meet him at Camp 31. Dan always liked to visit Joe Bauers, so he never cared if I was a little late. Dan had told me to keep on running the new main line with the time available as he wished to get the steel across Potato River to the camp site of Camp 45 before the fall freeze up. I kept at it until one day when I was about a mile from Potato River. It looked like a good course. I decided to run through to the river with a compass to see if we were going to hit the river at a good place for a bridge and to see how it would be on the east side of the river. I made the compass trip and it looked good to me as the river was not wide at the proposed crossing, with a high bank on each side so we would never have trouble with high water if we kept the driftwood moving. I went back to the picket line, worked the rest of the day, went back to Camp 41 that night, and called Dan on the phone. I told him to come the next day if possible. He said, "I'm free and I'll bring Ray Scribner with me so bring enough lunch for three of us."

The following morning I jumped on the speeder with the lunch and my axe, stopped at Camp 31 where they were to meet me, and had enough time for a visit with Joe when they arrived. The three of us started out together on a compass line to hit our pickets back far enough so we would not miss the line. I was in the lead, carrying the lunch. Since Dan and Ray were stopping every little while to talk, I said, "I will keep on going and if I get there ahead of you, I will set up a few pickets." The mosquitoes were bad and I wished to keep moving. Dan said, "Okay, go ahead. We will get there in a short time anyway." I walked on, reached the picket line, and went to work. I worked about an hour but no Dan or Ray showed up. I thought they might have gone over to where I spotted the bridge location on the river as I had told them I blazed up a few trees there. I set up pickets until about 11:00 a.m. and still they did not show up. I was sure they had gone to the river first, so I picked up the lunch and the tea bucket we used to boil tea for the lunch. I took off for the bridge location on the river. Still no Dan or Ray. By then I was puzzled so I made a bucket of tea and ate my lunch, of which I had plenty. After lunch I started back to the picket line thinking possibly one of them had an accident. I tried hollering once in awhile, with no answer, so I went back to the picket line but there was no sign of Dan or Ray. I set pickets again until about 3:00 p.m. When no one showed up by that time, I started for Camp 31 thinking surely they had gone back there and had taken the gas car on to Camp 41. When I arrived at Camp 31 Joe Bauers said they had not come back there and the gas car was setting on the side of the track. I told Joe I had not seen Dan and Ray all day. He laughed and said, "They must be lost. Let them go, they will come back when they get hungry." I said, "They should be hungry now as I have been carrying their lunch around all day." We visited awhile when Joe looked across the barnyard and saw them coming. One of Dan's pants legs was about torn off and they were bear-hungry. They had been lost or, giving them the benefit of the doubt, turned around. It seems while they were talking, in some way they got off the compass course and missed the picket line. Then before they realized it, were down in the big cedar swamp on the Tyler Forks River. By the time they wandered around the swamp for an hour, Dan said to Ray, "There's no use going to the picket line now. We may as well look around here for an hour as we will have to get a railroad along the edge of this swamp over toward Gurney next year anyway." Of course, they never did own up that they were lost, even though it was easy to do before fresh section lines were run out. Anyone can get turned around occasionally, especially in virgin timber. Dan and Ray took the gas car to Mellen and came back the next morning when we did make it to the picket line, looked over the bridge site and the area on the east side of the river where the railroad was to go. All was okay so we went on to camp and from that time on a helper and I continued the work on the railroad until the pickets were set to the end of Section 19.

A campsite was picked out on a nice level spot near a spring of good water for Camp 45. We picked out a spot to set the boarding cars near the river. The station workers and steel gang crew would be housed in the cars in the spring of 1925. The crew building Camp 45 would be housed there, as Camp 45 would not be used until the summer of 1925.

About the time I was finishing the running of new railroad lines during the last of September in 1924, Black Dan, the camp foreman who had replaced me while I was on the lines, was offered a foreman job with another company. Since he knew I was available for Camp 41, he took the job, so I was told to take over again for the winter. Camp 41 was keeping the sawmill in logs, loading out some peeled hemlock logs and one skidding crew decking some logs in the rough area of the Radar Tower Hill north of Weber Lake.

Camp 43, built in the spring of 1924, was about two miles east of Highway 122 on the center of Sec. 21-T46N-RIE where Henry Cronk was foreman. It now was in full operation skidding and loading out peeled hemlock logs for the pulp mill and decking logs on sleigh roads. Logs were being hauled over the bad hill mentioned previously, with the rod engine and 3-spot making the hill without trouble. The car camps were located on a kickback branch on the SE corner of Sec. 19-T46N-RIE to be used by Lee Scribner on a contract basis to cut, skid, deck and haul during the fall of 1924 and winter of 1925. Lee had a crew of about forty men and six teams until spring, getting out some nice hemlock and hardwood logs to be decked on the railroad, to be loaded out during the spring breakup. When Camp 41 started logging in 1923, there was solid timber stumpage from Weber Lake on Highway 122 north to the Freburg Road, east toward Kimball about three miles and west to the Potato River, except what had been logged off in clearing the small farms; good heavy timber of hemlock and mixed hardwood with an average of about 400,000 feet to a forty-acre plot, in addition to the cedar, balsam and spruce.

The forest growth is now coming back well but there will never again be a hemlock and hardwood forest with the kind of timber that was on it originally.

Back to Camp 41 logging as this was to be a memorable fall and winter. I am going into much detail on the logging of the Foster-Latimer Lumber Company in the area of Ashland and Iron Counties as it covered such a large block of timber logged before the advent of mechanized logging. This proved to be a period of big change from antique logging methods to mechanization, and automation began soon after.

When the company finished logging at Camp 39 north of Hoyt, I figured that from now on we would have less rugged country to log and for two years it worked out that way. We even had less snow those two years. In winter logging you did need some snow, but some winters we would get much more snow than was needed. The winter of 1924-25 was that kind of a winter, lots of snow and extreme cold at times.

　　During the late summer two young lads from Hurley showed up looking for a job and talked as though they really wanted to work. We were not short of men at the time but I guess what interested me most about them was their build, as they were the skinny type about like I always was. We hired them. These fellows were Stanley Organist and Joe Shelky. Stanley was anxious to drive team but Joe did not care about that so the first few days we put them swamping for two good teamsters. They were willing to work and got along fine as they would listen to the teamsters. After about a week at odd jobs of all kinds for experience, I put Stanley driving a fine but light team. They did make up for some of the lack of weight, being well matched and very snappy. After driving them a few days, Stanley was in love with the team and no team ever received better care. He watched so they would be in position to pull and would not hitch onto big logs just to see if they would be able to pull them. At night he spent a lot of time cleaning them and when he went home to Hurley the first weekend, he came back with spreader and hip straps decorated with colored rings. All went well until one weekend late in October. The weather was really nice and on Sunday the teamsters were turning out the horses one team at a time. When Stanley's turn came, he turned his team out and they rolled, ran around the yard awhile and then took off into the woods. We figured they would be back in a short time, but they did not get back for a month or six weeks. It rained hard that first night, knocking off what leaves were still on the trees and covering up all the tracks. On Monday morning Stanley and I took off, making a big circle that day but did not see a sign of them. We naturally figured they would come out at some small farm in the Saxon, Cedar, Gurney, or Upson area but they did not. The weather did not get too cold and very little snow fell, so the horses were able to find some grass and weeds to eat but when they did not show up any place nearby, we figured they either had trouble in some swamp or had slipped out toward Odanah or Hurley. After another week with no signs, the disappearance sure proved a mystery, since all the people in the area were watching for them. We finally just gave up looking. One day late in November the team came back, a little thin but none the worse off otherwise. The only solution we could ever think of was that the horses found some old barn with hay in it close to a wooded area and stayed there or were simply lost and kept circling around finding enough browse to live on. In a couple weeks they were back in working shape. However by the time the horses showed up, Stanley had taken a job in town and never came back except to visit once in a while.

　　By this time winter weather was appearing. It did get quite cold before the snow came, which was always a big help as the ground froze some and it was not so muddy skidding logs. Around December 10, the first really heavy storm moved in with about twelve inches of snow to start with. We were able to break sleigh roads at once and were hauling small loads of logs by December 20, so we had good roads by Christmas time. With winter setting in early, about half of the crew did not go to town for Christmas and we were hauling logs in pretty good shape by the 1925 New Year.

When I said we would have some rough hills to haul logs down I was putting it mildly. If you do not believe it, take a drive over Highway 122 from Saxon to Upson. Then watch where a fire lane road leads off to the east about 500 feet south of Sullivan fire lane road. Do not try to drive in unless you have a 4-wheel drive vehicle but take a hike and when you get near Weber Marsh, about one and a half miles in, turn right or south and follow the old road which circles around Radar Tower Mountain to the Radar Tower building. The Radar Tower has been abandoned as being obsolete now. Then if too tired, take the new road back down to Highway 122 near Weber Lake. It is not a hard trip but you will see some beautiful scenery on all sides of the mountain and if you travel in raspberry season, you will be able to get some nice raspberries. You may also have some help in picking the berries from creatures wearing bearskin coats -- no kidding either! However, they will not bother you if you let them alone. If you meet one in the berry patch, just let him have that patch and you move to another.

There was one difference in hauling logs on sleighs from the hills around Radar Tower Mountain than in the hills north of Iron Belt at old Camp 39. Here we had a 10-ton Holt Caterpillar tractor instead of horses to pull the sleigh loads. We didn't have to ice the roads as it was a short haul and all downhill with the logs going to Weber Marsh landing. This haul provided a good test for the 10-ton tractor to see how big a load it could hold back. We found it could hold back more than a team, but we still had to have ruts on both sides of the roads to hold the sleigh runners in and we had to use hot sand to provide traction the first few trips in the morning. We also could not put peeled hemlock or birch logs on the top wrappers for fear these logs would slide forward. It was, however, much easier holding the sleigh load with the tractor as it was much heavier than the team. It also proved safer for the driver.

I had my old sand hill man, John Koski of Iron River, Wisconsin, back again and we had no serious accidents, although it was a winter with a lot of snow.

I was beginning to find out that all along the Penokee Range was a snow belt covering a strip about thirty miles wide, from the Ironwood-Hurley area through Montreal-Pence-Iron Belt-Upson, north to the Copper Hill-White Cap Mountain area and south to the water divide where the streams running north empty into Lake Superior and south into the Mississippi tributaries. The heaviest snowfalls always occur here. From Upson toward Mellen, the belt tapers off into a more narrow strip running on the Penokee Range through Mt. Whittlesey, Penokee Gap, Guest Mine or Mineral Lake Tower on to Grandview. North from White Cap Mountain range and west to Birch Hill the belt tapers off to much less snow, with the Odanah, Marengo and Ashland areas generally having a very moderate snowfall.

It was not a moderate snowfall in the Camp 41, Radar Tower, White Cap Mountain area the winter I am writing about. It was snowing about fifty percent of the time with the other fifty percent very cold, making it an extremely tough winter. The extreme winter weather made it very difficult to hire and keep teamsters for skidding teams although we had good thick hardwood timber to cut and skid. We tried not to saw too many logs ahead because if we had too many cut ahead they would get covered with snow, making it more difficult to skid. By having just enough sawyers to keep the teams in logs the job was made easier for the swampers and the teamsters.

In the early part of the winter I had a straw boss named Ralph Mitchell, an old-timer, but the snow got too much for him so he left around February 1. I replaced him with Al Hunt of Iron River, an experienced camp foreman who had shown up looking for work. Al worked out well and became a camp foreman at Camp 44 the following summer. The only battle we had that winter was with the deep snow and we had a very weary bunch of horses and men by the time the camps broke up in late March.

During the fall of 1924, we had added another family to live at the camp which made it much more pleasant for my wife. A Mat Stark from the Marshfield area had been working for the company a few years as a piece worker, sawing logs first, then as a hooker on the loading crew. He loaded logs by the thousand feet, with the company furnishing the steam loader. Mat had married during the summer of 1923 and asked if he could build a cabin at the camp so he could live there. We all knew Mat would be a good steady man, so the loading crew gave him a hand in putting up a comfortable two-room cabin. He lived there for a few years after Camp 41 was through. Mat was a strong, active man and did not mind walking a couple of miles to work. The cabin centered the logging very well and, being on the road, helped Mat in getting supplies. His wife, Susan, was a very friendly person who was able to adjust to living at camp. They had a young son, Leonard, which helped keep her busy. After the Starks were well settled, Mrs. Stark also did some laundry work for some of the men, which was always welcome in a lumber camp. Mrs. Stark and my wife got along very well so it shortened the winter for the two of them.

One day in February 1925 we had a total eclipse of the sun which caused a little excitement. At the time of the eclipse, the advance news was not as widespread as it is today. With so few newspapers getting into the camps and with little time to read those we did have, very few men knew about it. The eclipse, when it started to get dark some of the men began to think of their pasts and some unbelievers began to believe that possibly there was a God after all. There was a sigh of relief by many when that eclipse was over and all felt better that night. It did not last long or we may have had a stampede of lumberjacks.

While we were breaking camp at Camp 41 in March, 1925, we had a couple of prominent visitors. County Judge James Flandrena and his wife stopped one day at meal time. He was running for a six-year term as County Judge of Iron County. He had been appointed judge in 1924 to replace Griff Thomas who had died in 1924. He was being opposed by Everis Reid of Hurley in the April election. We invited them in for a regular camp meal, which they thoroughly enjoyed as they both mentioned it to me many times in later years. After the meal, Judge Flandrena talked politics to the men of the crew at an outdoor meeting. It was to be the first election in which I voted in Iron County as my home had been in Mellen up until my marriage in 1924.

Since that time I have lived in Ashland County two different periods for a total of seventeen years with the balance of time, twenty-five years, in Iron County in four different periods, which shows how necessary it was to move around a lot when following a career in the forest industry. They say a rolling stone gathers no moss but it does get polished. If that is true, I should be well polished and I know the top of my head is at any rate. Looking back I will say the process was a lot of fun and in my moving around I like to feel I acquired many fine friends in the forest industry. One important thing I did find out for certain is that people are people wherever you are, and if you meet them half way you can enjoy living and working, wherever your work is.

14

Another Camp Move
Deeper In The Wilderness

Just after Camp 41 broke up, Dan McDonald came along one day with some news for me. He told my wife and I to prepare to move into the boarding car, prepared for us to live in the season of 1925. He informed me that the car would be moved to a siding on the east side of the Potato River near the new main line crossing going east toward Highway 122. All the boarding cars were going to set out at a siding for the summer of 1925 to hold the railroad crew while grading and building railroads in the towns of Saxon and Gurney. The car we were to live in would only be there until I could get Camp 45 built, which was to be located about one and one-half miles east of the boarding cars. I was to keep the camp building crew in the cars until we had a kitchen and men's camp built.

As soon as the snow was off and the spring high water danger was over, we moved the car camps to the new location. It was a welcome sight to me. I always liked a new campsite, so nice and fresh with virgin hemlock and mixed hardwood standing all around, and much wild game and birds of all kinds. Whenever I was foreman at a new camp, I started logging about one-quarter of a mile away from the camp and left the timber around the camp until just before closing out the camp. Of course we did clear enough so there was no danger of trees falling on the buildings. If a campground was all cleaned away, there was acute danger of forest fires. For that reason I disliked a camp with slashing all around it.

After a day spent getting the boarding cars all set for the summer on a siding on the river bank, I spent the next day picking up a camp building crew. I already had Tony Jesse and Max Organist, who worked together a lot. I then went to Saxon and hired Louis Rostollan, Archie Trudeau, George Villanov, George Marchant and John Wagner of Gurney. It was a good crew of experienced men with Trudeau, Villanov, and Wagner all carpenters. All I had to do was see that they were kept in

building supplies after laying out the different buildings for a crew of
one hundred men. With a crew of that kind working on the camps, I was
able to spend most of my time running out the section lines and new
railroad branches before the bark peelers felled the hemlock trees. All I
needed to complete quickly was the area we were to peel on during the
summer of 1925 as I would have time after bark peeling to run the lines
needed for the summer of 1926. When you could keep ahead one year
with lines, you were in good shape. With lines established, you could
look the ground over much better before setting pickets for the railroads. I always figured it was better for two men to spend some time
looking over the grounds that railroads or sleigh roads were to be built
on than to be in such a hurry that the roads might be in the wrong place.

Camp 45 was located in a good spot on high ground with a small
cedar swamp closeby where we could get the needed spruce and balsam
pole timber to be used for stringers and ridge poles, in place of 2x4's and
2x6's for walls and roof. The men building the camp all excelled with an
axe, or broad axe, and saw. It was no problem for them to build with pole
timber.

Foster & Latimer Lumber Company Camp 45, built in the spring of 1925 in a heavy setting
of good timber. The George Corrigans lived in high building on left side facing the
timber. A fine wilderness setting.

One day a comical incident happened. Tony Jesse, Max Organist,
and George Marchant were out in the swamp in the forenoon cutting
stringers and ridge poles. They had run onto some fine spruce for
stringers of perfect length and had peeled the bark off to make them
lighter to carry. After noon lunch I told the six men to carry in the

heaviest stringers and then four men could handle the lighter poles. After the heavier ones were carried in, I told Archie Trudeau and John Wagner to work on the carpenter work as John Wagner was an older man and Archie was deaf and dumb but a very capable worker. I had put the other four men carrying in the ridge poles. I followed them to the woods where the poles were located. I heard Tony say to Max, "If you can carry the small end, I can carry the big end." So they picked up the pole and carried it with the other two men walking behind. When they arrived at the building I said, "Okay, now you and Max may carry all the poles you can handle and I will keep the other two men to help at the building. There is no use of them walking back and forth just to see how strong you two are." The other two men were not able to carry the poles but were able to help on the camps. Incidents such as that showed me how much difference there is in men and confirmed why it is so important to pick the right men to fit the job. Dan McDonald said to me one time, "If you ever have a logging job of your own or are a woods superintendent and wish to pick a man from your crew to be a foreman, never pick the big strong hard worker because he will think every man should be as strong as he is, which is not the case. Pick a man who is a good worker and ambitious but is always looking to make the work easier so more can be accomplished." This proved true many times, as you often had good cant hook men who were not exceptionally strong; still they could roll more logs and do it more easily than some of the big men. The same thing happened with saw gangs, station workers, or bark peelers.

Camp 45 camp building progressed satisfactorily and in a few weeks the kitchen and one sleeping camp were ready. Then Louis Lesperance was moved to Camp 45 to cook for the summer and a young cook was put in the car camps as there was only a small crew in the cars. The camp builders at Camp 45 made a nice platform from the kitchen to the screen meathouse to make it easier walking for Louis Lesperance who was badly handicapped.

In a short time another bunkhouse was up so we were ready for a large crew of bark peelers. It was important to be ready to peel bark at the right time as there were no unemployment checks in that era. After a spring breakup of six to eight weeks, men were looking for work so if you were ready you could get the men who really wanted to peel bark. Ray Scribner went over to Hurley one day to hire bark peelers and when he came back he said there were as many "man-catchers" in Hurley as lumberjacks. This I could believe.

By the summer of 1925 the roads such as Highway 122 and Federal Highway 10 (now U.S. 2), were getting in better shape so you saw more cars and light trucks but they were still considered a luxury. My wife and I, living two miles off of Highway 122 with only a walking trail, decided to get along without a car and save to purchase one in 1926.

There was not a thing for my wife to be afraid of at Camp, as she had grown up on a farm in the wilderness same as I had. Of course, there were many lumberjacks traveling between camps in those days, but I have never known of real lumberjacks molesting women; in fact, the men at the camp always showed very much respect for the women who lived at camp. They even cut down on their "cussing" in the presence of women. The only danger was from some city tramp who might have decided to make the camps.

One day I was hiking down the track at a good gait as I was late for the noon meal when out came a big black bear onto the tracks just in front of me. We both stopped fast or we would have run into each other. He looked at me, I looked him in the eye, and he scampered away with no trouble at all. I have always respected bears and I continued to tell everyone they are wild animals so you must just leave them alone. If you meet a bear on the trail give him the trail and you go around. Do not try to drive him off the trail. When bears have cubs with them, give them all the room you can but do not run away or they may take after you, sometimes only to find out what you are. I have a funny thing going for me; I am afraid of dogs but not of any wild animals we have around here (except the grizzlies or brown bears). When I was growing up around Mellen, I often peddled bills house to house and almost every house had a dog, some not so friendly. In fact, I was nipped a few times, once pretty badly bitten through my rubber boot top into my leg. Now, of course, dogs sense that I am scared of them and they take advantage of it. On the other hand, I have talked to bears in an angry mood but so far I have not been bitten by one, for which I thank the good Lord who has been so good to me in many ways.

The bark peeling went along fine. The camp building crew stuck it out until all the buildings were completed, ready for a full logging crew to move in after the bark season was over. The company also had bark peeling crews at Camp 43 and 44, both on the east side of what is now Highway 122. The summer logging crew finished at Camp 41 in the fall. A small part of the crew moved to Camp 43 after bark peeling to skid peeled hemlock logs to the track in order to get the peeled logs and bark out to make room for hardwood log cutters when Camp 41 finished up. What horses were out on pasture were sent to Camp 45 to skid the hemlock logs and bark out to the railroad to be loaded out before the fall snowstorms hit. It was always better to skid peeled hemlock logs and bark on bare ground, especially in a snow belt area.

A very sad incident happened during the summer of 1925 at old Camp 31 on the Potato River just above Foster Falls. Joe Bauers, the faithful barn boss and horse pasture superintendent during the summer months, wanted to have a little vacation from the pasture job. He had not been to town during the spring breakup and was getting so dry the spring water we had at Camp 31 would not quench his thirst. Frank Capallen was shacking on a former car camp location about a mile from Camp 31. Frank was a woodsman who took a little time off during the summer to do some fishing and rest up some at his shack and Dan asked Frank to look after the horses while Joe was to town. Frank accepted since he always visited back and forth with Joe. Joe settled up and received a check for around six hundred dollars. He told Dan he planned to send five hundred dollars to a brother at Bloomer, Wisconsin, who owned a feed mill doing a good business. The brother could invest the money for him, and then he would spend the one hundred dollars. Dan told him that was a good idea. Joe's intentions were good but when he cashed the check, instead of mailing the five hundred dollars to his brother he put it on deposit at the Mellen Bank, probably already thinking the one hundred dollars was not enough to spend. The net result was that Joe started drinking and since he had been off of liquor for about ten months, it affected him fast so that he was not able to sober up again while in town. He drew out about one hundred dollars each day from the bank. He didn't spend it all . . . he gave some away and some was taken from him. After a week or ten days in town, Joe was broke and was a very sick man when he started to sober up. He met Dan on the street one evening and said he wanted to go back the next morning. Dan agreed. In the morning Dan sent the man driving the horse and wagon around the warehouse up to the tavern to get Joe and what items he had bought while in town. The man came back with Joe, who had a couple of quarts of liquor or moonshine to sober up on. He was put on the caboose and the train crew unloaded him at his shack on the Potato River around 10:30 a.m. Of course, he went to sleep right away but Frank Capallen was around and said, "Let him sleep. I will take care of the horses until Joe gets sobered up." Frank stayed all afternoon and Joe woke up at 5:00 p.m., when Frank gave him some good hot soup. Frank was a good cook. After supper Frank went back to his shack, telling Joe he would be back in the morning. The next morning he found Joe in a deep sleep so he stayed around all day and made some strong coffee and soup. When Joe woke up in the afternoon, he ate some soup, drank some coffee and seemed to be sobering up very well. Frank went to his shack again that night but when he went back to Joe's the next morning, he found Joe in bad shape, shaking all over and looking for snakes under the bed. Frank had hidden a little liquor the day before so he gave Joe a hot drink and some more hot coffee before he went out to take care of the horses. Frank gave them their morning oats, checked on the number, and found everything okay so went back to see how Joe was making it.

Frank Capallen had always kept a gun around him when shacking and had brought a 12-gauge shotgun over that morning and left it standing outside at Joe's shack. When Frank got near the shack, he saw the gun was missing so hurried to the shack and there Joe was trying to set the gun so he could pull the trigger with a string. Frank stopped that, then talked to Joe, but he was full of remorse about spending all his money. He said what a fine brother he had, but that he himself was no good, and other such remorseful thoughts. Frank cooled him down and stayed with him all day.

Dan, the woods superintendent also stopped in, so by evening they had him in fairly good humor again. Frank took the gun and went to his shack for the night. Early the following morning, Frank went over to see Joe but this time he found Joe hanging on the door of his shack with his feet about a foot off the ground. The old office was built up a little from the ground so it could not be reached by high water, with one step up before entering. Joe evidently figured it out that by placing a rope securely on the outside of the door, then throwing it over the top edge to the inside, he could tie the rope around his neck with his feet on the floor, then by swinging the door open his feet would be up high enough to not touch the ground. It worked as he had planned. It was the end of Joe. He always got those spells after a heavy spree and some of us figured he would make it sometime. It seems that once a person plans on suicide as the answer to their troubles that eventually they carry out their plan.

This was the second time Joe Bauers had made a suicide attempt by hanging. At Camp 37 a few years back he had placed a couple of planks on the benches, put a rope over the rafter, tied it on one end and had the rope around his neck when the chore boy happened to see what was going on from where he was chopping wood. He ran over to the barn and stopped Joe that time. I was at Camp 37 when this incident occurred. I also stopped at Camp 31 just after he was found dead. He was a fine man in every way once he got sobered up and had been well liked by all the crew.

Not all incidents have the sad story of Joe Bauers. I remember a humorous thing that happened with George Romanovich, the chore boy mentioned above. Dan McDonald came in to the camp one real cold day when the fire had burned down low in the big office stove. George, the chore boy, came running over to get the fire started and Dan said, "Run over to the barn and get a horse blanket." The chore boy went, coming back with the blanket. Then Dan said, "Now put it over the stove until the stove warms up." The chore boy, a little excited by that time as he aimed to please Dan, was actually going to put the blanket over the stove until Dan stopped him.

During the fall of 1925 I was fortunate in meeting a new man who had arrived in Saxon to teach school. He was V.J. Downey from near Ellsworth, Wisconsin. He liked the area so well that he stayed in Saxon from then on. Of course, meeting one of Saxon's prominent maidens, Annabelle Lauren, whom he later married, may have played a part in making Saxon more attractive to him. He became superintendent of the Saxon High School, a position he held until the Saxon High School consolidated with the Hurley High School. After the merger, he remained in Saxon as superintendent of the grade school until his retirement several years ago. It took men like him to make up a total community. We have always been the best of friends and for many years were hunting camp partners with a group of men from Saxon.

From 1925 to 1929 the economy was building up and the mines offered better working inducements for young able men than did the woods.

We started skidding and loading hemlock logs by the middle of August, hemlock bark shortly after, and by the end of November 1925, all the logs and bark within skidding distance of the railroad was out. The area was in good shape for the summer logging crew in 1926.

As Camp 45 was not going to run during the winter of 1925-1926, the crew was moved and split up between Camp 43 and Camp 44. I stayed on, running lines through December, 1925. McDonald came up one day and said, "I suppose you and I will have to make a decision on you for the balance of the winter." I said, "What do you have in mind?" He said, "How about taking over Camp 44?" This was a sleigh haul camp in the town of Kimball. Al Hunt, who had been my assistant foreman or straw boss the winter before, was running Camp 44 at the time and I knew he would have stayed on with me but I said, "Dan, I have been working steady for thirteen years now and if it makes no difference to you, I would like to take the next three months off. Al Hunt is located at Camp 44 and will get along okay as it is only a one-year camp. Let him finish it up." Dan said, "If you wish it that way, okay, as I do have an entirely new job for you April 1, 1926. Don't ask what it is as I cannot say now but I will say it may be the best job you ever had. I will tell you by March 15." "Okay," I said, "It's a deal."

After a couple of weeks visiting at Mellen and Ashland, I was rested up some and then helped my father-in-law, John Organist and the two boys, Max and Ed, on their logging job. I drove team hauling logs most of the winter. While it was work, there was not the responsibility that I had as a logging camp foreman, so I put in a good winter. My wife helped her mother with the cooking and housework.

During the winter I made visits to other logging camps in the Saxon-Gurney and Kimball area and found the pattern of logging to be about the same at all the camps. The camps were built in the same way, with equipment and machinery, what little they had, about the same. Horses and manpower were still predominant in all camps.

I did see Dan McDonald once in a while during the winter but nothing was said about the new position until around the middle of March when he called on me and said, "Have you had rest enough now?" I told him I had. Dan then said, "Get prepared to move to Mellen by the first of April as Mr. Latimer would like to have you take charge of the warehouse and do the buying of camp and mill supplies. You will be working directly under Harry Latimer but I will still give the orders about the camp supplies, which should be no problem as you and I have been working together now about fourteen years." I agreed. Dan told me that the salary would be about the equivalent of what I had been getting to start with and that I would be living in town for a change. I told him that was really no inducement as far as I was concerned as I really liked living in the woods, but I was sure my wife would be more satisfied. I therefore accepted the position. My experience as foreman and handy man around logging camps had certainly given me some training for the job, except for the mill and shop supplies.

15

A New Part Of A Logging Job

The next two weeks passed by quickly. We didn't have too much furniture as we had not needed much up to this time. We were able to leave what furniture we had in the car we were living in and the train crew took it to Mellen. The only drawback was that we were to live in a company house, which was not to be vacant until near the end of May, so we had to move into another house temporarily. The company moved just enough of our furniture for us from the warehouse track to our temporary house to get by for a couple of months. We were ordering some new furniture which we would keep at the warehouse until the company house was vacated.

The first day I started at the warehouse, Harry Latimer called me into the office to give me instructions about salesmen who would be calling on me. He also informed me that over the years they had found out that it did not pay to buy too much ahead when the salesmen had specials, as sometimes you gained and sometimes you lost, so you might as well buy as needed. It was good advice. Then he told me of some changes he wanted to make at the warehouse. He said if I picked a handy man for a helper, some of the changes could be made gradually. He told me to make a suggestion for a helper after first thinking it over. Since it was a responsible job, and I was new, I wished to have someone I could trust entirely. I mentioned Max Organist, who although a brother-in-law, needed no help to hold up his end at any job he undertook. I told Mr. Latimer to get Dan McDonald's approval of Max. Dan always thought a lot of Max and recommended him highly. Mr. Latimer told me to hire him if he would come. Max accepted for one year, but said he planned on logging on a small scale when he had saved up a little money. Max worked out well and was great help for me. Later, Mr. Latimer said he was a very able and conscientious worker and very handy. I told him that came from lumberjack training.

Mr. Latimer asked that I spend some time around the shop sawmill, planing mill, and flooring factory, learning the names of all machinery, equipment, greases, oil, etc., being used around the plant. He felt it would then be easier for me when ordering from the salesmen. He introduced me personally to the two men from whom they bought most of their heavy equipment and camp hardware supplies at the time. One of these men was Irvin Garnich of J.B. Garnich and Sons, Ashland, and the other was Jake Olson of Marshall Wells Co., Duluth, Minnesota. These two men appreciated the trust Mr. Latimer placed in them and were of tremendous help to me. Irvin Garnich turned out to be a good friend for many years.

Frank Huber was the sawmill foreman, a very capable man who ordered only what was needed, so I had no problem there. John Hoglund was the planing mill foreman who was also a very capable man and he and Mr. Huber worked well together. Joe Jordan, the shop foreman, also knew his business in every way, and was Dan McDonald's right-hand man on all the steam machinery. I knew Joe well, as I had worked with him a lot when I worked as an engineer on the steam loaders and skidder. Casimer Wasielski was now the Foster-Latimer flooring factory boss. We knew each other well, as he had been working there as a flooring machine operator, then as a flooring grader when I was there, in the 1912-1913 era. Julius Nordby was the superintendent of the lumber yard, planing mill and flooring factory which made a minor coincidence. My father, Pat Corrigan, piled lumber in the yard at Drummond, Wisconsin, where Julius Nordby was a lumber grader in 1890 or 1891, before my father and mother settled at the 160 acre Mineral Lake homestead in 1891.

Going to Mellen that spring was just like going back home after being away a few years. It did not take me long to adjust to the work as part of it was along the same line that I had been doing in the woods, looking after cook camp and wannigan supplies. I was really adding to my all-around experience and this position helped me very much when going into the contract logging business later on.

I wish to make a statement here regarding the management of the Foster-Latimer Lumber Company which played such a big part in its success. They always had a fine group of men in their top management, which carried on through their organization. After working under Harry Latimer a short time, I could understand why. He carried himself well, with a way of giving orders which demanded respect. His manner was just the opposite of Dan McDonald's. Dan was more blunt. I will say, all the old-timers, who came up the hard way in the woods had that fault, myself included, until I had worked under Harry Latimer a while. But both were successful, which is what truly counts. I had no trouble getting along with management and enjoyed the work very much as I was also very close to the logging end of the business.

Dan McDonald, Joe Jordan, Joe Landry, and the conductor on the log train generally stopped in the warehouse in the morning, as it was the headquarters. I always opened at about 6:30 a.m. and we would have a bull session before the work started. Another old-timer who always joined us in the morning was Peter Fischback, then the log scaler at the mill. Pete had formerly worked in the woods as a camp boss and scaler, but had the misfortune to have one leg injured and was never really strong again. Pete was a very sociable fellow with more than his share of wit. I particularly enjoyed Joe Landry, the railroad yard superintendent. While I did smoke a pipe and cigars some, Joe knew I did not chew tobacco, but he always said, "Hello, George, do you have some chewing tobacco?" It would be the same question if I met him a half dozen times each day; it was the same question he would ask others, although he almost always had some tobacco of his own. It was just a habit he had gotten into. One morning, Joe came into the office in an excitable mood. Some of our other morning members were in attendance. He said, "I had a funny experience during the night. One of my neighbors came home drunk and started to beat up his wife. One of their children came up the hill after me for help, but I said, "no thanks." I had done that once before and got the worst of it, so this time I called the police, who took the man in care until he sobered up." I said, "What happened the first time you were called in a like situation?" Joe said, "I was living in one of those houses across Hillcrest Drive from the Spa, when a child came to our door and said, "Come quick to our house, our father is killing our mother." I ran over there as fast as I could and the man had his wife on the floor trying to beat her up. I grabbed him by the shirt collar, pulling him to his feet. When he started swinging at me, I tied his arms up with mine by which time the woman was on her feet. Then she jumped at me clawing and scratching and said, "That is my husband. You let him alone!" Believe me, it was all I could do to get out of there without a good beating. I said to myself, "That will never happen to me again." We all sympathized with Joe that time. There was never a dull morning.

The latter part of May, the company house of Red Row became vacant, so we moved in, set up the new additional furniture, and were within a stone's throw of the warehouse and across the street from the main office. The houses were now painted white but the name Red Row stuck.[1]

On the south side of Tyler Street from Bad River to the company tracks, the main office building of the Foster-Latimer Lumber Company and the Mellen Lumber Company were located. Just across the company railroad tracks east from the office was the big warehouse where the camp supplies were handled. This was a large building with an upstairs and a handpower, rope-pulling elevator for handling supplies up and down. It also had a large ice box cooler with an ice house adjoining for storage of ice. We had a large meat block with all the necessary tools to cut meat into smaller chunks for small crews in the summer months. The company did not sell meats and groceries to families from the

[1]From Mellen Weekly of May 27, 1926 . . . Forest Fire May 20, 1926 -- Two million feet of hardwood logs, property of the Mellen Lumber Co. were destroyed by fire last Thursday, May 20, 1926, west of Mineral Lake.

warehouse, but did get calls regularly for meat in large quantities, such as a quarter of beef, a pork loin, a ham or slab of bacon and one hundred pound sacks of flour and sugar. All camp supplies went through the warehouse, except hay and oats, which were shipped out by the carload. We would have certain supply days for each camp, twice a week for kitchen supplies in the summer and early fall and once a week in cold weather.

The supply car had a well protected stove in it to keep perishable goods from freezing. Much care had to be taken of the perishable items in the cold weather or there would have been much waste, something Dan McDonald and Foster-Latimer did not believe in. Max and I had a full summer to get into the swing of handling the winter shipments.

The office and warehouse were steam heated, as was the machine shop and roundhouse on the track north of the warehouse. It was very comfortable and handy all around.

When we found out in March that we were going to live in Mellen, we ordered a new four-door Ajax (Nash) sedan through the William Burns Automobile Agency, Ironwood, Michigan. Bill Burns, the famous semi-pro range baseball player made the sale with the car delivered around June 1, 1926. I then had an extra way of spending my evenings in learning to drive. We found a good place for me to practice, the Mellen baseball park. It did not take too long, as cars were built more simply, with less power, but much sturdier. There was no use building for speed in those days as the roads were in no shape for speed. What was needed more on a car were good strong springs and shock absorbers. The old road which goes by the Richard Foley home, coming out near the John Tafelski farm, was the main highway out of Mellen, going south, now State Highway 13, with the hill near the Tafelski farm known as Camp Hill. Camp Hill was the real test for a car. A car which made Camp Hill in high gear would most likely be sold on the spot.

The route from Mellen that I traveled most at that time was what is now Highway 77 to Upson and then what is now Highway 122 from Upson to Saxon. This route has been changed very little since that time, nearly fifty years ago. There were two hills to test a car on on that route. The first was the Bruun Hill, as you leave Mellen on Highway 77, which was not bad at all, but the other hill on Highway 122, about two and one-half miles north of Upson was a real test. It is known as Copper Hill as a test pit was made for Copper at one time. Going north was not quite so bad, but the other side of the hill going south was more of a test as there was, and still is, a sharp curve at the foot of the hill. A car which would make the hill going south in second was considered very good. Of course, none of those hills are considered a test with today's cars.

The summer passed quickly. The highways were being improved right along, so we did get around a lot in the evenings by taking short drives. My wife had not seen much of the Mellen area before.

The machine shop crew, under Joe Jordan, consisted of Al Donais

- blacksmith, now living in Kenosha, Albert Amelung - blacksmith helper, who has a nice cozy home, well decorated with a flower garden on Highway 169 in Cozy Valley, about five or six miles out of Mellen. Joe Friemuth, Sr. - machinist and car repair carpenter, Louis Rebella - machinist and car repair carpenter. Their supplies were all ordered through our warehouse.

About every three weeks, I spent a day at the camps to check with the cooks and clerks about the supplies going to camp, with regard to the quality, brands, and amounts needed. One day, while at camp, Dan joined me in checking some gallon cans of fruit. The cook said the fruit was good, but there was not much fruit compared to the amount of juice. He said, "We have plenty of good water here and we have sugar." I said to Dan, "I should talk to the grocery salesman about solid pack fruit and vegetables. I know they have it, but it is much higher priced. How about trying a case each, of fruit and vegetables. We'll keep a record of the amount of sugar needed, then see how the cost compares with the cost of the fruit and juice?" Dan said, "Go ahead and try it." Tom Padjen was the cook we were talking with, so we told him to try it out fairly, keeping a careful check on the sugar used, and other details. Tom was always good about trying new methods to cut the meal cost and still feed satisfactorily. I talked with the salesman, Clayton Kellogg, of Ashland, who was representing the Eimon Mercantile Company of Superior, Wisconsin. He had been talking with me about solid pack canned goods for some time. We worked out a trial order which turned out much better than we anticipated; about a 33 percent savings according to Tom's figures. We then tried the other camps with the figures coming out about the same. From that time on, we bought whatever fruit and vegetables we could in solid pack cans. This is still good advice to consumers when buying quantities of fruit.

About the last part of October, Max Organist decided to go back to logging with his brother and dad. All the repair work was finished at the warehouse and he wanted to get home for the deer hunting season, which opened on November 10. Clifford Landry, who was working at the mill, had made an application for the job. I hired Clifford and it worked out fine. He was a very steady and capable young man. We got along well with no problem in the exchange of helpers.

After December 1, 1926, the road between Upson and Saxon became so undependable that we did not try to use our automobile. We set it on blocks, took the tires off, and did not put the tires back on until May. Most people followed this procedure at the time.

On December 8, 1926, I took one of my trips to camp on the logging train and when the train arrived back in the afternoon, Mr. Latimer was at the warehouse with a serious look on his face. He said, "What kind of a husband are you?" I knew right away what had happened. Our first child, Bonnie Mary Corrigan, had been born during the day. We were all prepared for the birth in advance. My mother, who had worked for years as a midwife for Dr. Lockhart, was there with us and Dr. Lockhart could see no reason for my wife going to a hospital, as so many mothers in those days would rather be at home. All turned out very well, with mother and child doing fine. In addition to my mother being present, we had fine neighbors. Mrs. Louis Moseler, living on one side of us and Mrs. Mat Jordan on the other, with all the other families in Red Row offering to help in any way possible.

My mother stayed on with us until spring and then spent some time with her daughters, Ann (Mrs. S.K. Carlin) at Winegar, Wisconsin, and Frances (Mrs. W.W. Powell) at Warren, Minnesota.

About the first Saturday in May, I had the wheels back on our Ajax and since my wife had been tied up all winter with our new daughter, Bonnie, she wanted to take a trip to her home near Saxon. So, shortly after noon lunch, my work all finished for the week, we took off. The weather was nice and we made it without incident, although some spots on State Highways 77 and 122 were rather rubbery. We knew there was danger of trouble before we would get back to Mellen on Sunday. How right we were! We started back immediately after the Sunday noon meal and made it to Upson without mishap. We then thought we were okay, but no such luck. First, we broke through a road boil on the east side of the Tyler Forks River. The George Lipske family was living on the hill on the west side of the river and had a team ready. They had pulled some other cars out of holes before we came along. They pulled us out and we then made it to about one mile west of the Ashland-Iron County line where six cars were already waiting in line. Another team was pulling cars through a bad mud hole and it was getting so bad that even the team needed help. I got out and helped push cars through, knowing the others would have to get through before I could, with the result that when my turn came, the other cars had pulled out and I had to make it with the team and what help I could give. I was already tired out. However, by taking a new rut, the Ajax which was not a heavy car, I was able to help the team by keeping in low gear so we made it to Mellen okay.

There was a sequel on the Lipske team help near their home on the Tyler Forks River which I did not know about until about twenty years later. One of the boys, Leo Lipske, worked for us a lot when Ed Organist and I were contract logging and then for me in the Bad River Timber Co. firm. One spring day, Leo and I were having a little road trouble on the Rouse Fire Lane with a pick-up truck and when we finally made it, I was telling Leo about the time I was stuck and their team pulled me out. He started to laugh, then said, "You know, we pulled a lot of cars through that spring for two or three weeks. We had two teams. We would keep the best team pulling cars through in the daytime and then use the other team at night for hauling water with barrels and dumping into the holes. It wasn't a bad system!"

George Lipske, the father, was a section boss on the Wisconsin

Central and was stationed south of Mellen so he only got home on weekends. One weekend during the winter of 1927, George Lipske told Leo to meet him at Mellen on a Saturday afternoon with the Model T Ford. By the time Leo arrived in Mellen, George had imbibed a little too much liquor and when he was in that condition, he got a little ornery. Leo picked him up and started for home with the road in a little rough condition from a recent snowstorm. George kept picking at Leo about not being able to drive a car and insisting that he never would learn, until Leo could take it no more. At the Ashland-Iron County line, there was a big snowbank piled up from plowing, so Leo turned the car and rammed it into the snowbank and then turned to his dad: "So I don't know how to drive? Well, now you drive it home!" With that Leo got out of the Ford, took off across country to one of the McClurg camps and didn't go home again for two years. His dad had to walk to his home near Moore about three miles away. Leo said, "If he had only told me once that I didn't know how to drive I could have handled it, but he kept on telling me and my temper got the better of me."

The warehouse duties were more routine in 1927, so it was no trouble for Clifford and I to keep the work up. One Sunday in July we were over to the farm where my father-in-law was having trouble getting the hay into the barn due to some bad weather and needed some extra help the coming week. Clifford and I had the supply car loaded and ready to go on Wednesday morning with only routine work which Clifford could handle alone. I asked Mr. Latimer if it would be okay with him if I went over to the farm to help haul hay into the barn. He asked if I could do some good and I said that I thought so or I wouldn't go over. To show you how reasonable a man he was, he laughed and said, "George, I know your work is all in shape and I also know when there is work to do, you have worked many extra hours without complaining so now when you have a day once in awhile where there is not much work and you want to take off half a day, just let me know you are going and see that your helper is going to be around." It worked out well and I did not abuse the right as I appreciated the confidence he placed on me. I have worked under and with many fine men, but Mr. Latimer was tops.

In the early fall of 1927, I went into my first business venture. Max Organist found out there was a forty-acre plot of timber stumpage for sale within a few rods of a Foster-Latimer Lumber Company railroad branch which would be pulled up the next summer. The land bordered Highway 122 which made the timber products easily accessible. I looked at it with Max on a Sunday. We worked out a price we would offer for the stumpage and Max was to log it the coming winter if our bid was accepted. The bid was accepted. Then we started looking for markets and naturally, I spoke to Dan McDonald about the hardwood logs, as it was good timber and could be landed on their railroad. He talked it over with Mr. Latimer who set a price for logs decked on the railroad track with the company loading out the logs. It was a good deal which we accepted. I then contacted the J.B. Nash Paper Co. which I had worked for in 1922 and 1923, about buying the hemlock logs and pulpwood. They set a satisfactory price so we were in business.

I didn't have to neglect my work in any way. In fact, I never spent a minute of company time on the venture. Max and his brother, Ed, took the job on a contract price for logging as the timberland was only one mile from their home. It turned out fine all around.

The boys did all right logging. Max and I made a profit and the two companies who purchased our forest products were satisfied with the quality and the manner in which the timber was cut. We called it a success and let it go at that.

Along toward the early winter of 1928, an amusing incident happened which concerned Dan McDonald, the woods superintendent. He got off the log train one afternoon, stopped in at the warehouse office where I was doing some book work. He had a big smile on his face, so I knew he was in good humor. He said, "George, I am in big trouble up in the woods." I said, "What kind of trouble can you be in when you are all smiles?" He said, "It is a long story."

"A short time after I joined the company in 1908, or 1909, a letter came to the office from a farmer in the Cedar-Gurney area that another farmer was trespassing on the company lands joining his farm. The letter stated he was building a house and barn from company timber when he had over three 40's of timber on his own farm. Mr. Latimer called me at that time and said there may not be anything to this, but we certainly will have to see what it is all about. Naturally I had to make a trip over there which took three days, as I had to take the train to Ashland then to Saxon. Then I walked out to the farm where the complaint came from. The farmer informed me that Joe Hodak was the man who was trespassing. I called on Joe Hodak to see what he had to say. He said, 'You know that section line was not very plain, so I may have taken a few trees, but not many! I said, 'Well, Joe, I have been sent here by the company. I will have to check on the trespass!' 'Alright' he said, 'Go ahead. I will help you.' We took off after Joe's wife had furnished a good lunch and the trespass was only a stone's throw from the house. I freshened the line up, then counted and measured or estimated from the stump what each tree scaled. There were a good many hemlock and spruce trees taken from across the line. I estimated the trespass would amount to $75.00 in money. Joe said, "That is a lot of money." It certainly was at that time, but he did not argue about it and just said he could pay $25.00 now and that he would pay the balance in sixty days. I agreed, gave him a receipt for the $25.00 paid, and walked back to Saxon. There I stayed one night as I wanted to talk with the assessor in Saxon anyway, and then went on to Ashland and back to Mellen. In sixty days, the balance of $50.00 was paid and I always figured that was the end of it.

This morning when I arrived at Camp 47 our foreman, Ray Scribner, said he was having trouble with a farmer named Joe Hodak. It immediately brought back memories of my trip to see Joe back in 1908. I asked Ray what the trouble was. He said, 'We are logging from the land joining his and when we made the log road to the timber we crossed a corner of one of his forties in a swamp where there is no stumpage value. I figured he would have no objection. Yesterday I sent a team and loading crew to haul logs from those forties. They loaded up a sleigh load which the Holt tractor went in to get, taking a few empty log sleighs in at the same time. When the load of logs arrived at the forty crossing Hodak's land, there was Joe Hodak sitting on a stump with a gun in his hands. I was following the load of logs out as it was the first load over the road and I wanted to see how the tractor made it. I asked Joe what the trouble was. He answered, 'About twenty years ago I was charged $75.00 for a trespass on the company land. It hurt at that time as cash was scarce in those days; now all I want is my money back with interest before a load crosses this land.' I told the tractor driver to unhook the load and leave it there until the trouble was settled. McDonald went out with Ray to where the load was and there was Joe with the gun. McDonald said, 'What is the trouble, Joe?' Then Joe told him what he had told Ray and McDonald said, 'Okay, Joe, I will take it up with the company when I get in this afternoon and give you an answer tomorrow.' After McDonald had told me, he went on over to the office to see Mr. Harry Latimer. The following morning Mr. Latimer arrived at the warehouse office with McDonald in time to take the train out to camp. He was all smiles too and said, 'George, these fellows get in trouble up in the woods and then I have to go out to help them out!' "

Mr. Latimer had figured out straight interest on the $75.00, added it to the principal making it around $125.00 in full, and made out a check. He went on out to camp with McDonald that day as he was really getting a kick out of it. He was a man who did not show it often. When they arrived at camp, Mr. Latimer walked out with McDonald to where Joe was guarding the load, greeted Joe and then said, 'What can we do to get those logs moving?' 'Mr. Latimer,' Joe said, 'All you have to do is give me a check for the principal and straight interest for the last twenty years.' Mr. Latimer then showed him the check and said, 'Is that amount satisfactory?' Joe said, 'That's fine. You haul all the logs you wish over the road and I will not bother you.'

Mr. Latimer and Mr. McDonald arrived back in Mellen in the afternoon in good humor and for Mr. Latimer it held over for some time; it really tickled his funny bone. I think he enjoyed it more because Dan was implicated.

Donald Meredith of Mellen started picking up livestock in the

Saxon area and was doing a good business. J.J. Defer and Pat Auger had been the big men at Saxon, not working together, but one trying to out-do the other. J.J. Defer had died a couple of years previously. His business, consisting of a saw mill, logging equipment and a general store being run by the estate with John Reid, president of the Saxon bank, as administrator.

John Reid became interested in the activity of Donald Meredith when he was picking up livestock in the Saxon area and found out that he had butcher training. He also knew I was married to a Saxon girl and that I had some buying experience so he approached Donald one day about Donald and I buying the general store. Donald listened to him and said he would talk to me about it, which he did. I do not believe I would have talked to John Reid at all about the deal, but I could see that the Foster-Latimer Lumber Company would be through in a couple of years as they were in their last logging camps and not planning to buy more stumpage.

Donald and I made an appointment to meet with John Reid on a Saturday afternoon. He showed us around the Saxon store. It was a very well built brick building with good living quarters upstairs, a well equipped butcher shop, and a general store with plenty of room for storage in the basement and an elevator from the basement to the first floor. After looking at it thoroughly, I said to Donald that it looked like a very big investment for the amount of capital we had but that we should ask him the price anyway. The asking price -- building, equipment, stock, and all -- was around $100,000 which, if business had stayed at the 1929 level, would have been a fair price as you could not put up the building for that price. But money was getting tight and Mr. Latimer and Dan McDonald told me it was going to get tighter. Donald and I informed John Reid that we could not handle the investment and I also told John Reid that I did not have experience enough in the general store business at the present time. John asked me to stop in again to see him. He tried to tell me they would make the terms to pay for the business so easy and charge no interest that we could not afford to turn it down. He said we would never get another opportunity like it. In fact, he made it look so easy we almost fell for it, but held firm. I then told him there was only one way I would even consider it and that was to manage it for a year to see if it was possible to make it go. Mr. Reid thought that over for a week and then called me in again and made me an attractive offer to manage the store for at least a year to see if we would be interested in buying at the end of the year.

What sold me on the job was that I would be allowed to deal in forest products with the loggers and farm wood lot owners, which would be credited to the store as long as I found markets for the forest products. This proved to be a business saver in the 1930-31 depression era. If I had known the depression was going to hit so hard, I never would have accepted the job. It proved to be a poor move. However, it may have made no difference as the depression of the early '30's hit everyone hard, rich and poor. I did dislike informing Mr. Latimer and Dan McDonald that I was going to make the move but they were very understanding about it as they would only be in business a couple more years themselves. However, Mr. Latimer said he was sure if I did stay with them I would get a job when they did close the operation. I, being a young man at the time, figured I should gamble on the proposition. I gave them six or seven weeks time to replace me as I was supposed to take over at Saxon on January 1, 1930.

We had one other important event in the summer of 1929. Our second daughter, Shirley May, was born on August 1, 1929. Again my mother took over the nursing help for Dr. Lockhart and we had no trouble at all. My mother was pleased to come from Chippewa Falls, as she had a chance to visit her Mellen friends again.

Even with the extreme bad luck my mother had at Mineral Lake and Mellen, losing two husbands through death, she always had a warm spot for Mellen. The Mellen people always treated her well through all her misfortune.

After my resignation from the Foster-Latimer Lumber Company in November, 1929, all my spare time was spent getting ready to move and getting pointers from experienced general store personnel and also salesmen.

The first job was an inventory and a big job it was at the time. Believe me, if I had taken the inventory before hiring out, I never would have made the change. Of course, in buying we would have taken an inventory. Anyway, it was too late and I never look back, only to compare the past with the present. The meats and groceries were not so bad, but the shelves, floor, etc., were in a very untidy condition. The dry goods, men's clothing, etc., were shopworn, faded and in a state of neglect. We had extra help for the inventory, but it took almost a week to complete as I wanted to know in what shape the store really was.

In the middle of the first week, while still taking inventory, a large carload of soft coal arrived with a bill to be paid C.O.D. We had no money in reserve. It was a new experience for me after working where all bills were discounted and no problem where money was concerned. I said to John Reid, "There is only one thing to do; put on a big sale at once, cut the price on the old dry goods to where we can move it." I got good support on that move by Julius Simon, a successful farmer and the chairman of the board handling the estate. He was also town clerk. He had been helping us on the inventory and could see those dry goods should be moved at once. It was wintertime and if not moved then, they surely would not go in the summer as there were a lot of woolen goods. John Reid told us to go ahead with the sale. We made up posters, as we did not expect to sell much outside of the local community. I had Guy Brown of the Mendenhall Grahm Clothing Firm, Duluth, Minnesota, help with the sale prices. He did a good job and spent part of two days at the store during the sale. Guy was a good natured, humorous fellow, always ready with a story or wit of some kind, so he kept the customers in good humor. We had a very successful sale which gave us some working capital. We followed that up with a few weekend grocery sales, which helped some more.

The next thing was finding markets for the surplus of hay, oats, vegetables, and forest products, especially pulpwood, ties, cedar poles and posts. My past logging experience helped me a lot to find markets. The salesmen I had been buying through while at Foster-Latimer Lumber Company helped too, as most buyers made the larger logging company headquarters. They helped us get hay, oats, farm produce orders, and the forest products orders.

The 1929 market crash was now showing signs of a real depression, which did develop fast during 1930, hitting its peak in 1931 and 1932.

By getting markets for forest products and farm produce, it helped our sales. A large percentage of the returns were taken out in trade. Joel Wickstrom, our butcher, took good beef, veal, hogs, and chickens in trade. The butcher was also good in making sausage, head cheese, etc.

After I had been at Defer's about two months, Mr. Latimer and Dan McDonald stopped in one day to see if I was interested in going back to Mellen. They had heard through the grapevine that I was not satisfied at Saxon, which was right, but I would not swallow my pride. I told them I had agreed to stay at the Defer estate one year at least, or until the store was sold. So I stuck it out, just to see what the store would do.

In the spring we had a couple of amusing incidents when it was time to load out ties, cedar poles and posts.

From 1923 to 1929 times were improving steadily and, of course, no one wanted to see hard times again like the early 1900's. During the 1929 period, workers were getting independent again; jobs were a little more plentiful, wages were fairly good. There was a good demand for forest products, so a worker would get the idea once in a while that he could fool someone. We had one producer who had put in some cedar poles and posts, peeled in April so they would not strip peel. The buyers of cedar products did not want strip peeled poles and posts. Strip peel is peeling when the sap is flowing freely. The bark peels off easily by getting a hand hold, then pulling off in long strips. Buyers prefer cedar products peeled earlier with an axe and a peeling spud, as the products last longer. Some of the poles in lengths of 35 to 50 feet had fairly large butt ends, which would have some rot, shake or worm holes. The producers were trying to get the extra five feet of length, so they would leave the butt end on until inspected, which was okay as he could always cut the butt off, but there was no way to add it on. This producer tried another wrinkle. He made cedar plugs which he drove into the holes tightly, then would cut a few inches off the pole. It would be harder to tell if the pole had been plugged. He had also plastered some mud on the butt to make it look like the pole had been dragged through mud.

The inspector arrived one morning to inspect and load out the cedar poles. He came in the store, told me who he was, and as the producer had not arrived with men to load the poles, he went out to the landing to size up the poles, taking his inspection and stamp hammer with him. The hammer had a stamp of initials on one side and a sharp side like a heavy screwdriver which he could dig into those rot or shaky ends to see how bad the ends were. The inspector was an old-timer who noticed those tampered ends. He then started digging with the hammer and by the time the producer arrived, he had knocked plugs out of several poles. After he had made the producer feel rather cheap, he said, "Never try that again, as now I will look hard at every pole and if there was any doubt as to quality, you will have to cut the pole off five feet each time." He also told the producer, "I bet it took you longer to plug those holes than it would have taken to cut a few more poles." The producer told me after that he was cured and would never try that again.

We had no trouble selling the timber products in the spring of 1930; but prices were declining during the summer of 1930, which meant that inventories were building up.

In the livestock market, grain fed steers and heifers held fairly steady, as did good butcher hogs, but canner and cutter cow prices declined rapidly in the fall of 1930.

Hay, oats and vegetable prices were dropping fast and we had to work harder to find markets at logging camps.

Money was getting tighter, which showed up fast on our credit accounts. Customers who had been paying their accounts in full started paying 50 percent to 75 percent which showed up in our working capital. More employees were being laid off temporarily at the mill, mines and road jobs.

Up until this time, I had always figured the big majority of people were honest and would pay up when they had a chance and I really believed they were all that way. But this depression coming on snowballed so fast that a lot of people got in debt so far and the depression lasted so long, they never were able to catch up. This was especially true for the workers who depended on their labor alone and did not have small farms to help out with much of their living expense. We had to barter more at the store, that is, exchange store supplies for farm produce, hay, grain, potatoes, livestock, etc.

It was now getting near the first year for me at Defer's, when I was to make a decision on whether to buy the store. Mr. Reid was pressuring me. I decided to ask a friend of three or four Corrigan families in the Sanborn, Marengo area who was operating a large general store at Sanborn to give his opinion. He was Harry Simon who just about all the people in Ashland and Bayfield Counties knew at the time. Harry came over and spent two days looking over all the assets, debits, kind of farms, people, etc., and then said to me, "George, if a man and wife took over this store with the intention of both working full time, they would have to gross $75,000 a year to make expenses. You have a well-built building, but not laid out right for a general store." He also said, "The highways are getting better now with more people buying cars and you are close to Hurley and Ironwood. It will be tough competition. We have noticed it at Sanborn now; we are too close to Ashland." He also gave me an additional point about the building, why was it built so you have three or four steps to go up before entering the main floor. He said some will say that is not important, but it is a very important part of shopping. He was right. How many modern markets do you see with steps up to get in?

After the report by Harry Simon, it was final. There was no way I would consider buying the Defer Store. I informed Mr. Reid and told him to look for a buyer. I told him I would stay through until spring or May 1, 1931, if he would guarantee me wages up until that time.

I had some big contracts for railroad ties through a couple of Duluth brokers to be delivered to Ashland. Railroads running into Ashland were Northern Pacific (N.P.), Great Northern (G.N.), Northwestern (C. & N.W.), and the Soo Line. I wanted to see those orders filled if possible.

We had made contracts with two large producers who logged and sawed their own ties. They were Frank Ansami and son, Arvo, Saxon, and Lawrence Peterson & Sons of Ironwood, Michigan. There were a lot of small producers and farm loggers who put tie cuts on the landing at Saxon. Adolph Kadlets and his son Bryon of Saxon took the contract of sawing those ties. We put in around 60,000 ties that winter, along with a few thousand cords of pulpwood, 300 cedar poles and 3,000 cedar posts. This was a lot of timber.

The hard part about the tie contract was that it called for 50 percent No. 3, 4 and 5, the larger ties and 50 percent No. 1 and 2, the smaller ties. It was not as difficult as it looked in the large mixed hardwood ties, as with average tie cuts you get near this percentage, but we did have a problem between the No. 2 and No. 3 grades. The contract called for about an equal amount of these two lower grades.

Ties are usually eight feet or eight feet, six inches long. If two inches longer than the length called for, they would have to be trimmed with a crosscut saw to the proper length. If more than one inch shorter, it made no difference how large the tie was, it would be put in with the U.R. class which was the lowest grade tie with a very low price, or the owner could take it back if he had other uses for them.

You hear people say or at least think that you did not have to know much to produce quality timber products. Those people should try it for a few years. Some of the owners of the large paper mills and wood using industries should try for a few years so they would know the cost of producing forest products. At least they should have logging operations of their own to get actual logging costs.

The ties also had to be peeled before sap stripping time, as pulpwood can be peeled by stripping the bark off. But the railroads preferred the bark off before stripping season. They gave as their reason that the ties would last longer if peeled before or after the stripping season which was the months of May, June, and July. That made some extra men labor that winter. You would knock the bark off with the back side of a single bitted axe and use the sharp side to peel what inner bark would stick on the tie. Many of the Saxon boys, 18 years of age and still in school, would peel ties on Saturdays and holidays. The hardwood ties produced that winter were a good grade. They did produce some minor problems according to a tie inspector of the North Pacific and Great Northern, a very fine man who had a good knowledge of ties. He had been a tie bucker for years. A tie bucker is a man who loads ties by the piece, carrying the ties into the car on his shoulder, using a shoulder pad to keep his shoulder from getting sore. A tie bucker has to be all man, as it is extremely hard work.

The tie inspector informed me that our No. 2 ties were running a larger percentage than the No. 3 ties. With the railroads demanding tight inspection, he said a lot of the No. 2 ties are very close to No. 3 grade; in fact, a year ago they would be No. 3. I am putting these kind into the No. 3 grade and I am asking no favor of you. But if some day when you are up here and a stranger would appear and ask you what kind of inspection you are getting, tell him not so hot; he sure holds to the specifications given him by the railroads. Be sure to not praise me up. Sure enough a few days later, a man who claimed to be a tie producer in Minnesota asked me about the inspection. I said it was much better last year, and the inspectors sure must be worrying about their jobs. When I informed the inspector he said, "Good, it may have been a checker on me and it may have been a producer, as when loading ties we always have some strangers around from local areas who are fascinated by tie buckers loading ties."

We did not use tie buckers. We had local men available who needed employment. We used three men with a stick crossways, two men on the front end and one man on the back end, with heavy planks from the ground to the boxcar door to walk on, as all ties were loaded into boxcars. It did not cost more to load with three men and it was much easier. Average men could not buck ties; it really took supermen. Tie buckers were used more where a railroad company had ties to pick up at many scattered landings, produced by many small producers. A tie inspector would generally have two tie buckers who would travel with him from landing to landing.

Some ties were still hand-hewed with a broad axe. It was generally cedar and hemlock ties. There were many good axe men in the woods who liked to hew ties.

About 10 years ago, I used to make a trip three or four times each winter to northeastern Minnesota as far as Grand Marais. I bought veneer logs and stopped in Duluth to see the owners of logging operations. I would stop by the employment office to see how many old-time woodsmen were still around. Very often I would see one of the old-time tie buckers who I could tell from a distance as the shoulder he used to carry ties on was a lot lower than the other one.

One told me he was retired and the one shoulder did ache a lot. I do not believe a man can carry ties over a long period without it taking something out of him. Many ties weigh up to 250 pounds each. There are very few tie buckers today as there is machinery equipment which can load ties.

In March, 1931, I was approached by Elmer Drier, manager and stockholder in the Persons-Freeland Company who operated a store formerly owned by Arthur Auger at Saxon. They operated mainly a grocery, meats and feed store, with a sideline of men's work clothes and shoes, also common hardware and dairy supplies.

Persons-Freeland had stores at the time at Saxon and Kimball in Wisconsin and Marenisco, Matchwood, and Trout Creek in Michigan. Gus Persons of Kimball was president and general manager. Gus was a good store man, but no man ever took over a group of stores at such an inopportune time as the depression was now in full swing. If I had not been such an eternal optimist, I would have stayed out of the store business at this time. Of course, there was very little logging either and only starvation wages. So I was talked into buying a job, as I was to be on a salary.

After Elmer Drier talked to me, I talked to Gus Persons and naturally, he painted a bright picture and about 75 percent of all people at the time did not believe the depression would be so bad or last so long. In the end I bought the Elmer Drier stock so was tied up again in a business I did not really like. Of course, one redeeming feature -- I was able to hold my forest products markets or I guess I would not have attempted another store. Another thing, the forest products industry as usual was the first to feel the depression, so I did not have another way to turn.

One thing about the 1930's depression days, you either had to work or go on the bum. I guess I would starve before I would bum, so I kept on working. I never worked as hard or longer hours for what I earned, but at that I was better off than a lot of people. I had steady work.

For pastime everybody in Saxon, Cedar and Gurney were interested in baseball. They had two baseball teams. The first team was a very good semi-pro team and played against all the better teams on the range. The second team was made up of dissatisfied players from the first team who did not think they were getting a fair chance to play. Among the young high school boys coming up, there was a lot of talent on the range in those days, as all kids were playing baseball in all cities, towns and villages as it was a cheap pastime and good exercise. Fishing and hunting were the other major sports.

A group of outdoor enthusiasts, not necessarily hunters, decided to build a hunting camp far enough away from civilization so they would not be bothered with many hunters. The group consisted of Vern Downey, Ed Schatzman, George Sullivan, Charles Steele, and myself. The next year George Meredith joined the group.

George Sullivan lived where the Sullivan Fire Lane leaves Highway 122 going west and he and I encouraged the group to go west on the old Foster-Latimer Lumber Company right-of-way about five miles to old Camp 29, where there was a good spring and high ground to build on.

George had a milk route so had a truck, which hauled the lumber, paper, nails, camp furnishings, etc., to our hunting camp location. Trucks in those days were still single wheels all around, no dual wheels.

We made sure to get our building supplies in while it was dry weather, although the right-of-way was in good shape. We worked hard each Sunday in September, October and November.

Hunting season was 16 days that year. I wounded one, but another hunter got it and I am sure Charles Steele got one. We called him Hank Ketchem, because he always got his deer and would not hunt on Sunday unless someone brought him a Sunday paper so he could see the Hank Ketchem funnies. Vern Downey got a deer also. It was good deer country, but very noisy that year with no snow until late in the season. George Sullivan always got a deer. We did have a lot of fun and to most of us that was the most important. I still believe an old-fashioned hunting camp is the only way you can enjoy a hunting season. As usual Vern Downey was the big winner in poker, with Charles Steele a close second. I was always good for a donation.

When we closed up camp at the end of the season, a snowstorm was brewing and it was fortunate we moved on that day, as it ended up in a two-day snowstorm and we would have had plenty of trouble getting out after the storm.

There were a few other tent hunting camps -- one at old Camp 31 on Potato River and one at the Tyler Forks River below Camp 23 Falls, who did fairly well that year.

16

The Peak Of The Depression

After the hunting season, it was back to lining up contracts for forest products to cover the winter of 1931-32. Also had a lot of hay, oats, potatoes and vegetables to move, with many logging camps not opening for 1932 as the depression was bad.

The winter of 1932 was a heartbreaker with despair showing on all the people, perfectly honest people getting farther in debt with the hope that times would get better, but times kept getting worse. Prices were dropping, wages were lower, and there was no work.

The mines, mills and woods operations were cutting down with many good men traveling around looking for work. There were jungles and soup kitchens all over. Men slept on the sawdust in mill boiler rooms, on the floor in the depots, jails or town halls, or wherever they could find protection from the cold.

I will say that 90 percent of the people responded in great style. Stores would give their scrap bones, old bread, pastry, vegetables, etc., to the men in the jungles. The logging camps fed the extra men in some way as there were no public relief stations.

After the spring breakup, the logging operations opened up some or the summer of 1932 would have been a disaster era, I am sure.

There were plenty of forest fires and if men had no woods work, chances are there would have been many more and larger fires.

We bought good steer and heifer dressed beef at $3.75 per 100 pounds, nice dressed veal - liver included - 5 cents per pound, dressed pork from 3 cents to 4 cents per pound, eggs 6 cents to 8 cents per dozen, with potatoes and other vegetables just as cheap in proportion. Most all of the purchases were paid for in trade. We bought everything possible from the local farmers.

It was a good thing we were able to get markets for forest products. It was a life saver in the Saxon, Cedar and Gurney areas. Most all the farmers had some timber stumpage or were able to buy some. I pulled every string I could to get markets, and my previous connections were a big help.

We managed to get tie orders, cedar poles and posts and conifer pulpwood. There was no aspen or mixed hardwood being used for pulpwood at the time.

During the spring of 1932, a man who had worked for me at the Foster-Latimer camps by the name of Mat Pellman from Iron River, Wisconsin, stopped at the store and informed me he had bought some stumpage on the lands of Foster-Latimer Lumber Company near Gurney. The company had logged all the sawmill material but did not touch the conifer pulpwood or cedar products, so he got some pretty good stumpage. He bought one of the company buildings to live in, fixed up a barn for one horse and was ready to go to work.

The hemlock stumpage and some high land cedar stumpage could be cut during the summer and skidded to the old railroad grades abandoned by the company where it could be trucked out.

We had a summer contract for hemlock pulpwood and hewed cedar ties, so I told Mat what we could pay him for the pulpwood loaded on cars and the ties piled on a railroad landing. Mat said, "I cannot do any better, but I have to ask you to advance me what supplies I need until I can ship some wood." I knew Mat was honest, so I said okay.

Mat took some supplies and started to work. He had one man with him, so after they both cut pulpwood a few days to get some cut ahead, Mat started skidding with the horse. Then one day when I was out there he said, "Where can I get a truck to do the hauling?" I told him I would have Jim Norton, who had a pulpwood truck talk to him. Jim did, and made a deal at so much a cord, loading in woods, trucking to the railroad, and loading onto a gondola car, all by hand loading. He was glad to get the trucking job as it helped to keep him busy. I do not remember the price he received, but it was around $2.00 to $3.00 per cord.

Mat worked steady until he had the hemlock pulpwood cut. He told me the man was going to start hewing the cedar ties.

After a few weeks on a quiet day at the store, I decided to visit Mat. I drove out to his shack after my noon lunch. He was in for lunch. I said, "What kind of wood are you working on?" "Oh," he said, "We are cleaning up the hemlock pulpwood and have started making ties." I said, "Let's go take a look at the ties." Mat said okay and started out to the woods. He walked me down one branch a short distance, then said, "We will have to cross over to the next branch." Then he said, "This is not the right branch either." I said, "Okay, let's go." He then turned to me and said, "George, the ties are not made yet." Well, it struck me so funny I could not help but laugh; here he had been walking me around for half an hour looking for ties which were still in the tree. Mat explained, "I am sorry, I thought you would give up and say you would look at the ties the next time." It was the only time he tried to fool me. He put out a fair amount of wood by the spring of 1933, then went back to farming near

Iron River, Wisconsin.

At about this time there was a Finnish fellow named Victor running the poolroom and confectionary store in Saxon. I stopped to chat with him a few minutes and while we were talking, a fellow sitting back in the room was talking to himself. Victor said, "Who are you talking to, Joe?" He answered, "Never mind. Can't a man talk to a sensible man once in a while?"

After my wife and I had a short vacation, it was back to the old grind again; first getting a car load of potatoes off for Chicago before the cold weather set in. We also moved some hay, oats, vegetables and potatoes to camps.

It was another tough fall, with men looking for work and families getting along without a lot of things they would like to have. I will say the people on the farms in the Saxon, Cedar and Gurney area were more fortunate than those in the cities. They at least had something to eat and were able to barter their surplus items to buy clothing.

The sawmill managed to keep running; although wages were very low, it helped a lot, especially for those who did not live on farms.

Adolph Kadletz and son, Byron, managed to keep their tie mill running. Herman Peterson had a logging job. Frank Ansami and son, Arvo, had a logging job and tie mill. Lawrence Peterson and sons were logging in the Little Girls Point area of Michigan and had leased the Saxon sawmill for the winter.

Between all of them, they kept most of the Saxon workers employed. We had some markets for forest products again, but it was a battle for all people, with some not having the courage to face up to the hard knocks, especially after the bank closing order of 1933. Our old hunting gang did not take time off to go hunting except Saturday evening until Sunday evening. We had a good time again, but the penny ante poker game was real penny ante, not many dimes and nickels any more.

Vern Downey, who would generally make a payment on a house he was buying out of his poker earnings, had to be satisfied with enough earnings for a payment on his taxes. Anyway, we had a good time, a fairly successful hunt which we were assured of whenever George Sullivan and Charles Steele were in the gang.

In the spring of 1933, we had a pile of nice white cedar poles and posts taken in on trade during the winter. With the demand for forest products dropping off fast, I started looking for markets early.

Two of the salesmen, Irvin Garnich and Guy Brown, were calling on the Christiansen Lumber Company at Phelps, Wisconsin, and found out they were buying poles and posts. The supply buyer advised Irvin and Guy to talk to the woods superintendent of the Christiansen Lumber Company by the name of Arthur Gustafson. He told them to have me write him advising the length and sizes of the poles and posts, then he would see what kind of a deal we could work out.

I made a report to Art Gustafson and he answered me that he was interested and would be up to see the cedar products on a certain day. He kept his word and arrived the day he said he would.

Arthur was a young man well trained in the forest products industry and we hit it off well; in fact, we are still friends. He was satisfied with our cedar products, so we made a deal. He said to let him know when the poles and posts were all peeled and trimmed to correct lengths and he would come back to load them out.

We put on a few more peelers so as to get the peeling done before the heavy spring farm work started. By this time, it was no trouble to get peelers; there were three or four men for each job.

Arthur Gustafson came back later to load out the cedar poles and showed me what they wanted in cedar posts. He then told me to check the posts whenever he sent an order.

While at Saxon, he told me about an incident at one of the Christiansen Camps while he was a foreman. The camp was on a railroad and when going to work or back, they would pass by a camp owned and run by another company. While going to work with some of his crew, one of the men said "this crew" has not started out to work yet, but Gustafson did not say a word. When going back to camp that night, the same men said this crew is at camp already. Gustafson spoke up, "They might beat us home at night, but I will guarantee you, we will beat them out in the morning."

Arthur Gustafson was a fair man to deal with. If you furnished wood up to specification, there would be no trouble. He was fair to his company and fair to his seller, which is all you can ask.

During the summer of 1933, I just about made up my mind that the store business was not for me. I missed being in the woods. I decided that once the depression hit bottom and conditions started to get better, I would try either to get a job or take a chance as a logging contractor. I started looking around.

When conditions are bad in whatever you are doing, they generally get worse before they get better, and that is what was happening in the year of 1933. After President Franklin D. Roosevelt took office, he did not wait long to try some remedies as it was very necessary at that time to get some wheels turning to stop the depression.

After the stock market crash in late 1929 and the rapid rise in unemployment along with a shortage of money, many banks were in trouble and those hardest hit started to close their doors. This made the crisis worse, as people who still had money in banks started to draw it out.

President Roosevelt and his advisors decided to call a moratorium on all banks, in order to keep the depression from getting worse and see if there were ways to help the banks solve their problems. It was a long slow process back up again with most banks paying creditors from 50 percent to 100 percent on the dollar over a period of years.

We kept up the depression battle in the summer of 1933, getting markets where we could for farm produce, hay and grain.

By filling our forest products orders the past few years, we were able to get some fairly good orders for pulpwood, ties and cedar products again. The Thilmany Paper Company of Kaukauna, Wisconsin gave us an order for 3,500 cords of Rgh hemlock pulpwood; it was a real help the winter of '33 and '34. We had good orders for ties, cedar poles and posts.

In September, 1933, Frank Ansami and son Arvo, who had been getting out mining timber, ties, and pulpwood, had a chance to get a block of timber stumpage on the Michigan side of the Montreal River near the power plant. Frank asked me if I wanted to join him for the winter of 1933-34, as a non-working partner to see how it would work out as to a profitable venture. I told Frank I would think it over.

Frank Ansami and son Arvo were experienced woodsmen, so it was no problem. We picked out a campsite to set up a small set of camps, put up a kitchen and root house, and then of course, needed a cook.

My mother and stepfather, William Brown, who was a hotel clerk at a hotel in Chippewa Falls at the time, applied for the job. Mr. Brown had been a restaurant man for years and was a good cook and my mother was a good cook. It was a nice job for the two of them, as we would not have over 25 men. We fixed up the kitchen so they were able to live in it and it worked out fine. We had no cook problems.

John Landon, general manager of the sawmill and woods operation of Marathon Corporation who had taken over the Scott & Howe Lumber Company Sawmill at Ironwood, Michigan, stopped at Saxon to see me. The Marathon Corporation had large land and timber holdings in Gogebic County, Michigan, and Iron County, Wisconsin. They had a large pulp and paper mill at Rothschild, Wisconsin.

Many of the stockholders of Marathon Corporation also had stock in other mills so were interested in keeping a large inventory of forest products at their mills at all times. He was looking for balsam and spruce pulpwood for his company. It happened that we had some, cut by Persons-Freeland suppliers, Ansami & Corrigan Logging job in Wisconsin and Lawrence Peterson and Sons at Little Girls Point in Michigan which had not been sold. The price was terribly low, but at least it was a market; balsam around $6.00 per cord and spruce $8.00 F.O.B. cars. I asked John how many cords he could handle. He answered right now any amount, but the company has other buyers in other parts of Michigan and Wisconsin picking up wood and we may be flooded with wood in a few weeks. I said, "Will you give me a few days to check the suppliers?" He said, "Sure, I will come back to see you by the middle of the coming week when I will make out a purchase order for what you can supply us." I checked up on it and came up with a promise of around 1,000 cords, with about 80 percent balsam, which was what he wanted. John Landon came back the next week and was surprised at the amount of wood. He said, "Now are you sure you will come anywhere near this amount? We would rather you would have a few car loads over what the purchase order calls for than to be too far under." I said, "If this works out to be a normal winter, I am sure we will make it. Of course, if we get an early breakup, it could cause trouble." He said, "That is an 'act of God'; neither you nor I can help a situation of that kind." So he wrote out a purchase order of 1,000 cords which we filled with a little extra, which they accepted.

The logging operation I was in with Frank Ansami went along okay, but there was not enough timber stumpage available in the Saxon area to keep a fair sized logging operation busy. Frank Ansami had a large farm to manage along with the logging operation so did not care to go away from Saxon. I then decided I would only stay with him until spring.

One day Art Gustafson came up from Phelps, Wisconsin, to check out cedar poles to be loaded. Max Organist was the top loader, Adelore LeGeault the cross haul teamster with Ed Organist and Walter Damgard hooking. All at once we heard some mild cussing by Max Organist up on the pulpwood car, so we turned to take a look and saw Max reaching in his shirt pocket for a package of cigarettes. He threw them as far as he could, then he reached in his back pocket, pulled out a box of snuff and threw that as far as he could. He never smoked or chewed again. He had been having some heartburn and laid it to the tobacco, which probably was the cause as he had no heartburn after. It seems that is the only way to quit a habit if you really wish to quit. Art Gustafson never got over that illustration of will power.

17

Contract Logging In Michigan

The next time John Landon was in Saxon, he started telling me about how many contract loggers the Marathon Corporation had in the Watersmeet area of Michigan who were logging Marathon stumpage. I said to him, "Would you have an opening for one more?" He said, "Is it you and Ansami?" I said, "No, it would be a brother-in-law, Max Organist and I." He said, "Is that the fellow top loading the cars on the landing, loading logs and pulpwood?" I said, "Yes"; he countered with, "He is a good able man, but I will not know for sure until the close of winter logging at the end of March." It was already late February when I was talking with him.

Around the middle of April, 1934, he stopped again and said, "We are going to have an opening for one more logging operation in addition to the 17 contractors we already have. It is not a good logging chance, but it is all we will let out this year. It is six forties we have, five miles northeast of Gogebic Station off the Gogebic branch railroad on the middle branch of the Ontonagon River. You will have to make a tote road two and one half miles from Stencils Camp on the railroad, which is two miles in from Highway 2." I said, "We will look at it when it dries up." "Yes," he said, "you would have to swim to get in there now, but I will let you know at the right time."

I went ahead, cleaning up in the forest products shipments and helped Frank Ansami load out the timber products on the landing.

In the early part of May, 1934, John Landon called and said we would be able to look at the logging job. He said for us to stop at the mill office and he would send orders to Stewart Baldwin, one of his assistant woods superintendents, to accompany us. One day we were to see the timber lands and one day to plan how we would haul the timber out in the winter, as it all would be a sleigh haul job.

We spent the two full days looking at the logging job and estimating the cost of building a set of camps for 30 to 40 men. We would have to tote the lumber in with a team and wagon from Stencil's Camp a distance of two and one half miles. When we were moving in with supplies from Saxon we would have to tote the first two miles down the railroad track, as the tote road from Highway 2 was through a large swamp which could only be used in the wintertime. The C. & N.W. railway company knew of the difficulties getting to Stencil's Camp, so they did not stop us at any time.

Max and I realized the disadvantages of the job. We also realized this was not ordinary times, so figured if we could make good wages the first year and build up our camp equipment to do a good logging job then we might have a better chance the next year. When we got back home, we notified John Landon to make up a contract. He had told us the logging prices and then said if you will take my word I will take yours and you can go ahead making your plans to get started at once as it will take a week to get a contract back from the Rothschild office. We took his word and never had a reason to regret it.

I informed Frank Ansami at once and he said he figured we would take the job and wished us well. We did not have any trouble on the job I had logged with him.

The first thing Max and I had to do was arrange our financial capital to start on a contract of this kind. The problem was made easier by getting a contract with a large company who owned the timber and were in a first class financial condition. They were willing to help finance loggers who were willing to help themselves.

With the Marathon Corporation, a jobber had to be able to start his job and have finances enough to operate his job the first 50 days at least. He had to be able to pay his men, pay for his supplies and equipment, etc., until he would get his first payment from the company.

At the end of each month one of the woods superintendents, either Stewart Baldwin or Len Damon, would come to our job and take an inventory of work accomplished during the month.

When starting a logging job, you would first be building camps, making log roads before bark peeling, and cutting pulpwood. Then they would estimate the amount of bark peeled, pulpwood cut, or cut and skidded. On or before the 20th of the next month, we would get a check for work accomplished during the previous month.

At no time was a profit figured on the estimate. Since it was a sleigh haul job, we would start work in May, 1934, work through to January 1, 1935, before we could move any forest products -- an eight-month period. You can see how important it was to be able to get a monthly advance from the company without paying interest.

Max Organist had a team and some logging equipment, also some cash. I sold some of my stock in Persons-Freeland to George Meredith, who with George Ansami took over the management of Persons-Freeland Company Store. I took out what I had in with Frank Ansami in the logging partnership. We were still short of cash for a safe working capital and if you think it is tough to borrow money now, you should have been around in 1934.

Max and I did not give up easily so we decided to talk to Ed Hagen of the Iron Exchange Bank at Hurley. Ed knew me from the time I came to Saxon in 1930 and he knew the Organist family well. He listened to our plans, then said, "How much money do you need and what security can you furnish?" We told him we needed $2,500 and would give all our logging equipment plus two teams of good draft horses and some other timber and farm land besides our signatures. John Landon informed Ed Hagen of the kind of contract we had with the company and the financial arrangement of monthly payments to their jobbers.

After thoroughly investigating our application, the loan was given an okay by the Board of Directors of the Iron Exchange Bank. We were then able to actively get started on our new job in Michigan.

Max and I made another two-day trip to the timber lands, looked up a campsite where water was available, and blazed out a tote road to the campsite.

We then signed up with Employers-Mutual of Wausau for Workmen's Compensation Insurance at the cost of $17.75 per $100 of earnings with a chance of getting a lower rate after a three-year period if we showed a good safety record.

Of course, you must realize that wages were low, but our logging price was low too, so the insurance cost was a big factor in our logging cost. It was necessary to have Workmen's Compensation Insurance to get a contract and we would not want to be without it either.

Mr. and Mrs. William Brown (my mother and stepfather) took the cooking job, with Mr. Brown going out alone to cook under a canopy until a kitchen was built.

We lined up two teams and heavy farm wagons with supplies enough for ten men, including a tent to sleep in, tools to work with, etc. We started the two teams out on May 24, 1934, figuring it would take two days as it was about a 60-mile jaunt on an all gravel road from Wakefield, Michigan where the teams stopped the first night.

Max and I left with seven men including the cook on the morning of May 25, with axes and crosscut saws to make the tote road from Stencil's camp on the Gogebic Branch to our campsite. Part of the road would go through some of the Stencil camp slashings.

The first part of the crew consisted of Adelore LeGeault and Walter Damgard, teamsters; Ernest Valkama, Ernest, Alfred, Elmer and Theodore Hill, John and Elmer Holms, with Max Organist in charge.

I looked after getting the lumber and other supplies toted in for the camp building crew. Mr. Brown, the cook, and myself had an early start from Saxon that morning and were at the Steve Damcheck shack on Highway 2 where the Gogebic Branch crossed the highway, by 8:00 a.m.

For the next year Steve was our host and a good one. He proved to be very accommodating with his shack always open for any worker who had to get shelter on a bad day.

We left William Brown, the cook, there to wait until the teams arrived as he would not have anything to do until the supplies arrived. The mosquitoes were terrible as there was a lot of swamp in the area.

Max and I took the seven men and hiked down the railroad track to Stencil's camp with the axes and crosscut saws where we started on the tote road at 9:00 a.m. and by 5:00 p.m. had the road brushed all the way, but only ready for the wagon about half way. When the teams arrived, we put the tents, kitchen range, blankets, cooking utensils, etc., on bark jumpers and went on through to the campsite so we would not have to set up the tents twice.

It made for a late supper when we arrived at the campsite. We all got busy setting up the canopy for the kitchen, the range, and a table of sorts, so William Brown could prepare supper. It was very welcome by the crew of hungry men at about 7:30 p.m.

It had been a very nice day, so the men were all in good humor, even if they had put in a long hard day. They were all fairly young men except Mr. Holms and Mr. Brown. The young men made it more of a picnic or camp-out which made a hit with me, as there is nothing worse in a situation of this kind than to have a griper in the gang.

While part of the crew was helping the cook, the other part of the crew was putting up the sleeping tent and building a big smudge fire to get rid of some of the mosquitoes, some of which were as large as humming birds. In fact, they were picking baked beans off the pan the cook was warming the beans on.

After supper which tasted mighty good, we spread straw on the ground in the sleeping tent, rolled up in a blanket and it was not long before we were all asleep. It was just cool enough to keep the mosquitoes quiet which was a blessing as we were all able to get a good night's sleep.

Bill Brown, the cook, was up early, heated up the old range and served hot cakes and sausage that first morning. This made a hit with the whole gang and they sure stored away the pancakes and sausage, after which they were ready to get started building camps.

Max took a few men out to finish the tote road so the teams could get in with the wagons. I took the other men to stake out a kitchen plot, which would be the first building to go up. There was a small grove of nice aspen or "poplar" near our kitchen site which would have to be cleared off before the other buildings could be built. We decided to build the kitchen out of upright aspen and it worked out well. We started in cleaning off the grounds and when the men finished the tote road, we put them cutting and peeling the aspen for the building.

John Landon had what lumber we would need loaded on a flat car at the Ironwood mill. This arrived and was spotted on a siding at the Stencil landing on May 26. One team was put pulling in the camp buildings' logs. The other team went back to the Stencil landing for a load of flooring lumber and made it back the same afternoon.

The only man we all felt sorry for was Bill Brown, the cook. He was an elderly man and had not been where mosquitoes were so bad for a good many years. The canopy covering the kitchen stove and table only covered overhead. With no mosquito netting, he really suffered. A smudge he kept going helped some and by mixing his bread or pastry batter in the evenings, he got by. The crew helped make it easy for him whenever possible.

We concentrated on getting the kitchen and meat screenhouse up first and by the end of the week were able to move into the kitchen, a big relief for the cook.

We set up bunks in one end of the kitchen and after sleeping five nights on straw and evergreen branches on the ground, the spring beds felt good. The men spent Sunday cleaning up, fixing up their bunks, etc.

Max and I made a trip to Saxon 55 miles for supplies we needed such as fresh meat and specialty items which we took back on Sunday afternoon. From that time on for a seven-month period, I never walked to camp from the highway without a loaded pack sack or knapsack. If I did not know how to carry one before, I sure had practice during the balance of the year 1934.

By January, 1935, the train was going in daily so supplies would be unloaded at our sleigh haul landing close to a landing of Victor Ahonen of Ironwood who was logging for the same company.

From the landing one of the teams would take the supplies to camp. At the start of the second week, we had lumber enough hauled so we built the men's camp out of all lumber. By the end of that week we were able to move into the men's camps, set up dining tables in the kitchen and were ready to start bark peelers on Monday, June 5.

We had been blessed with dry weather, so were able to put up the two buildings in ten days with a small crew. I assure you they were not insulated or all modern conveniences either, but they were camp buildings. With plenty of wood available to heat them in the cold weather, we would keep warm.

A very amusing incident happened that second weekend. Saturday morning an old-time lumberjack by the name of Frank Oliver, well known in the area, arrived at camp to peel bark. He was a very able man but a little hard of hearing. From where our camp was located, it was about a quarter of a mile from the river and we had blazed a trail hurriedly to the river until we had time to do a better job. Frank wanted to clean up, so shortly after noon lunch he started for the river and made it okay, but on returning got off the blazed trail and was lost for a couple of hours before getting back to camp. After supper, he started for the river again to see why and where he got lost and this time he did get lost. It became dark and he spent the night in the woods. When the kitchen horn blew in the morning, he found he had slept only a short distance from camp.

Max and I drove back to Saxon the second weekend with two cars so we could bring some men back to peel hemlock bark and cut and peel balsam and spruce pulpwood. It was a late start for peeling hemlock bark, but the company said to peel what we could, then ship the balance in rough logs.

My mother was now anxious to join and help her husband so I took her back on Monday morning and although 66 years old, she walked those four and one half miles of hard walking without flinching. She said it reminded her of the pioneer days at Mineral Lake and Mellen when she would walk to Mellen from our homestead at Mineral Lake eight miles and sometimes back the same day. They have lost the mold of some of those hardy pioneers.

This was the last camp where all the old methods of logging were used. It was also the first camp I actually worked in where hourly wages were paid and the minimum wage was 40c per hour. Most of our workers were pieceworkers; board and room was charged at $1.00 per day. The wage and hour law was now in effect.

We started putting peelers to work on Monday morning and by the end of the week had the camp full as there were many men looking for work, good husky young men as well as older men, a good combination. We kept four men building a barn and blacksmith shop and around 35 men working in the woods.

From that time on it would keep Max busy looking after the crew in the woods and I would check the pieceworkers with Max helping at the end of the month. I would keep the records, see that we had supplies, etc. During the summer months I would have to pack in fresh meat at least two times each week in my pack sack. The team would make one trip each week with the other supplies. Some were hauled from Highway 2 and some from Stencil landing.

We had to build the camps just as cheap as possible as it was a one-year setup. When a camp was for two or more years, you had a chance to do a better job on the buildings, but the first three years we were logging for Marathon we had to move each year. The next two moves we were able to build on a highway which was a tremendous asset.

After we started making roads, cutting and peeling hemlock logs, pulpwood, etc., the time passed away fast as we were all busy. The low piecework prices encouraged the peelers to work longer hours in order to have more satisfactory earnings.

The hard times put me in mind of the 1913 to 1915 era, which I had hoped to never see again. The 30's were worse in some ways. In the 1913 to 1915 era, there were lots more larger logging operations and they at least fed the transients free. In the 1934 era, they tried to make the transients pay for meals. It did not work out as no one had any money. We were very fortunate in one way in having a camp so far off of a highway and being a small setup. Only men real anxious for a job would take the walk in from Steve's on Highway 2. We also informed Steve to steer the transients away and only encourage men who had worked for us previously. If we needed a man or two, we would tell Steve who knew a lot of lumberjacks and it worked out very well.

Our crew did not change much during the peeling season and we kept picking up real good pieceworkers once in a while when I would be in Hurley or Ironwood on business. We had an awful lot of pulpwood to cut and skid in addition to the logs at this camp as there was a lot of swamp with good stands of balsam, spruce and cedar.

Our operations moved along smoothly during the late spring and early summer. We had all the peelers needed and a few men cutting and grading winter log roads so we could start skidding and decking the forest products when peeling season was over around August 1. All our hauling would be in the winter season.

I was perfectly at home again, the first time in eight years. I always had lived or worked in the woods until moving to Mellen to take the warehouse job in 1926. It seems I always have a real good outlook on life when out in the woods. The fresh air, plus the gaiety of the animals and birds, seems to put new life into me.

By the middle of July, 1934, our blacksmith shop was all ready and it was necessary to get a blacksmith who could wood butcher, as our crew was not large enough to employ two men. One day when I was going to Ironwood for supplies, I was talking with Steve Damcheck at the highway stopping place about a blacksmith. Steve said there is just the man you need in Marenisco. His name is Levi Haako; he is a first class blacksmith in all but horseshoeing and is able to get by in horseshoeing. He is also first class in wood butchering. I said, "Gee, that is what we need." Steve said, "He has one fault or he would not be in the woods and that is his likeness for liquor, but if you let him go to town for about a week every six to eight weeks he will do a lot of work for you." What an understatement that was!

I stopped at Marenisco on my way to Ironwood and located Levi, who was sober but very sick and shaky, so I bought him a drink, then talked to him about the job. He was very receptive and agreed to take the work. I picked him up the next day and while I had some difficulties with him and he tried my patience at times, he made money for us. He worked for us almost continuously for several years.

When I got Levi to camp, he was so sick for a couple of days I thought we would lose him, but by having some aspirins and pain killer at camp we kept him from going back to town. He swallowed two dozen aspirins the first night, then a bottle of pain killer which contained 67 percent alcohol and by the next morning his pain was gone. He was in a deep sleep and did not wake up for another 24 hours. I thought he was going to die, but he survived. When he woke up, he was feeling a little better and was able to keep a little coffee down. Then he walked around a lot that day, although still very shaky. He was able to sleep that night and the following morning said, "I may as well go to work. It is the only way to really get over a spree."

He did not work on iron much the first day, but cleaned up the shop, took an inventory, did a little wood work so as to sweat some and by evening was feeling much better. The following day he really went to work and for about three months stayed on the job, except to visit what he called his warehouse once in a while.

For about a week Max and Levi worked on getting equipment ready to start skidding and decking logs, fixed up a side horse jammer for decking the logs, eveners and singletrees for the horses, cant hooks, etc. We bought two teams of horses and hired one team in order to have a full crew of three teams skidding and one team in the cross haul with four single horses skidding pulpwood -- 12 horses in all.

We were able to get the log decking crew started around the first week in August and just had that nicely started when another problem turned up. Mr. Brown, the cook, began to have trouble with his feet and after a week of doctoring decided it was no use, he would have to give up the cooking job. I gave my mother some help so she could keep up the work until I could get a cook. She did not want to give up, as she liked it at camp very much, but she knew it was too much for her without him so I started looking for the right man.

One of the men working at camp had come from Ontonagon about a week before and he told me that Tom Padjen, who I had gone to logging school with at my first logging camp on the Mellen Lumber Company line was living in Ontonagon. He had just left a cooking job, so might be available. I lost no time and left for Ontonagon the next morning, as I knew if I could get Tom my cooking problem would be over.

Tom was at home and had been married since I last saw him. He and his wife Mary had Tom, Jr., about a year old. They asked me to have dinner with them which I did, then I told him what I came for. They were interested, but Mary was reluctant about being left alone with a young baby with Tom away out in the woods without even phone service. I said, "How about going out with Tom, you can help him." They said, "How about the baby?" I said, "We will fix up a room for you off the kitchen so you can take care of Tom, Jr. Many children have been born and raised in the wilderness. Look at me!" Mary, seeing me for the first time, took a good look. I could see she was not too impressed by the remark, but Tom saved the day. He said to her, "Why not, wherever I go it will be in the woods. It will not be too large a crew and we can easily do the work between us." She agreed.

Tom then said, "What wages are you willing to pay?" I said to Tom, "Wages? You do not talk wages in times like this, you know we have such a nice place out there in the wilderness, it is just like being on a picnic all the time. You are lucky we do not charge you board." "Yes," Tom said, "I know how much like a picnic any logging camp is." I said,

"Tom, I am not going to chisel at all. I know you and Mary can do the job and will stick with us until spring at least. We have a tough job this year. Max and I will have to get all the breaks in order to make wages so we cannot gamble on changing cooks often." I then told him the wages I had in mind for him and for Mary as a cookee. When the crew would be under 25 men, there would be no wages for Mary but she would get free board.

Fall of 1935 - Corrigan & Organist Camp 2 near Crooked Lake, Michigan. The kitchen built with logs. Mrs. Tom Padjen, wife of cook Tom Padjen, Sr. and Tom Padjen, Jr., 3 years old -- already a good lumberjack.

Tom talked with Mary, then said, "Your offer is fair; we will take the job. When do you want us to start?" I said, "How about you going back with me? Then I will get a room added to the kitchen for Mary and Tom, Jr. and will send a pickup truck for them as soon as the room is ready in four or five days."

Tom went back with me and Mary joined him the following week. It was a good deal all around, as the Padjens stayed through until the spring breakup at our Camp 1, then the C. & N.W. railway company let us use two boarding cars set out at the Sylvania Station while we were building our Camp 2 in the spring of 1935 on the Crooked Lake Road. Tom and Mary stayed through at that camp until the spring of 1936.

The wages we agreed upon for Tom was at a rate so he would clear $70 per month after board was paid. When Mary worked as a helper for Tom, she was paid so as to clear $35 per month.

Tom and I arrived back at camp before the evening meal, and Tom helped my mother clean up the evening chores and took over the kitchen the next morning. Later in the day, I walked out with my mother to the highway, then took her to our home in Saxon to join her husband, William Brown. After a few days at our home, they left for Chippewa Falls to make their future home where we visited them three or four times a year and they would make one trip each year to see us.

The next week Mary and Tom, Jr. joined Tom, Sr. and they settled down in their wilderness home like "three bugs in a rug." Mary and Tom were so much different in temperaments that you wondered if they would get along at all. Tom was always so cool and calm, never excited, but his work was always planned ahead. Mary was very industrious, also very excitable and of course, the work was all new to her but Tom would just laugh at her. "Calm down," he would say. "This world was not all made in one day. If we do not have a dinner ready for the crew, we will cut out one meal once in a while, etc." Tom did a great job for us all the while he was there as I was sure he would.

Tom and Mary both learned to talk English after arriving in this country from Austria so always had the Austrian accent, but Tom had a fine personality, very witty, and was generally well-liked by a crew, which helped a lot.

We were now well set at the camp, had a good crew all around -- about 50 percent older men and 50 percent young men, which is ideal.

We were able to make up a first class skidding and decking crew on the logs. A good crew of pieceworkers on the pulpwood and bark crew.

One day Levi, the blacksmith, said, "I can make you a good landing gasoline log loader before winter if you put a man helping me who can wood butcher." I had already been advised that he made such a loader for Arvey and Victor Ahonen. I said, "Where will you get the hoisting drums, motor, etc.?" He answered, "Me, from my warehouse." I said, "Where is that?" He said, "It reaches from Ironwood to Escanaba,

Michigan, east and north to Ontonagon, Michigan." I found out it was so. During periods he was not working and even while working he was looking and listening about some large logging companies who were finishing up their cut and would have some old steam loader hoisting drums and frames. He would use a Buick car motor for power as he had found the Buick motor to be the most dependable in that era. I talked the proposition over with Max and he was just as enthused as I was about it, so told Levi to start taking an inventory of his warehouse.

The first weekend Levi started out on Friday evening on foot for Iron River, Michigan with a $5 bill for expenses. I thought to myself, here's where we lose our blacksmith, but no sir, he came back Sunday evening without drinking at all and said he had located the hoisting drums, frame and all complete at one of the Fox Lumber Company abandoned camps. He wanted me to send a truck as soon as possible.

On Monday morning I told Walter Damgard to take Levi and the pickup for the machinery. That afternoon they arrived back at Steve's shack on the highway, near the Gogebic Branch with the machinery; then on Tuesday we sent Levi and a few men to meet the C. & N.W. switching crew and unload the machinery from the truck to a flat car which was taken to Stencil's landing where we loaded it onto our tote swing-dingle and hauled the machinery to camp. Levi was all smiles, then said, "Now get me a good used Buick motor and I will build you a good gas log loader for the winter." The next time I went to Ironwood I looked for a Buick motor and located a wrecked Buick car with the motor in good condition at the Burns-Chevrolet-Buick garage where the present Ottawa National Forest Headquarters is located. William Burns, the manager, and Lauri Lahti, sales manager, told me when the insurance claim was settled they would make me a good price on the motor and drive shaft. I contacted them the following week; the insurance claim had been adjusted and they made us a fair price which we accepted.

We picked up the motor the following week, got it into camp so Levi would not run out of work and you never saw a man go at a job with more enthusiasm. It seemed as though Levi had taken an interest in our logging job for which we were thankful as he was a great mechanic, one who had learned his trade in Finland. He could operate lathes, was a fine mechanic, as well as a good blacksmith except for horseshoeing.

When the camp buildings were completed, we put Ernest Hill in the shop to help Levi with the wood butcher work. A wood butcher is a man who made equipment for a logging job out of wood. Ernest Hill was a good, all-around handyman and worked for us steady for years.

With all the required machinery parts set out for Levi, I set out to get the balance of sleigh haul equipment ready for the coming winter. We had to make it all up and it seems from September to January 1 each year the time passes so fast, especially on practically a complete new logging job. We had to have seven or eight sets of heavy log sleighs, bark jumpers, pulpwood drays, team eveners, singletrees and cant hook stocks.

What made more of a handicap for our logging job was the fact we were not on a railroad spur or on any kind of a public road, just a tote road from the railroad spur to the camp. It was not a novelty to me but by the year of 1934 we were entering the new more modern methods of logging and I will always remember this camp as being the last one I worked in which could be classed with the old-time logging camps. We had no modern conveniences, no electricity, no telephone, no automobiles, within four and one half miles. We did have a battery radio or two.

What always gave me a lot of satisfaction at this camp was the way the younger generation accepted it. I always gave a lot of credit to

Gasoline Hoist Log Loader on landing at Rouse on State Highway 77 between Upson and the Tyler Fork River. This gas loader and many others built by Levi Haako, a fine mechanic, and a character in his own right.

the crew for the way they stuck it out. I know a lot of people will say, well at that time jobs were hard to get, but it is not the complete answer, as we did have a few who did not stick it out, especially when the late fall and early winter set in. But the big majority stuck it out and did a good job for us and from that time until we closed out the Corrigan and Organist partnership in 1950. Any man who worked for us any length of time at that first camp was sure to get a job if he was looking for one. We would always make room some way and many of those young men are still living in the area. There is not one but who will say it was a wonderful experience.

A frequent and always welcome visitor on weekends at the first camp was a William Nolan of Ironwood, Michigan, who was teaching school at Saxon, Wisconsin and had become acquainted with us. He was very much interested in our logging venture and would often spend a Saturday with us. He would then go on to Watersmeet, Michigan where he had a girl friend, Leone Kropp, who was a school teacher. They married later and have been good friends of ours since that time.

A big news item appeared on November 13, 1933, which gave Ashland and Bayfield counties a great boost in their economy.

President Franklin D. Roosevelt signed Proclamation No. 2061 establishing the Chequamegon National Forest. The act of proclaiming the Forest and giving it an official name was the culmination of many years of previous activity. It took over a large area of timber lands which had been burned over with delinquent taxes on a large part of it. Much of this land could have been bought up for back taxes, but very few individual people had money for investing in cutover hardwood timberlands which had gone through at least one major forest fire. Only a small start had been made in forest fire prevention. It also was in the middle of the serious depression of the 1930's with money a scarce article. Some land was available at less than $.50 per acre, but no one was buying it.

The 1934 and 1935 logging job was also a chance to see how I would react to the new logging era after spending seven years out of active logging. I never worked harder or longer hours than I did at this camp, but it was the first time I was really enjoying myself since leaving the Foster-Latimer Lumber Co. warehouse on January 1, 1930.

I was only able to spend weekends at home the first year and not all weekends either. I was always busy during the day, keeping the crew in supplies, men and horses, checking pieceworkers, etc., then in the evening doing the bookkeeping for 30 or 40 men. We had such a lively young crew of men including the cook and wife that there was never a dull moment.

Our skidding and decking crew in logs and pulpwood were piling up the forest products as fast and in as good a shape as was possible. Our log top decker was Pete Wierbas who took pride in putting his decks up so as to make good loading onto sleighs in the winter, as he planned to be loading out the logs.

One day the first part of October, 1934, I came by the log decking crew late in the afternoon, when Walter Damgard who was driving team said, "Who won the world series game this afternoon?" The St. Louis Cardinals were playing Detroit. I said, "St. Louis won, 4 to 3." He said, "Who pitched?" I said, "Paul Dean for the Cards and School Boy Rowe for the Tigers." It just happened to be the correct score and the right pitchers as I had not been near the camp all afternoon. Walter Damgard does not believe to this day that I had not heard the score. (It was October 8, 1934.)

The time passed quickly and soon it was November and deer season. With ten or twelve young fellows from Wisconsin with deer licenses working in Michigan and not one able to buy a Michigan license if he wanted to I began to have my first trouble. There was a large number of deer in that area and keeping those young fellows out of the woods on the two Sundays and Thanksgiving Day was an impossibility, some with no guns would do the deer driving. I told them, "If any of you fellows get picked up by a warden do not look for help as I have all I can do to support my family." It did not have much effect.

The net result the first Sunday of the season -- two nice bucks. They did not shoot does or it would have been more. Then what do we do with them? We did not want to see them go to waste and I did not want to see the boys arrested either. When Tom, our cook, came to the rescue, he said, "I will cook them up and feed them to the crew and no one will know the difference." He said, "I will mix it with beef and serve only at breakfast and supper. In where we are here, the only time there will be danger of a warden will be at the noon meal as we are four and one half miles off the main road, with the closest towns Marenisco about 30 miles and Watersmeet about 35 miles." There were no settlers around, and only two other logging camps with some men having Michigan licenses, but the camp near us was also mostly all Wisconsin crew from around Rosholt, Wisconsin and they were also killing deer, serving some at camp meals and taking a chance by transporting some to their homes.

Well, Tom was right. We had plenty of venison for a few weeks and he did such a good job of mixing it with beef and serving it only at breakfast and supper that only the men who killed the deer knew that venison was being served. In fact, Sim Johnson, who was part Indian and an old-time horse teamster and barn boss, said one day, "If I ever worked at a camp where they served venison, I would report them." He was eating it right along.

There was another thing in our favor and that was the hard times of the '30's as game wardens were more lenient, especially with un-employed heads of families who were living on small farms or around logging camps. The only time they would get hard boiled is when some people living out in the woods would go to town and after having a few drinks, brag about fooling the game warden. Just to give you an example, Joe Peterson in his early days as a ranger at Upson was out in the Potato River area below Foster Falls and decided to cross-country to

Highway 122 when he happened to pass a little crew of four men from Saxon who were shacking. They had just finished lunch but offered Joe a cup of coffee and told him to set on a heavy wooden box while drinking the coffee. Well, just after a cooked meal in one of those shacks, if venison had been cooked, a man with Joe's experience would be able to smell it, and he did, but he did not say a word to them about it. He thanked them for the coffee and went on his way out to where his truck was parked. The next day Joe stopped in Saxon to talk to Vern Downey, the high school principal, who was a good outdoor type. Joe told Vern about the incident and just laughed about it. Then a few days later those four fellows came to town and one of them met Vern on the street and told him how the ranger had set on a box with some cooked venison in it and did not know it. Vern said, you better notify your pals to keep their lips buttoned as Joe Peterson realized they had venison. It surprised the guy, and Vern said the four fellows did not brag about fooling the ranger anymore.

Just after hunting season, we began to get some snow and the better all-around lumberjacks, especially the cant hook men and teamsters, were looking for winter jobs in the sleigh haul camps. As I sat down at the table one evening, I saw my old buddy, Frank Banko of the Foster and Latimer Lumber Company days, the first time I had seen him in four or five years. Also at the table was Henry Gordon, an Indian from Bayfield, Wisconsin who had worked around Mellen for Layman, Meredith and Poundstone so I knew him although he had never worked for me. Needless to say, those two fellows got jobs and worked continuously for us for many years, two very versatile men. The first job I gave them was getting the landing in shape for the sleigh haul. They both knew what to do and I did not have to worry about the job and with the landing two miles from camp this was important.

The next day, Ed Organist who had been farming all summer and had the fall work completed showed up. I put him with Levi to get the gasoline loader completed as it would be needed right after Christmas. Ernest Hill, the wood butcher, was busy on the water tank and logging sleighs.

Ed and Levi made a great pair, as they would eat an early supper and away they would go and probably not get back until midnight but they would have what they went after. One morning after one of their trips, Ed said, "What a man. Where did you ever get him?" I said, "Sears & Roebuck." He said, "Send for some more."

They completed the loader by the middle of December and all put together except for the booms, which were ready. When they started the motor it worked like a charm. When we got back to camp Levi said that should be worth a drink; it sure is if that is what you want. He had over five months in at the time and had done a fine job for us. I settled up with him the next morning and said, "Try to get back by New Year's." He said, "I will be back," and he was. He had plenty of blacksmith work to do as the sleigh teams had to have sharp heel and toe calks for the ice road. Ed and Max both helped him shoe the horses.

During the week between Christmas and New Year's, it was getting cold so we had a couple of teams tramping the log roads, dragging logs cross-ways to drive the frost down, then we put another four-horse team on the water tank and started flooding the road with water. The Monday after New Year's we hauled the first loads, just light bunk loads, as we had to feel the road out, find the soft spots, get ruts made, etc.

It did not take long to get the roads in shape for hauling logs as there was enough snow and it was cold enough to make good ice roads. We were able to try out the new gas log loader with Joe Shaybel of Saxon. The hoister and the machine worked perfectly. The mechanic, Levi, and Joe, the hoister, were very pleased as we all were, because we had a lot of forest products to move by the middle of March, 1935.

After the first week of sleigh haul we found out we did not have the horsepower necessary to haul out the forest products. We had another decision to make in a hurry; whether to get two or three more teams and make an addition to the barn or get a couple of truck chassis, put a rack on the frame to hold a ton or two of weight and pull the sleigh loads with trucks. We heard Tom Ahonen and a brother-in-law, Jack Johnson, who had trucks at Ironwood, left a job and were looking for winter work. I made a hurry-up trip to Ironwood in the late afternoon, located the two men and made a deal for them to come down at once. They checked their trucks over one day and arrived at camp the next after a rugged trip in from Gogebic Station. They drove down the railroad track. After they reached the landing, there was no trouble in getting to camp as we had some ice on the main road.

We had Levi and Ernest Hill taking the horse tongue off the sleighs and replacing with a spliced tongue so it could be used for either teams or trucks. We planned to set the sleigh loads out to the main road with horses, then take them to the landing with the trucks one load at a time. We hauled an average sleigh load of 3,000 to 3,500 feet with two sleigh loads making a railroad carload of logs.

The Marathon Corporation allowed the loggers to cut the pulpwood in either eight feet or twelve feet lengths, so the eight feet lengths were loaded on the sleighs cross-ways on the racks.

None of my crew except Levi had experience in hauling with trucks pulling sleighs, so we listened to Levi and the truckers in lining up the equipment for the haul and they did a good job. It took about a week to get all equipment in shape when the trucks started to pay off in a big way.

Ed Organist took charge of the hauling and the landing, Max Organist, the skidding and loading in the woods; I checked the pieceworkers and took care of the bookkeeping besides attending to the supplies, the empty cars, billing out of loads, etc. We all were plenty busy, but did manage to do some joking and horseplay in the evening when the work was all running smoothly.

We had been gradually picking up some good steady men of all ages, some of whom had worked for me at the Foster & Latimer Lumber Company ten to twelve years ago. Others were farm boys from around Ashland and Iron counties.

We hired a team from John Kunz of Highbridge who sent a nephew of his, Charles Jack, to drive them. He was a very good, all-around workman at an early age. We also had Walter Damgard, Joe Shaybel, Ted Perlberg, John Holms, Elmer Holms, Ernest, Emil, Alfred and Hjalmer Hill, Adelore and Henry LeGeault from the Gurney-Saxon area. All young men but John Holms. We also had old-timers Fred Gigriere, John Wedin, Isadore Oakum and Ed Franzen, all very good pieceworkers who took pride in doing their work well. Of the others named above, some were pieceworkers, some were hour workers. Frank Banko drove the team setting out the sleigh loads. Henry Gordon was the top loader for Joe Shaybel on the gasoline hoist at the landing.

One day late in the afternoon, I saw five new men coming into camp looking for piecework. They had come up from Hatley and Rosholt near Wausau. We had just enough room in camp to sleep them and we had a lot of timber to cut. Two of them, Joe and Tony Flecs, were brothers who always worked together as a gang of log cutters, so we put them cutting logs. Two others were Joe and Tony Flees, nephews of the other two, young strapping fellows who would saw logs or cut and skid pulpwood. The fifth man, Tony Kudronowicz would take whatever job was available. We put the three young fellows cutting and skidding pulpwood. Those five men worked for us steady the next ten years, except for time out for service in World War II.

With the kind of crew we had built up, we had very little turnover of men that winter. In fact, John Landon, the general manager of the log and mill operation for Marathon, said he had never seen such a small turnover of men in a crew the size of ours and we had no labor trouble of any kind.

We also started getting some men from Watersmeet, Michigan. Harry Wright and William Brash showed up one day looking for piecework. We made room for them and it paid off for us the next winter.

All went well on the sleigh haul except for a couple of bad storms always unwelcome on a sleigh haul when the roads are all iced in good shape. But it was the same then as now, we can talk and complain about the weather all we wish, but seldom do much about it.

The snowbanks along the main road were building up, causing some trouble for our truckers. The area we were logging in was a combination of balsam, cedar and spruce, swamps and high ground of hemlock and mixed hardwoods with a branch of the Ontonagon River running through. This area contained a large amount of browse for deer in the Stencil, Ahonen area and also our cuttings. At times in early morning or late afternoon the trucks would see from fifteen to twenty-five deer while making a trip to or from the landing. They had to be on their guard at all times, but to their credit they never hit a deer but they did have some close calls.

Some of us went out to the deer yard a few times in the late evening on a moonlight night and without a doubt the estimate of 300 to 500 deer was correct. It was the largest deer yard I have ever seen. I have seen as many as 200 to 300 deer in yards in Ashland, Bayfield and Iron counties. It sure gave our crew of men something to talk about. The deer encountered very little coyote trouble so came out in good shape in the spring of 1935. It showed when they have enough browse there is not much winter trouble.

Eventually we finished our Camp 1 logging job. We did have one bad scare near the end of February when we had a real thaw, which held on so long it almost ruined our ice road. The only way we saved the road was by staying off of it a few days. We had our decked forest products mostly all hauled, but had one forty-acre swamp to be cut. With a thaw like that so late in the season, we decided not to take a chance on cutting the swamp but to cut what was left on the other five 40's so as to have a clean job. With the weather showing signs of an early breakup, the woods superintendent, Stewart Baldwin, advised John Landon he thought that was the most practical solution.

It proved to be the correct solution, as we did not get much cold weather after that and a creek crossing our log road started to raise very rapidly causing us to haul night and day. We finished the haul by March 15, 1935, with only the camp equipment to be hauled out.

We had some logs and pulpwood piled on the landing to be loaded out. The Marathon Corporation allowed us to keep on loading as our next camp was to be located on the Crooked Lake Road out of Watersmeet, Michigan about one and a half miles off U.S. Highway 2.

The C. & N.W. Railway Company loaned us three loading cars to be spotted at Sylvania Station to be used to keep our camp building crew in until we could build a couple of camp buildings at our new location. They spotted two of the cars at our Camp 1 landing so we could load the kitchen equipment and beds. On moving day we had breakfast at Camp 1, then dinner and supper in the cars at the landing, with Tom Padjen and wife, the cooks, taking the moving all in stride. We had breakfast the next morning in the cars at the landing. The train crew hooked onto the cars at about 10:00 a.m. and moved us to the Sylvania siding, a distance of about 25 miles, arriving there at about noon.

We had arranged for the landing crew to board at Victor Ahonen's camp about one mile from our landing and located on the railroad. Another three men stayed at Camp 1 to take care of the horses and tote out supplies and lumber to Stencil's landing.

18

Camp 2 At Crooked Lake, Michigan

Camp 2 was on a hard top town road leading to private resorts and the Sylvania Tract of timber owned by the Fisher Brothers' estate. This tract of timber and lakes has had the front lines in newspapers, television and radio the past several years.

When the administrators decided to sell the Fisher Brothers' estate, there was a big demand by large lumber companies that it be opened for bids. It was only natural. There was a good stand of timber on the land.

After a few years of controversy and debate, a plan was formulated that it be taken over by the U.S. Forest Service. It was to be made a part of the Ottawa National Forest, with headquarters at Ironwood, Michigan. The plan was accepted with the suggestion it be named the Sylvania Recreation area. It seems to have worked out well.

The new camp was located about 5 miles southwest of Watersmeet, Michigan at a nice spring just off the Crooked Lake Road about one half mile north of Crooked Lake and one mile northwest of Clear Lake.

There was a nice stand of hemlock trees near the campsite so we decided to build the kitchen out of logs. We had a few experienced men in log building who wished to help build one more log camp building. It worked out fine as it took only a few days to get it ready for our cooks to move in.

The Tom Padjens (cooks) with their boy, Tom, Jr., now able to walk in pretty good stride, was a busy boy with the novelty of a lot of action by the men in building the camp. Naturally, most of the men would give the boy a lot of attention as it was not often you would see a family in the woods with youngsters. During the spring of 1935, the Padjens had their second boy, James.

The kitchen was built so that we used the spring water runoff to make a water refrigerator where we kept butter, lard and other small perishable items along with cooking supplies. It served its purpose very well. We also had a screened-in meat house, as I described previously, and a root house for potatoes, vegetables, etc.

We had nice weather for building camps so the building went up quickly. We had a good experienced crew of men and had very little griping which always makes for a good atmosphere around a logging camp. It was also a good crew for horseplay in the evening when the day's work was done.

Our building crew continued to sleep in the car camps until a men's shanty was up as we hauled the men back and forth with a truck. Being on a good road helped out in many ways, and I really appreciated it. There was no more backpacking of fresh meat which I did so much of in the first camp. It sure was a relief.

By the middle of May the camps were ready to put on hemlock bark peelers as we had a lot of bark to peel. We also had a lot of pulpwood. Again we had a lot of mosquitoes. One thing they did not have around Watersmeet, Michigan, at that time was woodticks. Only one occasionally, where, as in Ashland and Iron County area, they had been bad for ten years.

I went into Kelly's store at Watersmeet one day and while in there, I felt one on my neck. I picked it off and said to Arnold Lundgren, the manager, "Do you know what a woodtick is?" He said, "No." I showed him and said we have to bring something over from Wisconsin for your people here. He answered, "I have heard that they are showing up around here and now they are in every state in the union." Personally, I dislike them more than mosquitoes. One thing, they make you think about taking a bath more often. If you do not get them off the first day, you may have a little trouble as they bore in and work their way under the skin where it is harder to get them off. One good thing to remember, do not jerk them off; it is better to soak them with a strong linament or rubbing alcohol first, let it sink in, then take a hold and pull steady, slowly until they let loose, then apply iodine or mercurochrome or other good disinfectant. Some lumberjacks tried drinking the alcohol and rubbing the bottle on the bite, but it did not help.

If it were not for the flies, mosquitoes and woodticks, etc., there would be two workers for every job in the woods, so the good Lord had taken care of that too.

After we got started peeling bark and other woods work, we still had a few men completing the camps, such as an office, blacksmith shop and barn, so we had a few men around the camps all the time.

On June 6, 1935, John Peterson, a salesman for E. Garnich & Sons Hardware Wholesale House of Ashland and Guy Brown, a salesman for Mendenhall-Grahm Clothing Wholesale House of Duluth, stopped at the camp. They had registered for a room at the Kelly Hotel and took orders at the Kelly Store in the afternoon, decided to go out to our camp for evening meal. They always did after that and being exceptionally good salesmen with fine personalities, we were always glad to have them stop. This night turned out to be a never forgotten night for members of our crew and the salesmen as well.

There were black bass in the little unnamed lake near our Camp 2, and some of the younger members of our crew could not resist the urge to fish for sunfish, perch and bluegills before the black bass season opened on June 15. The game warden, Hienie LaMue, warned them a couple of times, saying, "If I come along patrolling this road and catch you with black bass, I will have to take you into court."

The boys were a little careful for a few days, but on the night of June 6, 1935, Joe Shaybel, Ted Perlberg and John Wedin decided to go over to Clear Lake about a mile off the main road. It was really a bass lake with clear spring water. You could see bass swimming at any time of the day.

After the three men had been gone about an hour, I said to Ed Organist, "Let's test them out. They have been warned about fishing before June 15 and are on edge." He said, "Let's go." So we did. When we got near the lake, we walked very quietly until we were able to see John Wedin, a middle-aged man, in one direction and in the other direction there was a jog in the lake with a sharp point sticking out. Ed said, "I bet Joe and Ted are around that point. I will work around that way and when I see them, I will holler. I will get these two and you holler back when you will take the other one."

Ed made it around the point without being seen or heard and could see Joe and Ted. They had cut small saplings for poles and were fishing when Ed hollered, "I will take these two." They did not wait to see who it was, just broke off the end of their poles, wrapped the line around the broken end and took to the woods for the camp. I hollered, "I will take this man," but John Wedin recognized my voice and said, "Come and get me, Corrigan", and kept on fishing. Ed and I started back to camp figuring Joe and Ted would beat us to camp, but when we got to camp they had not arrived. We thought they were playing it safe and staying out a while. We visited with the salesmen a short time and when they left for town, we went to bed.

A short time later Louie Hines, our blacksmith, came into the office and said, "Joe and Ted are not back yet and it looks like rain." I said, "To hell with them; they will come back when they get hungry." But a couple of hours later, Louie came in again and said they were not back and it was raining, with some snow mixed with it. "Well," I said, "They sure cannot be lost with those lakes all around and if they do get turned around, will stop and build a fire," as there was lots of swamp land with many dry cedar windfalls on the area. We went back to bed.

At about 4:30 a.m. Louie came in again, said, "Those fellows are not back and we have about six inches of snow on the ground." It was not cold, but it was sure wet and we knew then that they were lost but figured they were not far away and would get back soon after daylight. But daylight came and no Joe or Ted until about 11:30 a.m.

I had stopped by a stump in the campground where John Wedin was filing a hand saw and there coming down the road were Joe and Ted. They were wet, of course, with their hats slouched over their eyes -- yes, hungry and tired. John looked at them and asked, "What happened to you fellows?" They said, "The game warden chased us." John, unconcerned, said, "I know! He stopped me, too. I did not have any bass and he just warned me that it would be much safer if I did not fish at all until June 15."

You know, it is hard to believe, but that crew of about 40 men kept it a secret for two weeks and would josh Joe and Ted about the game warden putting the run to them. Then on a Sunday, Joe Shaybel's father and sister Rose came down to visit him and he was telling them about the game warden chasing him and Ted. Tony Jesse, who had 40 acres of land near Shaybels, said, "Ach! That was no game warden. That was Corrigan and Organist who fooled you." Joe did not mind, but Ted gave us the cold shoulder for a few days but gradually got over it. The game warden, Hienie LaMue, got a big kick out of it. He said we did a better job of getting the boys away from the lake than he did.

With Camp 2 located on a good hard top road with some high ground timberland to log, we decided to do some log hauling with a truck and log trailer. We were able to use the hard top town road out to Highway 2, then the town road east to Sylvania landing, where we had the boarding cars in the spring while building Camp 2.

We hired Floyd Aldrich who, with his father and brother, Ray, had a fleet of trucks hauling for the Bonifas Lumber Company at Marenisco, Michigan, to truck the logs from the woods to Sylvania landing and he did a good job for us all summer and fall.

Levi Haako, the master mechanic, who had made our landing loading hoist at Camp 1, made us another one for loading trucks or sleighs in the woods and as usual did a good job. It was the only way he would do his work.

Ed Organist now looked after the skidding, trucking and landing. I took care of the bark peelers, pieceworkers, road builders and did the bookkeeping, bought the supplies, etc. We were both very busy as we had a crew of 40 to 50 men.

George Roberts who had scaled out our logs at Camp 1 during the spring breakup, was sent over to scale the logs and boarded at our camp. He was a character in his own right.

With our camp on a good road and only about five miles from Watersmeet with a chance of our logging being in the vicinity of Watersmeet for a few years, my wife and I decided it would be better to move to Watersmeet during the summer. I started house hunting and through the efforts of Frank McDonald, Gogebic County Highway

Commissioner, we located one in Watersmeet on old Highway 2. George Dellies, a C. & N.W. shop worker, and Harry McIver, a C. &. N.W. brakeman, or conductor, were our neighbors. We spent a pleasant five years at Watersmeet. I could spend most of my nights at home for the next two years. I could get out to camp by breakfast each morning and was able to do much necessary business by telephone in the evenings.

We moved soon After August 1, so as to be located by the time school started as our daughters, Bonnie and Shirley, would be going to school. We did not yet have son Clayton.

Our work progressed satisfactorily all summer. It was a fairly dry summer after one June snowstorm, so we were able to truck logs steady without too much lost time. We moved a lot of logs with one truck as it was a short haul.

There was a large C.C.C. Camp between Marenisco and Watersmeet, so we were able to observe the good work they were doing. It was a well managed camp, with the management taking the proper interest in the boys, which paid off with the boys doing a lot of work. They built many needed firelanes. There was much heavy timberland in the Watersmeet area being logged which made a dangerous fire hazard.

There was another C.C.C. Camp called Camp Bonifas near Watersmeet. Named after a prominent logging and sawmill family of Upper Michigan and Wisconsin who had sawmills at Winegar, Wisconsin and Marenisco, Michigan at the time we were logging at Watersmeet, Michigan.

There were also C.C.C. Camps at Upson and Clam Lake in Ashland and Iron Counties, in my native area, so naturally I observed the Upson Camp. I would make regular trips to Saxon with my family on weekends when the weather was right. With so many C.C.C. Camps in the area, I was very much interested in the work they were doing and I can say they did a fine job. The people who are living in northern Michigan and Wisconsin are now receiving the results of the fine work done by the C.C.C.

Many of those fine young boys come back to the area to live the days over and see the results of their work.

With the closing out of the Foster & Latimer Logging & Lumber Company at Mellen, Wisconsin in 1933, many of those employees ended up in the C.C.C. Camps. Some of the supervisory personnel of the Foster & Latimer Lumber Co. who took positions in the C.C.C.'s were Tom Leith, Ray Scribner and Arthur Woodward. Melvin Hovde, a real good mechanic, took a position in the shops. Basil Kennedy, the prominent attorney at Mellen, is a graduate of the Upson C.C.C. Camp where he was a cook. He learned the trade as a cookee from his dad, a long-time camp cook, George Kennedy. Basil still likes to talk about those days.

There was not much excitement during the summer of 1935, just plain hard work with long hours. With the coming of fall in a sleigh haul camp a little more excitement generally creeps in, with the weather having something to do with it. It had been a good summer and fall, weather-wise, and we were able to keep the log truck hauling most of the time.

A funny little incident comes to my memory. Oscar Barnhart, the old-time camp foreman who had taken such a dislike for me at the Foster-Latimer Camps, was foreman at the John Nichols camp only a short distance from our camp. He was logging for the same company as we were, and I would see him or his crew often. He had not changed too much.

Ben Green, part Indian and a good cant hook man who lived at Land O' Lakes, was tailing down logs for one of Barnhart's decking crews. One day Barnhart stopped at the decking crew and told the top decker what log road to move to when they finished the log deck they were on. When they were moving, the top decker got confused about which road to take. The result, it was the wrong road. Ben Green had to go back to the deck of logs they moved from for some extra tools when he met Barnhart, who said, "Where did that crew go?" Ben told him and then Barnhart said, "I told him to take the other road." Ben said, "I know you did, but he did not believe me, so the crew is over there." Barnhart took his hat off, threw it on the ground, and started jumping on it, which he continued for a minute or more, then started cursing. Ben then started jumping on the hat and asked, "How far do you want to drive that hat into the ground? I will help you." Barnhart started cursing again and walked away. It was an old habit of his.

In November, 1935, I had a good scare, health-wise. I had been having occasional stomach cramps which seemed to be getting more severe, so I began to think it may be chronic appendicitis. What a time of year to have something like that come up, but I kept praying it would not happen. Then one day while in Ironwood on business, I felt a cramp and then became a little dizzy, so I stopped at a store building corner to see if it would pass over. I almost fainted which really did scare me, so I decided not to fool around any more.

During the fall I had gotten acquainted with Dr. Maconi of Ironwood who had a cottage on Crooked Lake, so decided to let him examine me and went to his office at once. He took me in right away, gave me a good examination and my fears were verified. Dr. Maconi decided it was chronic appendicitis. Knowing what a bad time of year it was for a logger to go for an operation, he said that if I would watch my condition closely and diet, that I might possibly get by until spring without an operation, but if I should get some real bad cramps with dizziness to go to the hospital at once. The Good Lord was with me and I had only a few slight attacks during the balance of fall and winter of 1935 and 1936 for which I was very thankful.

The fall of 1935 was a fairly dry fall, so we had good luck in getting our timber products out and decked on the roads for the sleigh haul. It did not get cold enough to tramp the roads and get the water tank out to make ice roads until in January, 1936. This was bad as January and February were always the best sleigh haul months. My partner and I began to worry about what kind of a winter we were going to have. It did get some colder after January 1, 1936, and we started to tramp the roads, but it did not snow and did not get cold enough to make ice roads. We were also running out of timber for our crew. The general manager told his woods superintendent to let us cut on a block of timber being held over for the next year's logging. This saved us from laying off our crew and we were able to haul those logs with trucks. Then as it started to get colder around the middle of January, 1936, we started to get a little snow so put the water tank to making ice roads, but it was not cold enough to do a good job.

By January 16, we had completed the truck haul to Sylvania landing and would now have to do everything possible to get the sleigh haul started. The new landing for the sleigh haul was about one half mile west of the Sylvania siding, where we had plenty of room to spot loaded sleighs and set out empty sleighs. This was a very efficient way to haul logs, as we had found out the previous winter at our first camp.

We had to make a good crossing across U.S. Highway 2, east of where the town road left Highway 2 going to Crooked Lake. It is no easy job to make an ice road crossing a cement or black top highway, but on January 16, we fixed the approach to and away from the highway. We put the skidways in shape for unloading the sleighs on the landing as we were positive some good cold weather would surely come soon. The morning of January 17, we took some men and a team to complete the landing work. It was turning cold, also cloudy with some snowflakes in the air with a stiff wind developing from the northeast, a good sign of a snowstorm. We were very much encouraged, and how correct we were.

The winter of 1935-36 was a very cold winter with plenty of snow. From January 17, 1936, until March 1, 1936, it was below zero every morning -- a period of 40 days. Although we had some scares for an open winter the first part of January, once the cold weather did set in our troubles were over.

About the first or second day after the cold weather started, we had a close call to a bad accident. Frank Stolz, a teamster, was sent to the end of our logging job to load on a light load of logs to see how the road was going to hold up over some swamp land we had to haul over. It was not good swamp land, more of a bog, so we realized we might have some trouble until the road was frozen solid and iced. We had another team dragging a log crossway of the road to pack and fill some of the rough spots. We instructed that teamster to work toward the team coming with the load of logs, so he could help in case of trouble. The team with the sleigh turned around at the end of the road where we loaded on ten or twelve logs, about 1,000 board feet. The teamster got on the load and started off without trouble. He had gone only a short distance when he hit a soft spot which the team crossed but the back end of the sleigh broke through and started sinking. The teamster jumped onto the pole behind the team very quickly and unhooked the evener from the pole just as the front end of the sleigh started to sink. The team became free with the sleigh going down until only the top end of the sleigh pole could be seen with the sleigh and logs completely covered with moss and water. It was only the quick action of the teamster that saved the team.

We then poled the road in front of where the sleigh went down and after a few days of real cold weather, we were able with a block and line to pull the logs out one at a time as well as the sleigh.

From that time on we had real good luck and moved a lot of logs, pulpwood, ties, and hemlock bark to the railroad landing by March 1, 1936. It was such a steady cold winter with no thaws that we had all our decked timber products hauled by March 5. The Marathon Corporation then allowed us to cut an additional forty acres of timber which kept us going until around March 20, 1936.

With the extreme cold weather still holding on, there was a demand for stovewood in the Watersmeet - Land O'Lakes area. About ten or twelve of our real good year-round workers wished to work as long as they could, so I asked John Landon if we could cut wood from the cull logs and cull trees on the roads we had logged on during the winter. He said, "Sure go ahead, as it is impossible for you to clean campgrounds at your next year's job until we get some warm weather to take this snow away." I said, "This wood cutting job will sure help us keep down our camp expense and hold onto some good men for moving and building the next camp."

We really moved a bunch of stovewood as the cold weather stayed for most all of April and the ice road kept in good shape. With the heavy use in hauling timber products the frost had penetrated deep into the ground. By the latter part of April, we had the cull logs and trees all cut and the men wanted a short vacation before starting on a new camp.

At this time there was no unemployment compensation in the woods, so the men did not stay in town long as the earnings were so low in the woods, it was impossible to save much for a spring breakup. In fact, they did well to clothe and feed themselves. The logger was in the same boat at the time but conditions were starting to get a little better gradually, although it seemed to take a long time.

The period of 1931 to the spring of 1937, the work conditions in the woods compared with the work conditions in the woods of the 1907 to 1915 period except that men out of work were able to get aid for the necessities of life in the latter period.

Some men were capable of holding better positions but would let liquor get the best of them at certain times. The following shows that weakness.

A log scaler for the Marathon Corporation named George Roberts had scaled logs all fall and winter of 1935-36 until the sleigh haul ended on March 20. He had a good salary, at least much better than any other woods workers. He decided to take a short vacation in town. He had plans for putting some of his earnings in a savings account to be used for buying a piece of lake frontage he had in mind. John Landon, the general manager of the Marathon Sawmill & Logging Operations at Ironwood, Michigan had encouraged him to do that.

A couple of weeks later, John Landon informed me that George Roberts did fine the first week and was walking around Ironwood and Hurley dressed up and acting like a man of distinction and he could carry himself well and use good grammar. He started to take a few drinks each day, then he started to take a few extra each day. By the end of the second week he started drawing out of the bank account. At the end of the third week he was broke. In a talk with John Landon he was very repentent, sick and disgusted with himself and wanted to go back to work. John informed him there was no log scaler job open but possibly we could use him at some other job as he was working out a contract for us on a new camp location in the Tamarack Lake area northeast of Watersmeet, Michigan. It would be another one-year camp location but not a hard or long move as the new camp location would be on a hard top road, old U.S. 2 which made it possible for us to move camps by truck power.

George Roberts followed John's advice and showed up at our old camp the following week. It happened that our chore boy had been at camp all fall and winter and wished some time out so I asked Roberts if he would take the job. He readily accepted as we would have a small crew until the new camp was built. It was not a hard job, and Roberts was handy in getting things ready for moving to the new location as well.

During the summer of 1935, Ed Organist, my partner, had married Rosa Lee Kadlets of Saxon, Wisconsin and we had built an addition of two small rooms to our camp office for living quarters. When camp life would get too monotonous for Rosa Lee, she would spend a week at her parents' home in Saxon or Wakefield.

One day while she was reading in her room, she heard George Roberts come into the office with a pail of water and checked the stove. She heard him mumbling to himself, "George Roberts, you damned old fool, you should know better than to drink away your whole fall and winter earnings, then have to take what job is available, but it is entirely your own fault so take the consequences and keep still. Chances are you will do the same thing again as you never learn."

We had a big change in our contented crew which was a real loss and harder to replace. Tom and Mary Padjen, our cooks who had been with us for nearly two years, decided to leave the woods to try a small business of their own at Ontonagon, Michigan. Although we did not like to have them leave, we could understand the situation, as they now had two young boys and it was real hard for a woman with two small children in logging camps such as were prevalent at the time. There was practically no place to play outside that was not dangerous for small children.

They had saved about all the money they had earned in those two years. While earnings were not big, they had saved about $2,000 -- enough to buy out the stock and fixtures of a small beer tavern and lunch room in Ontonagon, Michigan. We wished them well and they made a success of it; although for a few years it was hard going as were all business ventures in the 1930's. They raised and educated three boys and one girl. They are now retired and live at Waukesha, Wisconsin.

The Padjens were anxious to get moved so we put Byron Bennett of Saxon in as cook. Byron had been the cookee for Tom the past year and he had listened to Tom and Mary, so was able to handle the small crew. When the new camp was ready to move into and start bark peeling, we would put on an experienced cook.

After the spring breakup of Camp 2 in the Crooked Lake area, we gave what members of our crew who wished a vacation a chance to go. Those who wished to work on our Camp 3 construction could stay.

Levi Haako, our blacksmith and mechanic, decided to take a vacation. He said, "I will be back in a week or two when I can be of more help in moving to the new camp." I said, "Levi, you have a fairly good paycheck coming. When you get to Ironwood, why don't you buy some new clothes, clean up, then take a little trip to see a little more of Michigan and Wisconsin." "Ach," he said, "if I clean up, put on a new suit, then walk down the street in Bessemer or Ironwood, Michigan or Hurley, Wisconsin, people will say, 'there comes dirty Levi all dressed up.' " He decided to stay greasy. After a few days in Ironwood he came back to Watersmeet and spent his time and money at the little tavern between Watersmeet and our Camp 2. It was okay with us, as we knew where he was if we needed him.

A few days later the foreman said, "You better stop to see Levi at the tavern about coming back to work. We have a lot of blacksmith work to do for the building of the new camp and to get tools ready for bark peeling." I stopped at the tavern where I found Levi sitting at a booth visiting with a woman I had seen at saloons or taverns in Hurley when picking up men from my crew. I told Levi we would like to have him go back to work. "Good," he said, "I will walk out to camp tomorrow." I bought him and his friend a drink, then stopped to visit the owner a while. Just when I was leaving, I heard Levi say to his lady friend, "What do you say we go and make a little blacksmith?" and away they went. Possibly Levi had a chunk of basswood he was going to make a blacksmith out of.

"What a man!" "What a card!" You had to know him to realize what a genius he was. Those kind were needed in the woods industry before woods work got so mechanized.

19

Camp 3 At Tamarack Lake, Michigan

While living at Saxon we had taken our two girls to Ashland, Wisconsin for checkups by Dr. Tucker. We were impressed by his thoroughness in the examinations. I decided to go to St. Joseph's Hospital with Dr. Tucker to be my doctor. After a thorough examination and reading report of Dr. Maconi of Ironwood, Dr. Tucker agreed that the safest thing to do was to have the appendix removed as it may cause me serious trouble at the wrong time.

I went back home to Watersmeet and started making arrangements to have the operation as soon as possible. After a week at the hospital, I returned home and thought my troubles were over. Although I did not go out in the woods too soon, I did over do it at home trying to catch up on the office work which had accumulated while I was in the hospital with the results that I began having serious stomach pains shortly after my first checkup after the operation, but I thought by taking it more easily, I would be okay but that was not the cure as I soon found out.

I began to have serious pains one morning which did not let up, even by staying in bed. By noon the pain was so bad that I thought my time was up and no fooling. My wife contacted our neighbor, Harry McIver, a brakeman and conductor on the C. & N.W. Railroad who was in from his day's run. He drove our car and took me to the hospital where Dr. Tucker diagnosed the trouble as serious adhesions and kept me at the hospital a few days until he had the trouble under control. He also advised me to watch closely if the pains should start again, but I got along good after that.

Miss McCulloch and Alice Sturgel, teachers in the Watersmeet school who had our 2 daughters in their grades, stopped in one day when I had a lot of bookwork on the table and one said, "Gee, I did not think it required so much bookwork to cut down trees."

By the middle of June when it was necessary to start scaling bark, I was able to do the bookwork but at a slower pace. This made no difference as we did not have a large quantity of hemlock bark to scale that summer.

This was the first logging camp I had been around that did not have good spring water for the camp so we had a well drilled by Harry Rice of Gurney, Wisconsin. We wanted the camp on the highway where it centered our logging job. Rice had to drill 80 feet to get good water but luckily it was sandy soil and easy to drill. The water level was 30 feet down, though, which made it hard pumping by hand power, but it was real good water.

We had been able to hire a good enough camp cook by the name of Dan Young from Ashland, but oh, what a crank. I do not believe he knew how to smile and a crank cook is never liked around a camp by the crew or those in charge. I decided to keep on the lookout for a new cook.

One day a couple of lumberjacks stopped from Iron River, Michigan looking for a job and we hired them. One of them mentioned in the men's camp about a cook Eugene Cameron from Iron River, Michigan, but they did not know whether he was on a leave or had left a job. I knew Eugene Cameron back many years when he was operating a small hotel at Mellen so decided to drive into Iron River to have a talk with him. He was on leave from a job but was also looking for a chance to change jobs. I told him what we had and the salary, which he accepted. He wished to go back to his present employer to give him a chance to get a cook. I agreed with that decision as I would like a cook to do the same. He thought a week or ten days would be about right.

I drove back to camp and was greeted by Frank Banko, a steady employee I have mentioned before. Frank usually worked outside as a teamster or cant hook man but we were only peeling hemlock logs and pulpwood until about the middle of July. I had induced Frank to do the chore boy work and help in the kitchen some as we did not have crew enough for two full-time cookees.

For some time, Frank had been having trouble with the cook about using too much water, which was so hard to pump. I had to agree that the cook was doing just that. He would scrub the kitchen floor, then take a pail and empty the hot water barrel by just splashing pail after pail of water onto the floor. Just before I arrived back at camp, the two men had an argument about this. Frank came into the office to quit but knowing the situation, I said, "Frank, how about staying another week when we are going to bring down a couple of teams from the pasture to get ready for the start of skidding logs." I talked to the cook about it. He admitted he had been wrong, but I guess he had about made up his mind to leave anyway as he realized the crew did not like him. He said, "I think it better for all concerned that you look for another cook. I will stay a week or more if necessary until you get a cook." This solved the problem nicely. Gene Cameron showed up in a week.

Gene Cameron was a good all-around meat and pastry cook. He was also strict, but not the crank Young was so it proved to be a very good change.

Another amusing incident happened at about this time. There were two other contractors for Marathon Logging between Watersmeet and Tamarack Lake, Victor Ahonen and W. C. (Cedar Pole) Smith from the Ashland-Saxon area, who had a foreman, Asa Allhiser, from the Eagle River, Wisconsin area. Asa was a fine, reasonable man who Ed and I got along with fine, but "Cedar Pole" at times was a little over-bearing and tried to be tough.

Due to the cold winter of 1935 and 1936, there seemed to be a shortage of potatoes with the price zooming upward. We had been lucky as Max Organist, Ed's brother, was on the old family farm at Saxon and raised an extra supply of potatoes, figuring on our camp. He also had a good root house, so we did not have to take a large amount to camp at any one time.

During the early part of June, "Cedar Pole" Smith's camp ran short of old potatoes and with new potatoes very high, asked Ed if he could borrow some old potatoes and pay us back when the price of new potatoes went down or when we would get short. We let him have potatoes until we began to get short. Ed advised Asa, his foreman, that we were running short around July 1, so the next week Smith started returning the potatoes according to our needs for a few weeks. After he returned about fifteen bushels out of thirty bushels we had furnished him, he told his foreman that we were now even as the new potatoes cost double the price of the old ones. I could not see the reasoning and told Smith we did not loan you money; we loaned you potatoes and we expected back the same amount we loaned you. After a little cussing, he agreed we were right. A logging contractor always had tough going.

I can think of very few logging contractors who were able to take annual vacations to California or Florida. It was hard enough to make a living, but I enjoyed it most of the time, except when we would get a January or February thaw with a lot of forest products on skids to be hauled. Then it was misery while the thaw lasted.

We had a fair logging chance with part of the timber on a sandy soil which helped for summer logging. Floyd Aldrich again agreed to do our summer trucking. We finished peeling bark in July, then got started skidding and hauling logs around August 1, 1936. We had purchased a Dodge truck and picked up a logging trailer which we used for trucking bark and pulpwood to Tamarack Spur on the C. & N.W. Another logging contractor lived there who was logging for the Fox Lumber Company of Iron Mountain, Michigan. The contractor's name was Al Raeck. He had part of the landing and we had part, but we had no problems. In fact, it was nice to have someone at the landing all of the time.

We had another weather scare in the fall and winter of 1936 and 1937. The summer of 1936 was warm with very cold nights. In fact, there was frost every month of the year of 1936. Very few gardens were able to take it. However we did not get snow to stay until after Christmas. I remember it rained hard a couple of days between Christmas and New Year's. It then turned cold followed with snow and it was a fairly cold winter with plenty of snow. From New Year's on, we had a successful sleigh haul, with some of the forest products loaded out as we hauled. The larger amount was decked on the landing as we had plenty of room with plans to load in the late spring.

In the summer of 1936, we joined the Michigan-Wisconsin Timber Producers Association which, I believe, had been organized in 1935.

The long depression of the 1930's had left the timber workers in a restless condition. The organizers of unions were working hard to organize the timber workers so the logging companies and the logging contractors figured they better have an organization to counteract the unions, at least be able to put the problems of the Timber Producers in proper perspective.

I believe the first president of the Michigan-Wisconsin Timber Producers was Albert Anderson of Michigamme, Michigan, who had a logging and sawmill operation at that location. Lawrence Walsh of Ontonagon was the first secretary-treasurer of the organization.

Some of the other charter members were:

Joe Carlson	Iron River, Michigan
Abbott Fox	Iron Mountain, Michigan
Louis Anderson	Wakefield, Michigan
John Landon	Ironwood, Michigan
Ray Aldrich	Marenisco, Michigan
Floyd Aldrich	Marenisco, Michigan
James Aldrich	Marenisco, Michigan
Lawrence Peterson	Ironwood, Michigan
John Hautenen	Ironwood, Michigan
William Lepanen	Ironwood, Michigan
Tom Nordin	Bruce Crossing, Michigan
Guy Nordin	Trout Creek, Michigan
Gordon Connors	Laona, Wisconsin
Victor Ahonen	Ironwood, Michigan
Arvid Ahonen	Ironwood, Michigan
Clyde Penegor	Ontonagon, Michigan
George A. Corrigan	Watersmeet, Michigan
Ivan Branham	Minocqua, Wisconsin
Cecil Branham	Eagle River, Wisconsin
George Banzhaf	Milwaukee, Wisconsin
Ed Organist	Watersmeet, Michigan
Joe Thieler	Tomahawk, Wisconsin
Clarence Weber	Shawano, Wisconsin
Howard Palmquist	Ironwood, Michigan

Earl Poundstone .... Mellen, Wisconsin
Harry Thieler .... Tomahawk, Wisconsin

In the short period of 1935 to 1937, after the organization got started, they did as well as anyone could expect. It was a very depressed period with the timber industry starting to show signs of working out of the depression and with the unrest of the woods workers growing each day, the loggers all knew that there were trouble signs ahead.

After the sleigh haul started the first part of January, 1937, all went very smoothly as we had an ideal winter until after the sleigh haul was finished around March 20, 1937.

A landing of logs at Pine Lake, Wisconsin. The logs were loaded with a cross haul team and a tip-up side jammer.

20

Camp 4 At Beaton Spur, Michigan

It was lucky for us that we had our forest products on the landing, but it did make a mess for moving to a new camp location, especially where there was no good hardtop road within three miles of the new camp location.

First we had to agree on a new contract with the Marathon Company on a longer term basis. We had at least satisfied the company that we were competent log contractors and could be trusted. With contracts in that period, both sides had to be trusted.

After a talk with John Landon about plans for 1936-1937, he informed us he had a block of timber plotted for us which would take at least four years with a crew from 60 to 75 men to log. He believed it could be done from one camp which would be an ideal setup. He showed me the marked map and said, "Of course, after you look at it, if you wish to add or cut down some, you have that option. You also have the option, if it is not suitable to you, to turn it down and we will show you another block." It was located on the Beaton Spur of the C. & N.W. Railroad. There was a flag station and a section boss with his family living there, with a two or three-man crew boarding with them. Beaton Spur was off of Highway 2 a short distance and about eight miles west of Watersmeet, Michigan. Our camp location would be about three miles north of Beaton Spur, with Beaton Lake on the west side, Crane & Sucker Lake on the east. A planned forestry road would follow an old log road from the campsite to Highway 45 coming out at a C.C.C. Camp, set up at a former Bonifas Lumber Company headquarters camp.

Ed, my partner, and I looked it over good on snowshoes. We were getting some slightly warm days, then cold nights which made good snowshoeing. It was a good block of timber, fairly level ground, but a big percentage of low ground which ran heavy to balsam, spruce and cedar. There was not much chance for summer trucking of forest products as the road costs would be prohibitive, so we ruled that out and figured out cost of logging on an all sleigh haul basis.

My early training at the Foster-Latimer Lumber Company and the Mellen Lumber Company where they always kept records of logging costs daily, came in handy now. After a good look and a complete estimated cost of logging, we decided on what price we would have to ask for at least the first year of operation. We also decided it would be necessary to have a clause in our contract to cover any wage or price increase on supplies, as the threat of a timber workers' strike was now a sure thing.

We picked out a campsite on the Beaton Spur near where the Forest Road was planned to cross the railroad going west along the north side of Beaton Lake out to Highway 2. The road was a sure thing as it was built that summer by the C.C.C. crew from Camp Bonifas. We were able to plan on a passable road by fall which, along with the good railroad location, was a plus for our logging operation.

A day or two later, about April 1, 1937, we met with John Landon about the logging contract. Without much alteration of our demands, we agreed on a contract. John Landon told us if we would take his word, he would take ours, we could then start building camps at once. The contracts would not be ready to be signed until around May 1, 1937, as they would make agreements with all the eighteen logging contractors before making out the new contracts. We agreed to that provision as we had no trouble on our three previous contracts and wished to get started building camps as soon as possible. We had a big move this time.

I contacted the Division Superintendent of the C. & N.W. Railway Company about letting us use a couple of boarding cars to cook and sleep in at the new location. He lost no time in granting our request. The two boarding cars were spotted at the Tamarack Landing before we even heard from him. We placed bunks and blankets for twelve men, kitchen equipment and supplies enough to handle the crew, camp building tools, etc. We notified the depot agent at Watersmeet to have the train pick up the two cars and spot them at the new camp location out of Beaton Spur.

The cars were spotted at noon on April 8, 1937, with the ten men for building camps, the cook, my partner, and myself. We had built fires in the cars the day before as it was really cold. It was eight degrees below zero the morning we moved and the next morning it was eighteen degrees below zero. It was nice sunny day which warmed up fast.

We needed some sunshine as there was over two feet of snow on the ground where we were to start building the camps. The hand-picked camp building crew in charge of our long-time chief camp builder, Ernest Hill, were anxious to get started so lost no time in getting at it the same afternoon we moved in. Some shoveled snow out of the campground, others started cutting and peeling ridge poles, foundation timbers, etc., all of which were handy to the campgrounds.

Ernest took a couple of men at once to start building a barn for the team coming in the next day and by evening Gene Cameron, the cook, had a real fine hot meal of fresh baked biscuits, pork chops and American fries. The crew went to bed in a hurry as with no banking around those boarding cars and eighteen degrees below zero weather, the floors were not too warm, but we had plenty of wood and blankets so kept warm.

The next morning right after breakfast of hot sour dough pancakes and pork sausage, the men went at the camp building with a vim and zest that only outdoor men can show. The train crew switched the lumber for the camps in before lunchtime the second day and could not help but be amazed at how much had been accomplished in one day.

The cook fed the train crew at noon and from that time on whenever the train crew was near our camps at noon or lunchtime, they were welcome to eat. We asked no special favors, but they always went out of their way to see that we were serviced properly and we sure appreciated it.

That first summer, with only a dry weather road, we had to transfer supplies at the Beaton Spur flag station many times from truck to railroad car. Sometimes on days the train had no switching on the Beaton Branch, the section crew would take the supplies in for us.

The next important decision we made was to put up ice from Beaton Lake one quarter of a mile away. Up until this time we had not put up ice for our camps, as we never knew in time where the camp was to be located. We were fortunate in having a cold spring with good clear ice on the lake.

Ed took a couple of men the next morning to put up an ice shed. I took the pickup from Beaton Spur as we needed some kitchen supplies from Ironwood, went to the Saxon farm where I got an ice cutting saw, some ice hand tongs, some vegetables and potatoes, as it had warmed up some. I was back to Beaton Spur in time for the section boss to take supplies and me to camp on the push car pulled by his track gas-powered vehicle.

The following morning, Ed took two men to clean off the wet snow on top of the ice where we decided to cut out a hundred feet from shore so would be away from weeds. The net result in a few days was an ice house filled with sawdust sent down from the sawmill. By April 18, 1937, the ice job was finished. It was a money-saving job, as the summer of 1937 was hot and dry. From that summer on, we always put up ice in our camps.

The camp building was progressing in good shape with the cook camp about ready to be moved into when we made a move to solve another problem which we had expected. What about water? There were springs in some areas but not near the railroad, so we decided to have Harry Rice, a friend and well driller from Gurney, come down to take a look at the chances of getting water. It was the time of year Harry was

Camp 4 on Beaton Branch showing a landing full of logs on Corrigan Siding, close to camp. A lot of logs, pulpwood, hemlock bark and cedar products were loaded from this landing in four winters.

not busy, so he came down at once, took his steel bar he used in spotting the right place to drill for water and after a short testing period, said, "I am sure I can get you water very quickly here wherever you want it." This was an understatement. We said how about moving your well driller in at once. You can drive it down to Camp Bonifas where we will have a tractor hook onto your machine while the frost is still in the ground. He said, "I will do it at once."

He drove home from Beaton Spur that evening and had his drilling machine down to Camp Bonifas the next afternoon where the tractor was waiting. The tractor was hooked to the drilling machine and they were at the camp location that same evening. Harry was set up for drilling the following morning and by night he had water. He tested it and said you have all the water you will ever need and it looks like good water. If I remember right, it was down only eighteen or twenty feet and in clear gravel. We decided to drill another well for the barn. Harry was sure we would have the same results. He was right and at about the same depth. He then took a sample of each well which was sent in to the state laboratory for testing and came back with an all safe test. Our water troubles were over which is a very important item in a camp where so much water is needed.

This set of camps was being built for a four-year setup. We planned to build them better and warmer, with double walls and roofs. We also knew of the demands to be made by the timber workers that there was to be all single bunks in logging camps.

We had put our old-time blacksmith or wood butcher cutting

down the double two-man bunks which were in good shape and making single bunks out of them. We also built little sections of two single bunks and a small table for each four men with a window on the outside wall in each section. It worked out very well. We also put up a "sauna" at this camp so the men would be able to take a bath when they wished. Some used it and some did not, which was not unusual.

We had the kitchen ready, a sleeping camp, washroom and office started when we found out for sure the strike was going to be called as scheduled on May 1, 1937. There was no way to avoid it but no demands had been made. There were no unions in the Michigan and Wisconsin camps at this time.

After the spring breakup in 1937, the union organizers of the American Federation of Labor (A.F. of L.) enlisted volunteers to help visit all cities, towns and villages where woods workers congregated as well as all camps who had a few men working in Michigan and Wisconsin informing them there was going to be a walk out of all woods workers in northern Michigan and Wisconsin on May 1. They told all the men there would be no trouble if all men obeyed the orders, but if they refused to walk out they would use force.

It worked out as planned. On May 1, 1937, there were four camps getting ready to start on the Beaton Branch and the organizers started at the end of the branch working out past our camp toward Beaton Spur. I was at the camp when they arrived. They were courteous, as was I. I informed them that we had no men working in the woods, only a landing crew at Tamarack Landing. I asked if it was okay to keep on building camps. They said it was. We could have a cook also, so we kept our small crew on until all buildings were completed. They did not stop us from working on the landing at Tamarack.

From that time on until the strike was settled in July, 1937, I was kept busy on the strike question, as I had been named to the Board of Directors in 1936. The Board of Directors, led by our serious, hardworking secretary, Lawrence Walsh, was in session most of the time during those two months.

I honestly believe the Board of Directors of the Michigan-Wisconsin Timber Producers Association did a remarkable job in settling that strike in such a short time. It was a benefit to the timber industry and workers as a whole. We were just starting to come out of a depression of six or seven years and a long strike at that time would have been a serious setback.

At the time the temporary agreement was made to settle the strike, around July 1, 1937, there were no complete demands made. They were more generalities with committees agreed upon by both sides to work out details.

The most important issue a demand was made for was the sleeping conditions. It was the number one problem which had to be solved before negotiations of any kind would get underway. They had a point in their favor and they used it. It was a demand that no logger who had worked his way up the hard way and had slept in the old-time sleeping shanties could oppose. The "oldtime wool clothing and wet socks perfume" had left its mark. The demand was made for single bunks, although they could be two bunks high, with a mattress, blankets, and a pillow.

A separate washroom with good drying facilities was asked for. It could be attached to the sleeping shanty.

A bathhouse of some kind. This was settled where no power was available, by putting up a "sauna" steam bathhouse for those who would use it. A bathtub was also furnished with plenty of hot water.

The demands were not excessive and were granted. One old-time woods superintendent for a large company put it this way: "It is a demand that should have been taken care of years ago. Without a doubt, it was the worst condition imaginable and the cost to remedy it was not excessive."

We had started to make our double bunks into single bunks and had a washroom planned along with a sauna. It was the first chance we had to put a little extra investment into our camp buildings.

The first three camps were each a one-year setup in the middle of a serious depression. We did real well to make enough profit to build up our equipment and have some working capital.

From July 1, 1937, we started to see some improvement in the economy and were planning to stay in the contract logging business, which we did. The forest industries were in my blood. Even the first three years of contract logging, when no one worked any harder than we did was fun for me. We were meeting a challenge and making a success of it.

The forest industries were having a new look. With the successful work of the C.C.C.'s in northern Michigan, Wisconsin, and Minnesota, it helped fight the depression of the 1930's by building fire lanes into inaccessible locations.

The states were starting to make gains in appropriating money to prevent and fight forest fires.

The owners of timber stumpage began to see reforestation of our forest lands was possible.

The Federal Government started to take over cut over timber lands and started more National Forests. The states and counties followed the lead, as did private capital.

With the cooperation of all those organizations working together, real progress was made in forest preservation. It gives me a great deal of pleasure and satisfaction to feel that I had a part in the program. I still continue to take part in all phases of reforestation.

Forestry has been a part of me since I was a young boy living on a homestead and an abandoned sawmill village at Mineral Lake, Wisconsin. Mineral Lake and our old homestead are now a part of the

Chequamegon National Forest.

The Chequamegon National Forest personnel are now cooperating with the Mellen Lion's Club in setting up a marker where an old large white cork pine tree stood until cut and hauled to the Mineral Lake sawmill in the early 1890's. It is at a corner where three roads branch off, between Marengo, Sanborn, and Mellen. The old stump has been used as a road directive sign since about 1900.

As time goes on, history will record more and more events of the earlier days of logging.

The first thirty days after the walk out of timber workers on May 1, 1937 were hectic days. Many of the workers did not know what it was all about and the Timber Producers were in the same boat.

The officers of the Timber Producers Association went to work at once. It was very important to do so, as there were many hardwood logs decked on landings at that time of the year.

Basswood logs deteriorate very fast and should be cut into lumber or veneer by the first part of July, or a loss will have to be absorbed. Other mixed hardwoods should be cut into the finished product by the first part of August or take a loss.

The agents for the A.F.L.-C.I.O. Union were not too much interested about the company side of the coin until they began to realize it was a two-way street.

I was named to the committee of the Timber Producers Association to get together with the Union Agents to work out a settlement. It was time consuming but a great experience. Neither side trusted the other until we had completed a few meetings.

A negotiator was sent in by the National Relations Board from Washington. He was an expert, always cool and fair. He had a way about him that demanded respect and after the first two meetings we began to show progress. A Timber Producers Union was new, especially in the area we were in. It was not easy.

There was no way you could start a union of workers when you had no crew. After both sides understood this, we were able to get at the problem of getting the men back to work.

It did not take long to settle the camp conditions. The log contractors were willing to improve camp conditions when they were assured of getting the cost added to the cost of logging.

The Marathon Corporation, who we were contracting for, were always fair on their logging contracts.

We were coming out of the depression where we had learned some lessons. One good lesson was that it was necessary for all of us to work together toward better conditions for all of us.

The company put an escalator clause in our contract. If costs went up, they would raise our contract percentage-wise to cover. If costs were going down, it would work the same way. It was a successful arrangement for both sides. The company did not change contracts very often.

After it was impressed upon the Union that we had to have a crew before we could have a Union, it didn't take long before we had a settlement. In fact, they allowed us to put on loading crews immediately. It took a little longer to put men back to work peeling hemlock bark and logging.

A nice load of logs pulled two miles to landing on an ice road. A truck chassis was loaded with 2,500 lbs. of sand. A heavy truck was able to haul a big load, about 4,000 or 4,500 feet on this load. Ed Organist, my partner, on the load.

Tanneries

One of the consultants on my manuscript took note of the description of hemlock bark being shipped to the tannery at Mellen. Then when I visited him at Madison, he asked me, "What tanneries?" When I told him there were many tanneries in northern Wisconsin in the first part of this century, he said, "You know, I have never read any history on tanneries. Could you write a short resume on tanneries in northern Wisconsin?" I told him I could and here goes.

It seems the tanneries were all owned by the United States Leather Company who had been operating tanneries in the East previous to coming to Wisconsin. They extracted an acid out of the inner part of the hemlock or oak bark (only used hemlock bark in Wisconsin). The acid was used in tanning leather from mostly cattle hides for leather products, etc. Tanneries were a big business in Wisconsin when I was growing up and I took an active part in supplying bark for tanneries from 1913 to 1945, although the Wisconsin tanneries closed out in the 1920's.

View of the U.S. Leather Co. tannery in Mellen. Note the piles of hemlock bark in the background. This bark was hauled directly from the woods with four-horse teams.

In 1896 the Fayette-Shaw Tannery came to Mellen, bringing about one hundred workers into town. The tannery was later taken over by the U.S. Leather Company who increased the capacity of the plant. From 300 to 400 men were employed most of the time. It became a very prosperous industry. A big boost for Mellen until the middle 1920's.

A notice in the Mellen Weekly Files, March 16, 1922. Tannery closes indefinitely. Superintendent Kumm receives orders to report to Cumberland, MD to take charge of operations there.

The U.S. Leather Company operated tanneries in northern Wisconsin from 1885 to 1922 in the following cities or towns: Mellen, Medford, Phillips, Prentice, Rib Lake, and Tomahawk. Most of them would need 10,000 to 12,000 cords of hemlock bark annually.

I cannot help but add a narrative on the wages of the good old days in 1916. During the summer of 1916 when unemployment was coming out of its lowest ebb, the tannery company was paying common labor at the rate of $.15 per hour on a ten-hour day and a six-day week, or a weekly rate of $9.00. They paid weekly with one week's wages held back.

One man, I will not mention his name although I could, had been receiving the weekly check of $9.00 for some time. He received his first check of a raise in wages of one and one-half cents per hour or $.15 per day or check for the week of $9.90. He looked at the check for some time and could see the figures were different. He took the check back to the office for an explanation. The office man tried to explain, but the worker said, oh, make it out the way it has been. I know how much it is. It is hard to believe, as $.90 was a lot of money at that time.

George Kennedy, Camp Cook

There is another man who lived in Mellen many years who no one would be able to leave out of a logging history of Ashland and Iron Counties.

George Kennedy, one of the better camp cooks of that era. Not only was he a good cook, but he was one of the most dependable cooks who ever entered a camp. George did not cook for me until near retirement age, but I knew him as a fine family man of sterling character.

The first time I ate a meal at a camp where George was cooking was in November, 1913, when he was cooking at Camp 1 of the Mellen Lumber Company at French Lake, now Hanson Lake, part of the Louis and Martin Hanson property.

A Mellen Lumber Camp out of Glidden, Wisconsin, around 1920. George Kennedy, a famous cook of that era for 40 to 50 years, is pictured with the cook's apron on. His son, Basil Kennedy, is a long-time attorney at law in Mellen.

The Mellen Lumber Company had logging headquarters at Foster Junction out of Mellen and at Glidden. J. D. Twomey of Mellen was logging superintendent of both operations with Gust DeLene in charge of woods operation out of Foster Junction and Elmer Bergland in charge of woods operations out of Glidden.

The Mellen Lumber Company generally had three to four camps running in each operation with the hardwood logs going to the Paine Lumber & Manufacturing Company at Oshkosh and the conifer or softwood logs going to the J.B. Nash Paper Company at Nekoosa and Port Edwards. The Nash Paper Company was changed later to the now well-known Nekoosa-Edwards Paper Company.

With that many camps running in the wartime years of 1917 to 1918, it was hard to keep good steady camp cooks, so J. D. Twomey decided on an experiment which paid off. He made George Kennedy a traveling cook. That is, he had no regular camp to cook for but when a camp needed a cook in a hurry, George would have to take over until another cook was hired. Needless to say, it was not very often that George had a few free days; more often he was cooking for two camps at a time and one period for three camps.

George Kennedy was one of the fastest camp bakers of bread and pastry I have ever been around. When he would be short of two cooks or three at one time, he would always try to have a second cook or an experienced cookee at those camps who could at least cook meats and vegetables, etc. and George would bake at one camp in the morning, then hike when no railroad ride was available to the other camp where he would bake in the afternoon; when a third camp was short a cook on the same operation, which happened at least once, he would go there and bake after supper. George told me once it worked out well; the only trouble would be when short a cook at Mellen and Glidden at the same time.

I have heard a good many yarns about some incidents at camps where George was cooking, and one of the best he verified for me. The following rules were in use at all large logging camps:
Rule 1 -- No talking at the table, only to pass food.
Rule 2 -- Keep your regular place at the table.
Rule 3 -- Pass or eat food from your setup of six men only.

Rule 3 was the one neglected the most or taken advantage of by one member of the setup. In this instance, it was pie -- always a favorite food in camp except when oatmeal pie. One day a cookee told George that a certain man was coming to the table who would eat a piece of pie first, then his regular dinner, then another piece of pie, so George watched the next day and sure enough, it was so. George said to the cookee, "We will fix him tomorrow." The next day George had pumpkin pie and he let the man eat his second piece of pie and just as he finished, George walked over with a whole six-piece pie in one hand and a meat cleaver in the other and said, "Here is some more pie for you." The man said, "No, me full." George said, "You eat this pie or I will use this cleaver." The man ate the pie but no more at that camp. The point here was when a man ate the second piece of pie, it left some other man in that setup short of pie.

During the depression year of 1931 -- to be exact, April, 1931 -- Keith Jesse needed a job and did not care what kind of work. He heard that the Roddis Company was putting on cedar pole and post peelers at one of their camps on the logging railroad out of Sells Spur, Wisconsin. Keith hiked across from Mercer and was hired even if there were around 100 men working with more men traveling looking for work in logging camps than there were men working.

Keith said the work was okay but the board was terrible. The only supplies were blue beef, potatoes, navy beans, cabbage, beggies and onions and flour with no cook to cook what they had.

The foreman told the woods superintendent he would have to get a cook if he wanted any work done. The superintendent said, "I can get you a cook at Mellen, as he has applied for a job." The foreman said get him as soon as possible. A few days later George got off the train at the camp as the crew was going in for the noon meal. George went in to dinner and when he came out, he said to the conductor on the train, "Do not leave until I have a chance to talk to the foreman, as I may wish to go back with you." George had a talk with the foreman who took him to the store room and roothouse. Then George told him there was nothing to cook, but the foreman said we have a telephone here and that he would call in asking for the supplies George needed. George said, "I will stay until tomorrow. If no supplies come, I will go back home to Mellen." The supplies came the next day and George stayed on and the crew started to get something to eat.

Acknowledgements

This book is the result of the desire to record the heritage of the logging era from about 1890 to 1937. It was the time between the logging of the pine and the beginning of the logging of the hemlock and the hardwood species. After World War I or around 1918 saw the start of the mechanized age of the crawler type tractor, trucks and trailers, and the power saw.

Many people made valuable contributions to this book. Especially:

1. Jasper Landry, Editor of the Mellen Weekly Record, Mellen, Wisconsin, who urged me to write this book.

2. Orton Henning, Shawano, Wisconsin, veneer log purchasing agent for the Weber Veneer Company of Shawano, Wisconsin; vice president of the Michigan-Wisconsin Timber Producers Association and a member of the State of Wisconsin Forestry Advisory Committee.

3. Howard J. Krauss, Ellsworth, Wisconsin, director of field services for Wisconsin Farmers Union, who worked with the author on many important projects and decisions in forestry.

4. Mrs. Patricia Carlin Grahm, Oakdale, California, niece of the author, who along with a cousin of the author, Diane Fairchild Beck, Oakdale, California, made recommendations as to how to start the writing to get it into book form.

5. Dr. Margaret Mary McCarthy, Mellen, Wisconsin, who advised the author on writing up early history of northern Wisconsin.

6. The typists of the manuscript:
Margie Clawson, Oakdale, California
Shirley Sukanen Meredith, Ashland, Wisconsin
Karen Krankkala, Iron Belt, Wisconsin
Tammy Lundberg, Iron Belt, Wisconsin

7. My wife, Lillian Lindsay Corrigan, who gave me valuable suggestions, proof reading, typing and encouragement.

8. L. G. Sorden, Madison, Wisconsin. Retired from the University of Wisconsin Extension Service, who worked many days over a three-year period with the organization, structure, and editing of this book.

He is the author or co-author of five Wisconsin books including *Lumberjack Lingo, I Am The Mississippi, Wisconsin Lore, The Romance Of Wisconsin Place Names, Family Record Book*.

9. The following newspapers, whose files provided information for this manuscript:

Ashland Daily Press - Ashland, Wisconsin
Glidden Enterprise - Glidden, Wisconsin
Iron County Miner - Hurley, Wisconsin
Mellen Weekly Record - Mellen, Wisconsin
Ironwood Daily Globe - Ironwood, Michigan

10. I wish to pay tribute to Roy Welch, who has encouraged me constantly during the writing of this book. He lost his father when he was just a lad. That did not stop him. He made up his mind to get an education and did not let little obstacles stop him.

The summer of 1913 immediately after school let out for summer vacation, he was successful in getting a clerk job in the railroad construction crew for the Mellen Lumber Co. out of Mellen, Wisconsin. Roy held a job for the Mellen Lumber Co. each summer after that while going on to higher education until his graduation from college.

After graduation from college, Roy hired out to the Marathon Corporation of Rothschild, Wisconsin as a salesman in the finished paper division, where he worked up to sales manager. When Marathon Corporation sold out to the American Can Co., Roy stayed on as sales manager until his retirement at 65 years of age.

After a few weeks, retirement was too much for him. He then hired out to Cadillac Associates, Inc., Chicago, to locate top executives for the paper packaging industry. He now lives in Winnetka, Illinois.

George A. Corrigan, author, on the tree farm where he now lives 3 miles west of Saxon on U.S. Highway 2.